Building Scalable Database Applications

The Addison-Wesley Object Technology Series

Grady Booch, Ivar Jacobson, and James Rumbaugh, Series Editors

For more information check out the series web site [http://www.awl.com /cseng/otseries/] as well as the pages on each book [http://www.awl.com/cseng/I-S-B-N/] (I-S-B-N represents the actual ISBN, including dashes).

David Bellin and Susan Suchman Simone, *The CRC Card Book*
ISBN 0-201-89535-8

Grady Booch, *Object Solutions: Managing the Object-Oriented Project*
ISBN 0-8053-0594-7

Grady Booch, *Object-Oriented Analysis and Design with Applications, Second Edition*
ISBN 0-8053-5340-2

Don Box, *Essential COM*
ISBN 0-201-63446-5

Alistair Cockburn, *Surviving Object-Oriented Projects: A Manager's Guide*
ISBN 0-201-49834-0

Dave Collins, *Designing Object-Oriented User Interfaces*
ISBN 0-8053-5350-X

Bruce Douglass, *Real-Time UML: Developing Efficient Objects for Embedded Systems*
ISBN 0-201-32579-9

Desmond F. D'Souza and Alan C. Wills, *Objects, Components, and Frameworks with UML: The Catalysis Approach*
ISBN 0-201-31012-0

Martin Fowler with Kendall Scott, *UML Distilled: Applying the Standard Object Modeling Language*
ISBN 0-201-32563-2

Martin Fowler, *Analysis Patterns: Reusable Object Models*
ISBN 0-201-89542-0

Peter Heinckiens, *Scalable Object-Oriented Database Applications: Design, Architecture, and Implementation*
ISBN 0-201-31013-9

Ivar Jacobson, Maria Ericsson, and Agenta Jacobson, *The Object Advantage: Business Process Reengineering with Object Technology*
ISBN 0-201-42289-1

Ivar Jacobson, Magnus Christerson, Patrik Jonsson, and Gunnar Overgaard, *Object-Oriented Software Engineering: A Use Case Driven Approach*
ISBN 0-201-54435-0

Ivar Jacobson, Martin Griss, and Patrik Jonsson, *Software Reuse: Architecture, Process and Organization for Business Success*
ISBN 0-201-92476-5

David Jordan, *C++ Object Databases: Programming with the ODMG Standard*
ISBN 0-201-63488-0

Wilf LaLonde, *Discovering Smalltalk*
ISBN 0-8053-2720-7

Lockheed Martin Advanced Concepts Center and Rational Software Corporation, *Succeeding with the Booch and OMT Methods: A Practical Approach*
ISBN 0-8053-2279-5

Thomas Mowbray and William Ruh, *Inside CORBA: Distributed Object Standards and Applications*
ISBN 0-201-89540-4

Ira Pohl, *Object-Oriented Programming Using C++, Second Edition*
ISBN 0-201-89550-1

Terry Quatrani, *Visual Modeling with Rational Rose and UML*
ISBN 0-201-61016-3

Yen-Ping Shan and Ralph Earle, *Enterprise Computing with Objects: From Client/Server Environments to the Internet*
ISBN 0-201-32566-7

David N. Smith, *IBM Smalltalk: The Language*
ISBN 0-8053-0908-X

Daniel Tkach and Richard Puttick, *Object Technology in Application Development Second Edition*
ISBN 0-201-49833-2

Daniel Tkach, Walter Fang, and Andrew So, *Visual Modeling Technique: Object Technology Using Visual Programming*
ISBN 0-8053-2574-3

Available Summer/Fall 1998

Grady Booch, James Rumbaugh, and Ivar Jacobson, *Unified Modeling Language User Guide*
ISBN 0-201-57168-4

Ivar Jacobson, Grady Booch, and James Rumbaugh, *The Objectory Software Development Process*
ISBN 0-201-57169-2

James Rumbaugh, Ivar Jacobson, and Grady Booch, *Unified Modeling Language Reference Manual*
ISBN 0-201-30998-X

Building Scalable Database Applications

Object-Oriented Design, Architectures, and Implementations

Peter M. Heinckiens

ADDISON-WESLEY

An imprint of Addison Wesley Longman, Inc.

Reading, Massachusetts • Harlow, England • Menlo Park, California
Berkeley, California • Don Mills, Ontario • Sydney
Bonn • Amsterdam • Tokyo • Mexico City

Many of the designations used by manufacturers and sellers to distinguish their products are claimed as trademarks. Where those designations appear in this book and Addison-Wesley was aware of a trademark claim, the designations have been printed in initial caps or all caps.

The author and publisher have taken care in the preparation of this book, but make no expressed or implied warranty of any kind and assume no responsibility for errors or omissions. No liability is assumed for incidental or consequential damages in connection with or arising out of the use of the information or programs contained herein.

The publisher offers discounts on this book when ordered in quantity for special sales. For more information, please contact:

Corporate, Government, and Special Sales Group
Addison Wesley Longman, Inc.
One Jacob Way
Reading, Massachusetts 01867

Library of Congress Cataloging-in-Publication Data

Heinckiens, Peter M. (Peter Marc)
    Building scalable database applications : object-oriented design,
  architectures, and implementations / Peter M. Heinckiens.
        p.   cm. — (The Addison-Wesley object technology series)
    Includes bibliographical references and index.
    ISBN 0-201-31013-9 (alk. paper)
    1. Object-oriented methods (Computer science)   2. Client/server
  computing.   I. Title.   II. Series.
  QA76.9.O35H45   1997   97-44555
  005.1'17--dc21   CIP

ISBN 0-201-31013-9

Text printed on recycled and acid-free paper.
1 2 3 4 5 6 7 8 9 10 - CRS - 02 01 00 99 98

First printing, February 1998

For my great mentors

Ghislain Hoffman,
for guiding me through my profession

My parents, Jeannine Fiers and Marc Heinckiens,
for guiding me through life

Contents

Foreword

A fundamental trend in computing is the evolution of applications from monolithic codes to component-based systems. Evidence of increasing software modularization and distribution is clear. The typical design center for application software has evolved from a huge mainframe orientation to a two-tier, client/server perspective, in which user-interface logic resides on desktop clients and the balance of the application executes on remote servers. The server commonly supports large, well-established databases and is accessed by a variety of applications. This two-tier, client/server model is evolving further to a three-tier model, with legacy databases remaining on centrally administered servers and application logic executed by mid-tier departmental servers. The next step is even more completely distributed applications. We are creating a new understanding of what an application is. That is, an application becomes a collect of well-modularized applets that interact in a network computing environment to accomplish the work of the application.

Designing client/server and distributed applications is a complex, challenging proposition. There are so many variables to consider and variants to analyze. If you've been faced with this challenge, you may have found it difficult to leverage the experience and expertise of others in the area, partly because so little has been published. This book should help to make your job easier because it shares real experience and expertise on how to design client/server applications.

Coupled with the trend toward modularization and distribution is that of more often using object technologies for designing and implementing applications. These two trends are quite synergistic and complementary; each reinforces the other. Object technology is well-suited for distributed environments, and distributed applications are well-served by object technology.

"Object-oriented" has become one of the more popular adjectives of this period in computing. At today's computer-industry trade shows, an amazing percentage of products are boldly labeled "object-oriented," to the point that the term is becoming a bit empty. In fact, however, object technology is exceptionally important. It encompasses object-oriented analysis and design techniques and methods, object programming languages, object database management systems, object request brokers and services, and so on. This book explains an approach for building robust applications by leveraging a stable and reusable business model that is developed using principles of object modeling.

The approach of Peter Heinckiens advocates separating not only an application's user-interface from its logic, but also separating the application's logic and its data persistence (or database) aspects. This additional cleavage plane is analogous to the extension of a two-tier client/server to a three-tier architecture. Not only are the user-interface modules separated from the application logic, but it also is easy to isolate the persistence mechanism. This approach is especially applicable in situations in which you want to build an application using an object programming language and want that application to access data that already resides in a non-object-oriented persistent store, for example, in a relational database or a conventional file system.

Peter's approach is not entirely new. For some time, others have been designing and implementing three-tier client/server and distributed applications using object modeling and object programming languages with relational database management systems. However, not much of that experience has been captured in the printed word. In contrast, Peter's book is rich with code examples that will help you understand exactly how to follow his footsteps in order to get a working system.

Building Scalable Database Applications discusses a variety of topics of importance relative to object-oriented application design. Here's a partial list of what it does:

- Presents a persistence architecture that allows for clear separation of object-oriented business models and relational database models.
- Shows how to abstract the details of database concepts and terminology so that you can concentrate on the fundamentals of persistence.
- Explains how to approach the design of reusable business objects.
- Shows how to approach the design of systems that are open and extensible.
- Emphasizes the pragmatic aspects of designing applications.
- Focuses on leveraging relational databases into object-oriented programming environments.
- Not only offers theory, but also shows how to apply that theory in practice.

Although I don't necessarily agree with everything Peter says in this book, I find it interesting and thought-provoking. It is definitely a step forward in the purveyance of practical information about how to combine notions of object-oriented programming and relational database storage. It should prove to be a valuable resource for many designers and implementers of modern applications.

Mary E. S. Loomis, PhD
Palo Alto, California

Preface

Perhaps the biggest problem the software industry has been coping with is the inability to travel in time, both forward and backward. Forward, because it would be nice to know in advance what our system specifications will end up looking like. Backward, because then we could change the mistakes we made and now have to live with. Thus our present is dictated by our past, and in its turn, our present dictates our future. So, we had better make sure that the choices we make today are well considered, or we might regret them for years to come. However, since we cannot predict the future, we must try to make our choices in such a way that our options stay open.

This situation is even more prevalent today. Because of the rapid technological advances the software industry faces, continually bigger demands are made by customers of software products. Those same customers are also experts in adding or changing "some very minor points" to the program requirements that often result in a programmer having to rewrite almost the entire program. This problem is often the cause of frustration between developers and customers. Developers get frustrated because the customer's modifications come so late in the project that major reprogramming is needed. Customers get frustrated because they had expected a more flexible collaboration.

Database Applications

The observation in the previous section particularly holds for many of today's management information system (MIS) applications. Most of these applications have very long life cycles, often spanning several technological waves in the fields of both programming and database technologies, and they often require extensions or modifications. It is impossible to rewrite the software every time the technology changes. However, at the same time, customers want to use the latest technological evolutions (just think of the World Wide Web, for example).

Traditionally, database applications were designed using programming languages such as COBOL or, in the best case, C. The main objections to these approaches have been that writing an application takes far too long and that afterward it contains too many bugs and is not sufficiently maintainable or portable. The portability issue is very important. Often, the (potential) customer already possesses a database system and wants your application to work on it. If that system differs from the one that your library of reusable routines was developed for, you might have a problem. An even more frustrating situation occurs when you demonstrate one of your applications to potential customers, and they agree that it is just what they have been waiting for all their life—if only it had not been written for a different database system than the one that they are currently using.

To increase software development productivity, Rapid Application Development (RAD) has become very popular and has given explosive birth to fourth-generation language (4GL) systems. However, being able to develop applications fast is one thing. How do we cope with the entire software life cycle, particularly maintenance and extensibility? Recent study has shown that in several companies, more than 93% of all software efforts go to program maintenance. And this figure is increasing.

The current silver bullet to conquer the software werewolf [Brooks87] is said to be object orientation. As a result, most RAD products got an additional label stuck on them: *object-oriented*. But what does *object orientation* really mean? Does it mean we should be able to draw or inherit fancy user interfaces? Does it mean we have to program in Java, Smalltalk, or C++? Or does it perhaps mean that we should migrate to an object-oriented database system?

Database technology, too, is an area in which rapid advances are being made. As a result, we are stuck with a mixture of several technologies: network databases, relational databases, flat-file systems, object-oriented databases, and so on. How do we integrate these? If we need to buy a new system, which technology do we choose? What if this choice turns out to be wrong? Or what if, in a couple of years, we have to migrate to a new technology?

The database is playing an increasingly important role in software design. However, what is a *database application* exactly? Does the database really play such an all-important role in these applications that it justifies letting it dominate the entire software approach?

All of these questions, and plenty more, are being asked every day by application developers. These developers need a database in which to store their data, but they are finding it increasingly difficult to present a suitable solution to their customers' ever-growing software demands.

To survive the explosive technological evolution in the software industry, we need an entirely new view of the concept of databases or, rather, of persistence as a whole. The concept of persistence has to be abstracted from the actual persistence technology.

What to Expect from This Book

In this book, I sketch a picture of the issues concerning database applications and how to handle them in an object-oriented way. The concepts and views introduced here are illustrated by the use of a persistence architecture called Scoop, short for *scalable object-oriented persistence*. I describe the fundamentals of the Scoop architecture and use it to explain how to develop database applications using object-oriented techniques.

The main objective of this book is to present the concept of object storage from an application developer's point of view. Somehow we have to manipulate persistent data. How do we do this, and, more important, how do we do this without having to throw out the tools we already possess?

Various aspects of software design are covered, including

- Determining the position of the database
- Developing an object-oriented view on the database
- Designing reusable business components
- Modeling and implementing associations
- Separating the user interface from the business model
- Designing database applications in such a way that maximum reuse and openness are achieved

I emphasize how to write software that conforms to a three-tier, client/server architecture. That is, I focus on how to obtain maximum separation and independence between the user interface, the application logic, and the storage.

A case study of a real-world application illustrates the concepts and techniques presented in this book. This study is interesting in that it describes an application that has been implemented in multiple versions. One version was implemented using the Scoop architecture, while others were developed using a number of 4GLs. This case study allows you to compare the object-oriented approach to the data-driven approach offered by most 4GL systems.

Intended Audience

Many application developers are committed to relational database management systems (RDBMSs). Although they may be interested in object orientation, they are often hesitant (or unable) to throw out existing relational or legacy products. This book shows how they can continue using their existing products and still benefit from an object-oriented approach. More generally, this book is of importance to anyone interested in object-oriented design and is unwilling to be committed to a specific database system. On the contrary, by using the techniques described here developers will be able to run their applications on a wide range of low-end and high-end database management systems (DBMSs).

Although some parts of this book are quite technical, several chapters should also be useful to managers. They will provide managers responsible for directing the information systems strategy of a company with some insights in and background about issues relevant to "modern client/server software." Especially of interest to them should be Chapters 1, 2, 3, 4, 11, 12, and 13.

Another target group is the designers who need access to database systems for applications that are not really database-related. This book will show them how they can eliminate most of the details concerned with databases and thus be able to focus on the fundamental parts of their programs.

Although the examples are given in C++ and the reader is expected to have some familiarity reading C++ code, the reader does not have to be an expert C++ programmer to benefit from the book. Knowledge of object-orientation is helpful; however, the reader need not be an object-oriented specialist. All that is required to benefit from the book is an open mind.

Feedback

Comments, criticisms, and suggestions about this book are greatly appreciated. They can be sent by e-mail to Peter Heinckiens at *Peter.Heinckiens@rug.ac.be*.

Acknowledgments

Many of the ideas proposed in this book originated from the experience I obtained working with Professor Ghislain Hoffman. It was he who, many years ago, sparked my enthusiasm for object orientation, and he is one of the first people I met who seemed to fully understand this concept and its implications for today's software systems. Working with him not only provided me with an invaluable experience, but also taught me a necessary lesson in pragmatism.

This book has benefited substantially from many fruitful discussions I had with Philippe Van Damme, Herman Tromp, and Johan Hoffman. They served as sounding boards for my often only partially formed ideas, and they meticulously reviewed my draft manuscript. I am particularly grateful to Philippe, who not only reviewed my final draft, but who read and reread my manuscript from its early days. His comments led to often heated discussions, but they were of immense value and resulted in many improvements to this book.

The detailed reviews by Rick Cattell, Margaret Ellis, John Lakos, and Mary Loomis are greatly appreciated. Margaret and John not only went into the technical aspects of my manuscript, but also did a very thorough job of polishing my English. Mary and Rick provided some very pertinent suggestions. Mary's offer to write my foreword was a big encouragement for me, not only because of my respect for her professionally, but especially because of my respect for her as a person.

I received helpful comments and support from many of my friends and colleagues. I particularly want to thank Bob Adams, Peter Arnold, Kris Carron, Daniel Chang, Patrick Delbeke, Hendrik Devos, Martin Hedley, Michael Hoffman, Rony Lanssiers, Geert Premereur, Herman Steyaert, Misty Taylor, Bart Van den Berghe, Bart Van Renterghem, and Richard Wiener.

I want to give special thanks to my family—Michelle Van Hollebeke, Marc Heinckiens, Jeannine Fiers, Masha Heinckiens, and Mo Khalfa—for their love, support, and understanding.

They not only supported me morally, but also helped with another major task I undertook during the writing of this book: renovating a house. Without them, I would not have been able to finish both of these jobs successfully.

Finally, I want to thank Katie Duffy, Mike Hendrickson, Marina Lang, and Marilyn Rash at Addison Wesley Longman and Laura Michaels of Montview Publications for their very professional and pleasant way of working with me. Katie, Mike, and Marina have been very supportive and helpful throughout this whole project. Marilyn made sure that I (almost) made all my deadlines, and Laura did an excellent job of copyediting.

About the Author

Peter M. Heinckiens holds the Belgian equivalent of an M.S. degree in electrical engineering. He works for the Information Technology Department of the University of Ghent, where he is responsible for coordinating the strategic planning and deployment of software technology throughout the university's administrative section. His function at the University puts him in the unique position of being able to do research while also confronting the real issues and problems that business faces today.

In addition, he often teaches and consults for industry. As a consultant, he has been involved in introducing object-oriented techniques in large-scale projects. Many of these projects were designed using the techniques described in this book. He is also a frequent speaker at international conferences and is a contributor to several technical and scientific magazines.

Part One

An Object-Oriented View on Persistence

Chapter 1

A New Generation of Software

1.1 From Data to Information

One of the most fundamental changes in software technology is the transition from data manipulation to information manipulation. In the past, software design essentially centered on how to manipulate elementary pieces of data, such as a name, an address, or an invoice number. None of these pieces contained much information. A name was just a string of a certain predefined length; an address or an invoice number, too, were just strings of some length. There was no fundamental difference between the three strings, at least as far as the data was concerned.

When we speak of information manipulation, we are, of course, still manipulating this elementary data. However, that manipulation is on a much higher level of abstraction. We do not work with the data as such, but rather with the information it represents. The name is not just a string anymore. Instead, it represents, for example, a person with a certain address, typical habits, and so on. Thus that name has become some data with a certain meaning attached to it. An even more striking example can be found in multimedia applications, in which a musical object is asked to play itself or film objects are integrated into text documents. All of these things have thus become much more than just ordinary data.

Another example is the concept of object linking and embedding (OLE) in MS-Windows. Consider, for example, an Microsoft Word document in which you embed a certain illustration that was drawn in CorelDraw. To edit this illustration, you need only double-click it; CorelDraw will automatically load the picture and make it ready for editing. If, further on in your document, you want to include the financial results of the last quarter from an Excel spreadsheet, you can embed the file containing those results as an Excel object. Double-clicking that object will take you into Excel, from where you can alter the data. In classical data-driven systems, all of this information is nothing more than a collection of characters and digits, none of which have any further meaning.

1.2   Improving Software Quality

The evolution from data manipulation to information manipulation has significant implications for the software designer. It has made modern software systems many times more complex. Add to that the explosive evolution of available hardware resources, ever-growing user requirements, and the demand for graphical user interfaces (GUIs). Further add the need to stay compatible with old character-based terminals and the demands for openness, portability, and extensibility. The result is a situation that holds many advantages for end users, but that also holds all of the necessary ingredients for a wonderful nightmare for the unsuspecting application developer.

Managing that complexity while still delivering robust software is a major challenge for the developer. Modern software problems have become so complicated that traditional procedural methods for designing software are no longer adequate. Conquering this explosion of complexity requires an entirely new level of abstraction, one that clearly separates all software components from their actual implementation.

Object orientation has emerged as an important enabling technology to ensure software quality, reusability, portability, maintainability, and extensibility. It allows developers to decompose their problem domain into a set of objects that offer a well-defined interface to the other components of the system, while keeping the objects' internal structure hidden. The implementation of these objects can be fully verified and validated. Moreover, by using inheritance mechanisms, one can derive specialized objects from more generic ones. This leads to optimal software reusability. Hence, application developers can design software with minimal effort. Further, they can do that reliably because they build an application on top of an object space that has been validated independently and that offers a high level of abstraction.

Portability also is a major asset. Operating system and user interface dependencies can easily be hidden within objects. If the software is to migrate to a different platform, only the internal structure of a limited number of objects must be modified. As long as the objects' interface to the outside world is left unchanged, they can be incorporated in the new software system without a major disruption of the system's operation. In this way, existing investments in software development are protected and reliability is enhanced.

1.3   Databases Everywhere

Much of today's business applications can be labeled *database* applications. Indeed, the ever-growing need for the storage, retrieval, and manipulation of large amounts of data has led to database systems' becoming an increasingly important subsystem of modern software systems. No matter which application you are developing, at one point or the other, it becomes necessary to store data to or retrieve data from disk.

This situation has led to a proliferation of database software of a varying degree of complexity and an overwhelming variety of application program interfaces. On the one hand, this variety of choice is an advantage: The potential user has a wide range from which to choose. On the other hand, this diversity holds an inherent danger: It can cause confusion. "Which system is best?" is an often-asked question that, unfortunately, seldom has a unique answer. Its answer depends largely on the application for which it will be used. Another question often is, "Will it be portable?" A database system available on one platform is not necessarily obtainable on another.

1.4   To Have and to Hold

Application developers who must use a database system for their applications are confronted with an enormous responsibility. Although the choice of the database system is not really related to the application, which system is used often is mission-critical. A system selected early in the design phase might become a serious burden later. Many of the programming language interfaces that these database systems provide create problems in that they force programmers to write their programs according to a certain framework. Another problem is that this framework is different for each system. Thus once you have chosen a certain database interface, it is difficult to switch to another, since switching would require you to rewrite much of the software. Portability is thus strained.

You have to choose a system knowing that it is possible that a better system will pop up after the project is under way. Even upgrading to a new version of the same system can pose problems, as the new system may contain some "minor" alterations in the programmers' interface that are incompatible with old application code.

So, the choice of the database system is a little like marriage: Once you have chosen a certain system, you may be "stuck" with it for the rest of your life, so you'd better make sure you have made the right choice. Of course, a divorce is not impossible, but the question, as always, is whether you can afford one. Divorces tend to be cumbersome and to take a long time to complete. Above all, they are expensive. The price you pay in this case is a total rewrite of all libraries and programs that are based on the discarded system. In the best case, this task means substituting all old database calls for new ones. In the worst (most) cases, it involves a complete redesign of your program. This is a huge and almost impossible task.

1.5   Concentrating on the Essence

The result of all of this database trouble is that the developer far too often must cope with details of the structure and manipulation of the persistent data structures instead of being able to concentrate on developing the application itself. This is in sharp contrast with the paradigms of modern software design practice. From the point of view of the application developer, data storage should be nothing more than a technique for storing objects. The developer's view of the data is essentially object-oriented and should be strictly separated from the actual mechanism used to store and retrieve the data. That mechanism may range from a simple file structure such as standard C-ISAM, to a simple database interface such as Btrieve and Codebase, to a relational database system such as Sybase, Informix, and Oracle. It might, however, also be a fully developed, object-oriented database system.

Although the database subsystem is important, it often is only a minor concern to the developer. Consider a CAD system in which the emphasis clearly lies on the design and simulation of, for example, a mechanical object or an electrical circuit. It would be a shame to waste the time and knowledge of the CAD professional and limit portability by drawing that person's attention too much to a routine task, such as data storage. In addition, because of the framework imposed on the developer, the developer has to spend considerable time on such tasks as selecting the correct indexes, the opening and closing of database files, ensuring the number of open files does not exceed the system limit, and so on. As a direct result, the developer cannot fully concentrate on the real essence of his or her work—the design of a CAD system.

1.6   The Importance of Scalability

When talking about databases, and certainly about object-oriented ones, people tend to think about relatively expensive, high-end products such as DB2, Oracle, Informix, Sybase, and Ingres. However, they often also tend to overlook the fact that a very significant part of contemporary software design is directed toward low-budget markets. Indeed, a key achievement of the personal computer (PC) is that it brought computer systems within the reach of the masses. As the PC became more powerful, small businesses became more and more dependent on PC-based products. Database applications such as MS-Access, dBase, Foxpro, Paradox and similar products have become very popular. Consider, for example, a simple invoicing system for a small business. Small businesses are not looking for a full-blown, state-of-the-art database system that can serve hundreds of users at the same time and that possesses the latest technology in distributed systems. All they want is a program that allows them to efficiently create invoices and that handles their customer and stock databases. Such applications are typically based on inexpensive low-end database systems.

Those kinds of applications are still often written in languages such as Clipper because these languages allow the designer to work with relatively inexpensive database systems and because they often do not require runtime licenses. However, although these languages are simple and easy to learn, they are not always the most robust, from a software technical point of view. They also are not appropriate for programming an application if the database system is to be used for a task that is not really database-related. You would not want to write an entire CAD package in Clipper just because you need access to a component library that happens to be stored in dBase files. It would be nice if you could use languages such as C, C++, Java, or Smalltalk to access these database systems.

If developers thus decide to design a database interface, a design goal must be to make it applicable to small database systems as well as large. In this way, the applications you write become truly scalable and will run no matter which database system is used. You will be able to use the same object library to develop either an inexpensive and simple customer database for the hairdresser next door as to develop a full-blown, state-of-the-art accounting program for a major company.

1.7   Application Program Interfaces

As mentioned in the previous section, it would be nice if you could access database systems from languages such as C or C++. And indeed, there are several very good program libraries available for managing data stored in database systems. Almost every major large database system offers a C application programming interface (API). There also are a large number of APIs for low-end, file-based storage systems. For such systems, you could use, for example, Codebase, a popular C-library for accessing dBase- and Foxpro-compatible files.

However, the problem with these libraries is that they do not hide the database concept at all. Some are even closely connected to the file concept, which means you must take care to open and close the files, not exceed the maximum number of allowed open files, and so on. Other approaches allow for embedded Structured Query Language (SQL) in your program. An interesting concept in this regard is Microsoft's Open Database Connectivity (ODBC). This approach offers an extended SQL standard. Programs that are ODBC-compliant can work with any database that supports the ODBC API.

Although SQL to a certain degree already abstracts the file concept, it still does not hide the database concept. Also, an SQL-based interface is often less efficient than a more low-level approach, such as that offered by a C-API.

No matter which approach you choose, it will force a certain framework on you in which the database-related topics not only remain apparent but, even worse, also often dictate the entire software approach. This framework has implications on portability and the freedom of choice of the data structures.

1.8   The Road to Follow

To obtain complete portability, the developer must design a persistence architecture that is the same for any available database interface. In this way, the developer can make the application independent from the underlying database system, as well as make it feasible to port the application program between platforms and from one database system to another. The same application can be used, without any changes, on low-cost platforms, such as a PC using a simple and inexpensive file system to store the data. It also can be used within sophisticated client/server architectures based on high-end relational or object-oriented DBMSs. In this way, applications become truly scalable, as far as their database interface is concerned.

However, this solves only part of the problem. Developers still must be concerned about a number of routine jobs, such as the opening and closing of the databases. And because of the framework imposed on them, their choice in the use of data structures is limited. They will, for example, be hesitant to use linked lists, knowing how difficult it often is to store them in databases. So they need a system that completely hides the database concept from the programmers. They must be able to develop their software without having to worry about the database. One can even go one step further: The programmers must be able to develop their software without having to know whether a database is involved.

A system that fulfills all of these requirements places us in the domain of object-oriented databases. There is one distinct difference when compared to object-oriented databases, however: This system is able to work with existing database systems. This is a very important feature, since in several application areas, using object databases today is not feasible. Especially in the administrative (MIS) sector, relational systems will stay around for a long time. The reason for this is simple. Companies have invested far too much money and effort in relational systems to be able to throw them out in favor of object-oriented ones. Imagine the amount of software that is still written in COBOL just because it would cost too much for a company to rewrite its existing programs in a more modern language. There are actually more lines of COBOL being written today than there were in the 1970s.

By applying the techniques for object-oriented database application design described in this book, developers obtain the best of two worlds. That is, they get the power and flexibility of object-oriented techniques, while still being able to use existing database systems, thereby protecting often phenomenally large investments. A perfect collaboration between the "old" and the "new" software technology becomes possible, even within the same application. This means we have created a way to move gradually to object orientation. The migration to object orientation no longer has to be a leap into the unknown [Cox86].

Chapter 2

The Database Community
Today

This chapter offers a brief overview on the status of the database community today. It looks at the trends in this community and examines some of the problems involved in designing database applications.

2.1 Walking among Dinosaurs

Few of us are destined to become creators. Most must be content to be modifiers of the past. To become creators, we must create twice: the first time to design our creation and the second time to build a bridge from that creation to our heritage. It is this second creation that is so hard to achieve and that prevents us from becoming creators in the first place.

When developing new applications, we must always keep in mind that there already exists a huge installed software base. Of course, this existing software is developed using the latest state-of-the-art techniques, but those techniques are often those of two or three generations ago. And that software is here to stay for many more generations to come.

For a new technique to be truly accepted, it must be gradually integrated into our existing world. The new technique must be implemented as an improvement of the existing technology, not as a replacement of it. Of course, the technique sometimes requires that we make some trade-offs. Nevertheless, we are always better off with a simple but handy system that works than with a sophisticated state-of-the-art system that cannot be integrated with existing products.

As mentioned in Chapter 1, relational database systems are far from dead. On the contrary, given the market penetration those systems have, one can safely state they are still very much alive. In addition, a large amount of data is still stored in network databases. It is important to be aware of these "elders" and to respect them, as it is they who are still in charge, for both financial and political reasons. So we had better know how to get along and communicate with them. Generational conflicts have no place in software.

This integration with existing products is one of the most fundamental changes of the software industry. Hence, it is a key concept that appears throughout this book.

2.2 Database Usage

Existing software can be separated into two large categories of applications that use DBMSs. The first is traditional data processing, in which, over the last 15 years, relational databases have become the de facto standard in both the high-end and low-end markets. The success of relational databases has largely been due to the flexibility they offer over network and hierarchical database systems, and, of course, also to the availability of a large number of powerful RDBMSs. It is this success of the relational databases that will probably delay the general acceptance of object databases in the data processing sector.

The second category of application consists of the more sophisticated applications such as engineering applications, CAD packages, and office automation systems. These applications can be characterized as consisting of objects that have often complex interrelationships. They are much younger than those in the first category. It is especially for this category of applications that true object databases will serve a significant role. It is also the area in which most object databases are targeted today.

2.3 Database Users

Like the applications themselves, the users of DBMSs can be divided into several categories. The first category consists of the database administrators. These administrators have a thorough knowledge of database systems and the issues involved in working with these systems. This knowledge makes them the most suited to choose the database system, to design the database layout, and to make sure the system stays operational and consistent at all times. They also have knowledge of reporting tools, and they are the people to go to when one needs support in designing complex reports. Most database administrators, however, are less skilled in programming and software analysis.

The second category consists of the application programmers who use a database system to store their application's data. Those users communicate with the database from their programming language by means of a C application programmer's interface; they can use embedded SQL or can develop their program in a fourth-generation language (4GL). Although the programming team needs to be able to store its data in the database, team members often lack the knowledge either to adequately choose the database system most suited for their application or to design the optimal table layout.

The last category consists of the end users. End users do not use the database directly. Rather, they use the applications written by the programmers. They perform two types of operations on the application: data navigation (including data entering and editing) and querying. Data navigation should be completely covered by the programmer. Many of the standard reports a user might want to generate can be anticipated and thus developed by the programmer. However, the end user also may want to perform an unforeseen query, so there has to be a query system. Through this system, the end user can communicate directly with the database system instead of with the application. Also, the end user is often computer illiterate. Indeed, most end users know how to use their system, but they have little knowledge (nor should they) of either the database system, database layout, or programming techniques. So the query system must be very user friendly and as simple as possible to operate.

A first way to query the database is by using SQL. However, SQL is not simple for inexperienced users, so many user-friendly relational query tools have popped up. These tools allow the user to graphically and interactively model the query and generate the necessary SQL statements. Also, a large number of report writers are available that offer a user-friendly environment in which users can generate sophisticated reports.

A problem with these systems is that the users must still have some knowledge of the database layout. They must know which data is stored directly in the database and which has to be calculated. If they have to join two tables, they must know the primary and foreign keys of those tables. This not only is confusing, but also requires the end users to have at least a basic understanding of database technology.

A better approach would be to hide database concepts from the end user as much as possible. Chapter 13 presents a method that shields end users from the database layout, while giving them the opportunity to continue using their favorite query tools and report generators.

2.4 Designing Database Applications

An examination of how software is often designed reveals that much discussion still revolves around topics concerned with the database layout, such as what tables to create, how many characters to reserve for a certain database column, which primary key to choose, which and how links should be made, and which indexes should be created. Although such discussions are necessary, they tend to lead us away from the real problem: the development of an application. They also often occur on the management level, thus creating a Babel-like confusion among managers and engineers. Even on an engineering level, decisions about database-related topics should be avoided in the early stages of a project. However, since the outcome of those decisions often has a fundamental impact on the application design, database issues can dominate the project from its initial phase. The only way to avoid them is by abstracting the data structures, or the objects on which we have to work, from their representation in the database.

Suppose, for example, that you want to develop an invoicing system. Using classical approaches, you might start the design process with certain database-related questions. For example, how will the customer data be stored in the invoice table? Do you want to store all data or just use a join to the customer table? If you use a join, what will be the foreign key and how many characters will it consist of? Will it have a numeric or alphanumeric data type? As you can see, you must look at the customer table first. But what if later you find that you made a mistake and you want to add or change a link?

What about the set of stock items, which represents a one-to-many relationship? How will you implement this? In memory, this would be no problem, since you could simply use a linked list. However, you are not working in memory, so how do you map this linked list onto your relational (or any other) database structure? How do you store the stock data? Do you use a join to the stock table? What about the sales price? Do you store this inclusive or exclusive of the sales tax or value-added tax (VAT)?

It is much simpler to say that an invoice consists of a customer name, a shipping address, a set of stock items, and a total price. The stock items consist of an article and a price. How everything is implemented is of no importance; that is the responsibility of the person creating the customer, stock, and price objects. How is this data stored in the invoice? That, too, is of no importance to you. All you care about is that the invoice is made persistent. The mapping on the underlying database is something that has to be totally transparent.

2.5 Relational Databases

Because of the still-growing importance of relational systems, it might be useful to take a brief look at their most important characteristics. The most striking feature of the relational data model is its simplicity. It is based on the concept of the *table*. A table consists of a specific number of columns and an arbitrary number of rows. Each column contains data of a specific type such as strings, integers, and/or dates.

The relational data model consists of three main parts: structural, manipulation, and integrity.

2.5.1 The Structural Part

The structural part concerns the database layout. It consists of the different tables, the rows (the records), the columns (the fields), the primary and other keys, and so on.

As an example, consider a database consisting of two tables: an employee table and a department table (see Figure 2.1).

Every table has a **primary key** The primary key is a column or a combination of columns that are unique for each record. The primary key uniquely identifies a record. Certain tables also contain references to other tables. For example, the "Department" column in the employee table in the figure is a reference to a record in the department table. This column thus contains the value of the primary key of the corresponding record in the department table. A column that contains this value is called a **foreign key** to the department table.

2.5.2 The Manipulation Part

The manipulation part of the relational data model deals with the operations on the database. Typical operations in relational algebra include selection, joining, union, and intersection. This section briefly discusses the two most important of these: selection and joining. A complete discussion of all aspects of relational algebra is outside the scope of this book; for more information, see [Date95]. Note also that all examples in this section are in SQL, the accepted de facto language for relational database management.

EMPLOYEE

ID	Name	FirstName	Department	Salary	...
0001	Brown	John	01	75000	
0002	Robinson	Joe	01	49000	
0003	Jones	Claire	02	89000	
0004	Thomson	Bill	03	43000	
0005	Butchers	Andy	02	60000	
0006	Aladin	Jim	03	79000	

DEPARTMENT

ID	Name	Boss	...
01	Engineering	0001	
02	Sales	0003	
03	Marketing	0006	

FIGURE 2.1   Relational data model example.

ID	Name	FirstName	Department	Salary	...
0001	Brown	John	01	75000	
0003	Jones	Claire	02	89000	
0005	Butchers	Andy	02	60000	
0006	Aladin	Jim	03	79000	

FIGURE 2.2   An example select operation result table.

Selecting

The select operation allows the user to select those records in a table that conform to certain selection criteria. Its result is a new table that contains only the selected records.

Say you want to select all employees earning more than $50,000. You could use this SQL statement:

```
SELECT * FROM Employee WHERE salary > 50000
```

which would result in the table in Figure 2.2.

Employee.Name	Employee.FirstName	Department.Name
Brown	John	Engineering
Robinson	Joe	Engineering
Jones	Claire	Sales
Thomson	Bill	Marketing
Butchers	Andy	Sales
Aladin	Jim	Marketing

FIGURE 2.3 An example join operation result table.

Joining

The second fundamental operation in a relational database system is the *join*. A join allows the combination of two or more database tables.

Say, for example, that you want to know the department name and the address for each employee. To retrieve this data, you must combine—join—two tables: the employee table and department table. You can do this by using an SQL statement of the following form:

```
SELECT Employee.name, Employee.FirstName, Department.Name
FROM Employee, Department
WHERE Employee.Department = Department.ID
```

This join is made by expressing in the WHERE clause that the "Department" column in the employee table corresponds with the column "ID" in the department table. This selection results in the table shown in Figure 2.3.

2.5.3   Integrity

The integrity part of the relational data model consists of two domains: referential integrity and entity integrity. **Referential integrity** is ensuring that no table ever contains references to rows that no longer exist. In the previous employee-department database, for example, if you want to delete a row in the department table, you must make sure that there are no employee rows that reference this row.

Most database systems allow the database administrator to specify such referential integrity rules on the database level. The database then ensures that a row is deleted only if it is not referenced by other rows. In certain low-end systems, however, this integrity is the responsibility of the programmer.

Entity integrity is ensuring that a record always remains in a consistent state. A record might become inconsistent in a number of ways. For example, the user might enter data that is semantically incorrect. Providing a mechanism to check for semantic correctness is clearly the responsibility of the programmer. Another way the database might become inconsistent is if two users are simultaneously updating the same record.

An important concept to ensure integrity is transaction management. A transaction can be considered to be an elementary unit of work. Although within a transaction a database could be in an unstable state, before and after each transaction, the database is guaranteed to be in a consistent state. This topic is discussed further in Chapter 10.

2.5.4   Normal Forms

To remove redundancy, you can *normalize* the database. In this regard, reference is often made to the "normal forms," of which the first three are the most important. Each normal form offers a decreased level of redundancy [Date95]. Although most databases start out in third normal form, they often end up in first normal form because of efficiency reasons. Implementing these schema changes, however, often requires serious programming efforts.

2.6   Client/Server Systems

In a client/server model, a software system is modeled as a set of loosely coupled processes, all of which can function independently in their own process space. They ask or perform services by sending messages to each other [Tromp92]. The following sections discuss in depth first the server side of the model and then the client side. It then explains how the client/server model works in information systems.

2.6.1   The Server

A **server** manages a resource on behalf of multiple users (clients). This resource can be one of a wide variety of things; for example, a screen driver, a printer, a database, or a communication facility. It is important to note that the server is the only unit that can make direct use of the resource it manages. All other units can access this resource only by issuing requests to the server. This server has a uniform interface regardless of the actual implementation of the resources it manages.

The server does not have to be on a separate computer from the clients it serves. It is a logical unit, so it can run on the same machine as the clients that use it (for example, the printer server in MS-Windows). Both the client and server might even be part of the same process. In sophisticated database applications (still one of the most important client/ server application areas), a request to the database server could put several other computers to work. In this way, the data server becomes, in its turn, a client to other (lower-level) servers.

2.6.2   The Client

The **client** invokes the services provided by the server. It does this by sending a request to the server and then waiting for an answer (see Figure 2.4).

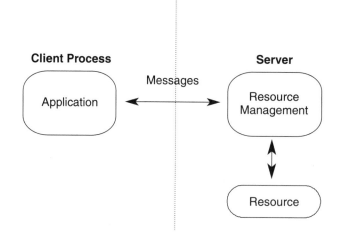

FIGURE 2.4   Client/server architecture. A client accesses certain resources by sending messages to the manager of these resources: the server.

2.6.3   The Client/Server Model in Information Systems

In the past, most large database systems could be viewed as consisting of one big mainframe to which several dumb terminals were connected. This configuration typically ran under a character-based user interface.

This situation has changed tremendously over the last few years. An important reason is the tendency to decentralize information systems. This has been done for two main reasons. The first has to do with geographical considerations. Companies are becoming more dependent on information technology. Also, a company can be very geographically distributed; consider, for example, a bank that has branches in several cities and sometimes even in several countries. Hence, data becomes increasingly more distributed over multiple systems. This data distribution poses several problems. One is whether you will store data locally or in a centralized location. The latter is often impossible (for example, for a banking company that has branches in the United States, Europe, and the Middle East). However, localized storage raises important considerations about the integrity of the data.

A second reason for decentralizing information systems is the trend towards downsizing (or better, "rightsizing"). Thanks to the phenomenal price–performance ratio that the typical PC offers and to the availability of many very powerful and relatively inexpensive applications (word processors, spreadsheets, and so on), the traditional mainframe has been left in favor of a more flexible client/server architecture build around a PC network. In this approach, a number of inexpensive and intelligent clients (often PCs) are connected through a relatively inexpensive local area network (LAN) that has a number of servers. Each server can be designated to perform a specific task, for example, central data management or the execution of calculation-intensive applications.

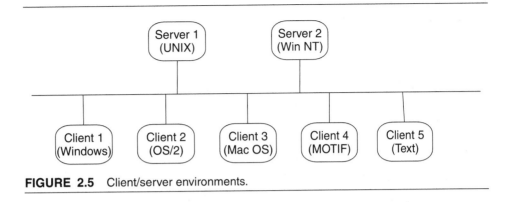

FIGURE 2.5   Client/server environments.

Providing user-friendly software has become more important, thanks to the availability of the PC and modern operating systems and user environments such as OS/2 and Windows. Many users have grown so accustomed to the ease of use of GUIs that they consider the ability of their software to run in a GUI environment as a prerequisite to their purchase of the software.

Openness has become very important, too, on both the hardware and software levels. On the hardware level, users do not want to be bound to a particular hardware vendor anymore. They want their application to be able to run on many different hardware platforms. They also want to be able to connect hardware from several vendors in the same network.

On the software level, users are demanding that their software be able to communicate with one another (*interoperability*). They want to use their favorite spreadsheet to evaluate the results obtained with another application, and afterward, they want to copy this data to their word processor in order to write a report on it. Indeed, this cutting and pasting between applications has become a must-have feature. There is even a tendency to build custom software using a number of standard packages. One could picture, for example, writing an accounting program but using MS-Word to print the invoices and Excel to analyze the data and create graphics.

The data processing world is more and more moving to a client/server environment. A number of central servers running, for example, UNIX or Windows NT, are used for data storage. Connected to these servers are several clients, most often low-cost PCs, running a graphical user environment such as Windows or OS/2 (see Figure 2.5).

It is important to realize that each of these clients and servers can run a different operating system and can be obtained from a different vendor. The result is a very flexible heterogeneous computer network that can be custom built and easily extended as needs (or technology) change. This is contrary to the classical mainframe situation, in which users were stuck with the same technology and vendor for many years. Note, however, that downsizing does not necessarily imply the death of the mainframe. Rather, the mainframe gets to play a different role. It can become, for example, a data server or a communications hub, or it can be used to process the largest applications.

So we've moved from having one processor per company to having one processor per user. At least one, as the tendency to multiprocessing becomes more and more apparent.

2.7   Distributed Software

The increasing importance of data distribution has made itself felt in several ways. First is the trend toward creating distributed database systems [Andleigh92]. These systems can be homogeneous, or they can consist of database systems from multiple vendors (see Figure 2.6).

Second is the efforts of several organizations to develop methods and standards for developing distributed software. One such standard is CORBA, short for Common Object Request Broker Architecture [Siegel96]. This is a standard for the environment-independent exchange of objects in a client/server system. It was developed by the OMG (Object Management Group), a consortium of hardware and software companies. This standard describes the way objects and calls for operations on objects have to be transferred to an implementation of CORBA so as to create a fully environment-independent exchange of data. Programs written in a library that is CORBA-compliant can share data relatively easily with other processes that are running either on the same computer or on a computer thousands of miles away. In addition, those applications do not have to be written in the same language in order to interoperate. Hence, for example, C++ applications can share objects with Smalltalk or Java applications.

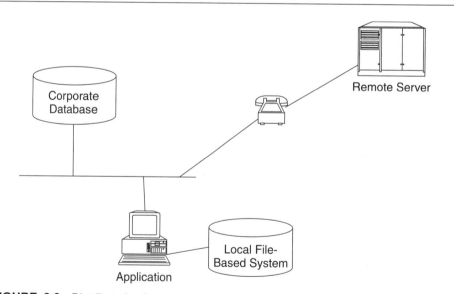

FIGURE 2.6   Distributed software systems.

Third, distributed software is also important in client/server architectures. An important consideration in developing client/server applications is what to put on the client and what to put on the server. There are typically three approaches to consider: the fat server, the fat client, and the truly distributed application. In a fat server approach, all processing is done on the server. The application is run on the client as a Telnet session. In other words, the client plays the role of a terminal. In the fat client approach, the entire application runs on the client and the data resides on the server. This time, the full power of the client is used, but running the application might result in a lot of network traffic.

The ideal case is the truly distributed application. Here, the application runs partly on the server and partly on the client. In this way, the application can be designed to optimize the network traffic. Many database systems support stored procedures as a technique for implementing application partitioning. Another way to design distributed applications is to use remote procedure calls (RPCs). This approach, however, does not always work well with objects. In such a case, an object request broker (ORB) might be more appropriate.

2.8 Problems with Traditional Systems

This section looks at the main problems encountered when designing database applications using traditional software design techniques [Loomis95].

2.8.1 The Impedance Mismatch

One problem encountered when designing database applications is that in traditional systems, the programming language and the database system are two completely different environments. To use database constructs in, for example, a C-program, you often have to use embedded SQL. This means you are using two different languages at the same time.

An even worse problem is that more often than not, there is a complete mismatch between the data constructs used in the database and those used in the programming language. This phenomenon, called the **impedance mismatch** [Keene93], means that to make your variables persistent, you have to map them onto the database environment. Those who have ever tried to store, for example, a linked list in a traditional database system will no doubt agree that this mapping is often far from straightforward. Solving such mapping problems wastes a significant portion of development time (sometimes more than 50%) and accounts for many program bugs. Figure 2.7 depicts a classic database application design.

2.8.2 Schema Changes

Another problem encountered when designing database applications is that the database layout (the database schema) does not always remain static. The layout may have to be changed because of changes to the application requirements or because of demands made by *other* applications. Then, of course, all program fragments of all applications depending on this layout have to be altered. These modifications often require a substantial amount of work and result in a very high software maintenance cost.

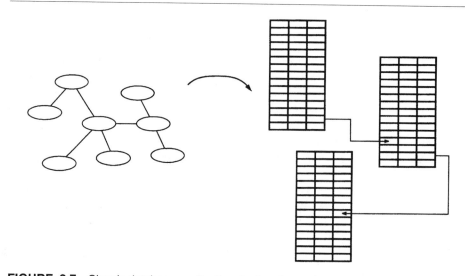

FIGURE 2.7 Classic database application design. A very large portion of the development time goes into disassembling the various objects and mapping them onto the database layout.

2.8.3   Separation of Concerns

To resolve all of these problems, we must try to obtain a conceptual separation between the database system and the application. This means that the application must not depend on the layout of the database. You must be able to safely change the database layout without having to worry about the implications on the software that depends on the database. If you succeed in making the data storage independent of its representation in computer memory, then you are free to construct the most exotic data types without having to worry about whether you'll be able to store them in the database afterward. You can leave this storage problem to the database specialist. Note, however, that this does not mean you're shifting the hard part to this person. The database specialist, too, is free to choose his or her own database layout, without having to worry about the programmer. It is the task of a (preferably automatic) mapping mechanism to ensure that the programming language world and the database world can communicate. A total separation of concerns is achieved.

2.9   4GL: The Solution?

Fourth-generation languages have been increasingly successful in the database community by offering an environment that allows us to quickly and easily develop database applications. However, they have their drawbacks.

Most 4GLs are centered around the design of the user interface of the data-processing application. They allow you to design various dialog boxes and attach some code to those boxes. For certain applications, such as a customer database, this approach can be sufficient. These applications consist mainly of navigating through the data, a typical user-controlled operation. These applications can be called *user-centered*. This contrasts with more sophisticated applications that have a much more complex business logic. The user interaction is minimal compared to the amount of program logic that has to be executed. These applications could be called *algorithm-centered*. To represent the complex business model in a robust way, these applications require substantial capabilities concerning data abstraction and structured programming, something most 4GLs do not yet offer.

To control the explosion of complexity and maintain a high degree of extensibility, we have to cut the dependencies between the various software components as much as possible. A first way to achieve this is to separate, on a conceptual level, the user interface, the database (or rather the persistent storage mechanism), and the application.

Most programs written in 4GLs still depend on the database layout. As explained earlier in the chapter, this holds the danger that changes in this layout may result in significant changes in the program. Also, as already mentioned, 4GLs are suited mainly for developing database applications. Many programs, however, are not pure database applications (for example, CAD packages), although they may make extensive use of databases. 4GLs are in no way adequate for developing such applications.

Further, when choosing a 4GL, you commit yourself to a single vendor. Many people feel a bit uncomfortable knowing that their entire software system (and thus often their entire company) depends on a single software vendor. A huge advantage of languages such as C or Smalltalk is that they are supported by several compiler vendors.

Another problem with many 4GLs is that they require relatively expensive runtime licenses. Especially for the lower-end applications, these licenses can become a very high cost overhead. The overhead that 4GLs introduce is not limited only to their cost. The runtime efficiency of applications developed with most 4GLs also is remarkably lower than the efficiency of similar applications developed in, say, C or C++.

2.10 Object-Oriented Databases

In this book, object-oriented databases are called object databases for short. Object databases evolved out of the need for a better integration of the object paradigm and databases. Originally it was thought that these databases would become the replacements for their relational counterparts. However, as relational technology is also evolving to objects, it is likely that both technologies will have their own place in the market.

2.10.1 Object Databases Support a Single Data Model

The most important feature that object databases offer is that they support the same data model in both the programming language and the database. The notion of persistence is considered to be an extension of the programming language. Because object databases support a single data model, the impedance mismatch of a relational model does not exist here (see Figure 2.8).

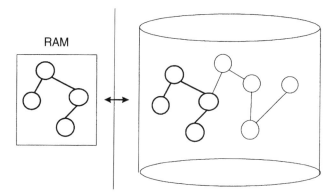

RAM

FIGURE 2.8 Object databases have no impedance mismatch. Object-oriented databases support a single data model on both the database side and programming language side, so there is no impedance mismatch between the objects stored in memory and those stored in the database.

2.10.2   The ODMG Standard

One fundamental requirement for a technology to become widely accepted is the presence of standards. Luckily, the Object Database Management System (ODBMS) community realized this early on, and the major vendors of object databases formed the Object Data Management Group (ODMG). The ODMG is a commercial organization whose purpose it is to build a de facto standard for ODBMS through vendor cooperation. ODMG members hold over 90% of the ODBMS market. At the time of this writing, the voting members of the group are GemStone Systems, IBEX Computing, O2 Technology, Object Design, Objectivity, POET Software, UniSQL, and Versant Object Technology.

In 1993, the ODMG came out with a first release of an object database standard, ODMG-93 [ODMG93], that specified to what an ODBMS should conform. This standard is intended to play the same role for object databases that the SQL standard played for their relational counterparts. It consists of two important parts: an object model and a set of programming language bindings. The latest version of the standard is ODMG 2.0, which came out in 1997 [ODMG97]. Currently, programming language bindings are available for C++, Java, and Smalltalk.

2.10.3   Existing ODBMS Products

Several commercial object-oriented databases are available. They fall into two broad categories:

1. Those built around a relational database system such as Persistence, Ontos*Integrator, or NeXT EOF
2. The true ODBMSs such as ObjectStore, VERSANT, and POET

Both categories have advantages and disadvantages. Those built around a relational technology have the advantage of being able to cooperate with many existing products, thus allowing for a smooth migration path. Furthermore, they are based on a stable and well-accepted technology. This can be a great comfort when choosing a database system that will play a key role in an entire company.

True ODBMSs, on the other hand, have the advantage of being many times more efficient when modeling complex relations. In relational systems, these relations are implemented as joins between tables, and when tables are too deeply nested, performance is dramatically reduced. Thus true ODBMSs are especially well suited for storing the data of complex applications such as CAD systems and office automation systems.

A popular alternative to ODBMSs are object-oriented wrappers of relational database systems. One such example is RogueWave's DBtools.h++, which offers a C++ wrapper to SQL-based relational databases. Many traditional relational database vendors are also adding object-oriented extensions to their products.

2.11   Preserving Openness

More and more, the software community is moving to open systems. Software is becoming distributed over multiple platforms, and different software products are working together. An example of this tendency is software built using Microsoft's COM and OLE architectures. Different products, often from different vendors, are integrated into one software package. This movement toward openness is apparent in the database community too. Just look at report writers, which often are third-party products, or at ODBC and JDBC, which offer database independence.

For us to use object-oriented database technologies, it is important that we preserve this recently won openness. But preserving openness is still a problem with many ODBMS products. They are sometimes hard to integrate in the existing world. This is because the (software) world in which we live does not yet know that those products exist, and consequently it has not yet provided any hooks for them. Thus we have to adopt a different approach: If the mountain will not come to Mahomet, Mahomet must go to the mountain. That is, since the world does not know yet that we exist, we have to appear to the world like something it does know: a relational database, for example. We have to do this, of course, without losing the advantages of the new technology.

As a matter of fact, this approach fits perfectly well in the object-oriented philosophy. That is, hide all implementation aspects of a product and make the product accessible only by means of a well-defined interface. One implementation aspect of this is the technology in which our software is written. The outside world has little interest in whether this technology is state-of-the-art object orientation or good old COBOL. It just wants to use it, and in a way that it understands.

Of course, when *implementing* this product, we are very much interested in which technology is used. The point here is that the technology is of interest only to the team implementing it and not to the outside world (as long as the product behaves correctly, of course). This philosophy also will allow us to integrate our new software with existing products.

2.12 Summary

This chapter gave an overview of today's database world. It looked briefly at the main concepts of relational databases. It also introduced the client/server model and looked at its application in distributed information systems. Also covered were the main problems with traditional database systems—impedance mismatch and schema changes—and how to guard against them, by obtaining a conceptual separation between the application and the database system.

Also discussed were object database systems and their main benefits; that is, they provide a single data model for persistent and transient objects. Finally, this chapter stressed the importance of designing open systems.

Chapter 3

An Object-Oriented View
on Database Applications

Many of today's applications are labeled "database applications." These kinds of applications are often treated differently from other software applications. Usually the database is considered to be the central and most important element in the design of database applications. This chapter examines the central and all-important role that the database plays in business software design and examines whether it can justifiably play that role.

3.1 Data-Driven Software Design

A popular approach to mastering software complexity, or at least to assisting Rapid Application Development (RAD), is offered by 4GL tools. Most of these tools allow the designer to specify both the GUI and the database layout (in the form of an entity-relationship diagram, for example).

The first step in application design is often the creation of a user interface. Next, the database schema is designed. The user interface is then mapped onto the database by attaching the necessary statements in a query language, such as SQL, to the user interface forms. Thus a program becomes merely a collection of screens with some attached code (see Figure 3.1).

Although this approach leads to rapid development times and easy programming, it also tends to lead to unstable solutions. This is because the user interface and database layout are completely interwoven (see Figure 3.2). The slightest change in, for example, the database layout may have potentially drastic consequences on the code attached to the user interface forms. Changes to the user interface or additions to the program requirements can require a redesign of the database tables. This redesign may affect the user interface, which, in turn, may seriously affect the programmer's sanity.

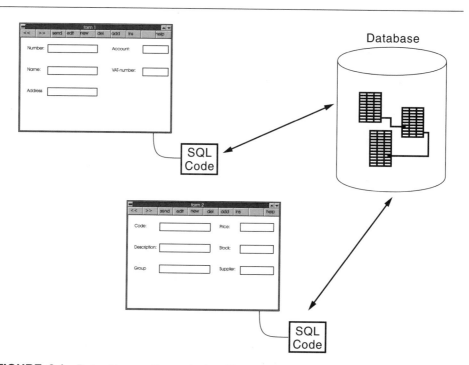

FIGURE 3.1   Data-driven software design. Many applications are designed as a collection of user interface forms with some SQL code attached to them. Because this approach depends heavily on the database layout, it can lead to programs that are very difficult to maintain.

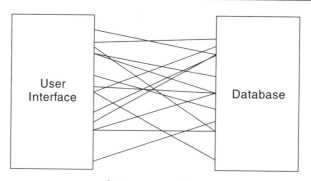

Interconnections

FIGURE 3.2   Data-driven programming. Direct mapping of the user interface on the database layout results in a web of interconnections. Every change in the database layout can result in drastic changes in the application code.

An example of data-driven software design is the following typical 4GL program fragment taken from a large 4GL application:

```
ON CHOOSE OF BUTTON-DELETE IN FRAME FRAME-A
DO:
  DEFINE VARIABLE tmp-logical AS LOGICAL.

  IF BROWSE:NUM-SELECTED-ROWS = 0 THEN
    MESSAGE "Select a category first"
        VIEW-AS ALERT-BOX INFORMATION BUTTONS OK.
  ELSE
    DO:
      tmp-logical = BROWSE:SELECT-FOCUSED-ROW().
      MESSAGE "are you sure you want to delete" CATEGORY.CAT_CODE
        VIEW-AS ALERT-BOX QUESTION BUTTONS YES-NO
        TITLE " " UPDATE choice AS LOGICAL.

    IF choice = TRUE THEN
      DO:
        DELETE CATEGORY
        {&OPEN-BROWSERS-IN-QUERY-FRAME-A}
      END.
    END.
END.



ON CHOOSE OF BUTTON-OK IN FRAME DIALOG-CANIAD
DO:
  IF CATEGORY.CAT_CODE:SCREEN-VALUE <> " "
  AND CAT_NAME:SCREEN-VALUE <> " " THEN
    DO:
    CREATE CATEGORY.
    ASSIGN CAT_CODE.
    ASSIGN CAT_NAME.
    changed = TRUE.
    APPLY "GO" TO FRAME {&FRAME-NAME}.
  END.
    ELSE
      DO:
        MESSAGE "You must enter a category (code & name)"
                VIEW-AS ALERT-BOX INFORMATION BUTTONS OK.
      END.
END.
```

(1)

```
ON CHOOSE OF BUTTON-NEXT
DO:
  DEFINE VARIABLE age AS INTEGER FORMAT "99"
  VIEW-AS FILL-IN SIZE 42 BY 1.                              (2)
  FIND NEXT customer USE-INDEX cust_name.
  RUN convert_bdate_to_age(INPUT customer.birth_date, OUTPUT age).
  DISPLAY customer.name age.                                 (3)
END.



ON CHOOSE OF BUTTON-NEW-CUSTOMER
DO:
  CREATE customer.
  UPDATE customer.name customer.birth_Date.                 (4)
END.
```

In this sample program fragment, the user interface code and the database layout are tightly interwoven. In (1), there is even a direct mapping of the input fields of the dialog box onto the database fields. In (2), the variable age is declared, and a display format is attached to it. The situation is even worse with the database field name of the customer table, which has been assigned a display format on the database level. Issuing the display command in (3) results in customer.name and age being displayed using formatting information stored in either the database table (name) or directly connected to the memory variable (age). The update command in (4) displays the database fields customer.name and customer.birth_Date on the screen, allows the user to modify them, and writes them back to the database. Thus the user interface comes in direct contact with the database layout. However, since both the database layout and user interface can change often, this approach can never result in a stable and robust program.

3.2 Supporting Multiple Applications

Often the situation is even worse than that pictured in Figure 3.2. In many organizations, several applications have to operate on the same database. When traditional data-driven design techniques are used, several applications may thus become interwoven with the database (see Figure 3.3).

When a new application is added, changes to the database schema are often required. These consist partly of adding new tables to support functionality that is specific to the new application. These types of changes normally do not influence the other applications. However, adding the new application may also result in having to modify the existing database layout—for example, for reasons of efficiency or to maintain consistency. These types of changes can often have drastic consequences, forcing a rewrite of all applications that depend on the database.

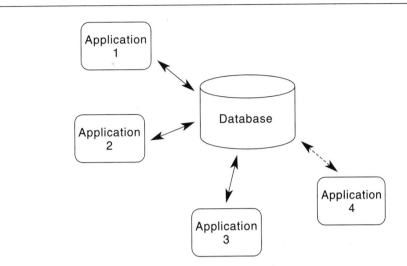

FIGURE 3.3 Supporting multiple applications. Adding a new application (*dotted line*) to the database often requires changes to the database schema. These changes may result in having to modify all of the other applications that operate on that database.

3.3 Object-Oriented Software Design

The main problem with the approach described in the previous section is that the resulting design relies solely on *operational* information as it is observed in the *application domain*. The entire design is centered around the question, "How is an application developed?" In other words, "What are the user's wishes, and how can a program be written to meet those wishes?" However, such an approach tends to lead to programs that are too application-specific and that are not robust enough to survive changes in application requirements. Indeed, these inevitable changes often require a redesign of large parts of the application.

In contrast, the approach offered by object-oriented methodologies concerns the *problem domain* (business domain). This time, the question to start with is, "How do we best model our *business?*" In other words, "What are the business entities and business processes?" This model should be independent of the application and user interface to be designed. By modeling the business, you get a framework that is relatively stable, since the business domain (the way people work, what they do in the business) is less likely to change. Indeed, you may want to migrate to a new and more efficient database system or use a fancier user interface technology. However, people are generally much less willing to drastically change the way they operate their business.

Only when you have designed a good business model (which can result in a set of C++ classes, for example) should you pose the next question: "How do I use these entities to build my application?" This task now not only is much simpler than when you start from scratch; it also allows reuse. The application can be built using an existing set of business components, which may be developed in-house, but which also could be shared

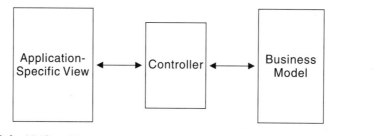

FIGURE 3.4 MVC architecture.

with other businesses. Indeed, although the actual applications that companies want to use may differ considerably, the entities that most companies use are similar.

It is at this stage that you start to design the user interface. You then map this interface onto your business model. The corresponding mapping code can be regarded as a controller that projects a certain application-specific view (defined by the user interface) onto the business model. This kind of architecture is often called a model-view-controller (MVC) architecture and is popular in the Smalltalk world (see Figure 3.4).

Since an object-oriented design is started from the relatively stable business model and only the (relatively small) user interface and controller are application-specific, the final programs will be many times more robust, thereby providing some protection against changes in the application domain.

In contrast, most applications designed around 4GLs implement only views. (Note that this is not a criticism of 4GL systems, but rather of how they are used.) Since both the database layout and the user interface represent a view in the MVC architecture, RAD approaches thus actually call for the design of applications by mapping two views onto each other. A fundamental characteristic of a view is that it often can change, so this approach can never result in stable and robust programs.

3.4 The Object Model

It is beyond the scope of this book to be a tutorial on object-oriented programming. However, it might be of interest to look at the basic principles of the object model. Several (similar) definitions of this model have been proposed. To standardize the concepts concerning object orientation, the Object Management Group (OMG), which was discussed in Chapter 2, was created [Siegel94]. This group came up with its own version of the object model.

Booch, for example, defines the object model as consisting of four fundamental components: abstraction, encapsulation, modularity, and hierarchy. He defines these as follows [Booch94]:

> **Abstraction** "An abstraction denotes the essential characteristics of an object that distinguish it from all other kinds of objects and thus provide crisply defined conceptual boundaries, relative to the perspective of the viewer."

Encapsulation "Encapsulation is the process of compartmentalizing the elements of an abstraction that constitute its structure and behavior; encapsulation serves to separate the contractual interface of an abstraction and its implementation."

Modularity "Modularity is the property of a system that has been decomposed into a set of cohesive and loosely coupled modules."

Hierarchy "Hierarchy is a ranking or ordering of abstractions."

Abstraction and encapsulation are the most important components and offer two of the greatest benefits of the object-oriented paradigm. Using them, you can offer to the outside world a view of an object that presents only its essential behavior and characteristics, independent of its implementation. This contrasts with more classical programming paradigms, where behavior and implementation are interwoven, and the software programmer must know (and even worse, understand) many of the implementation details in order to use data structures and their associated behavior. This separation of behavior and implementation guarantees that you will be able to use the objects without having to worry about inevitable changes to the internals of these objects. This, is turn, will lead to much more robust programs.

Inheritance allows developers to derive more-specific objects from general ones. Behavior that is common for a range of different objects can be implemented once. Each different class of objects can add specific behavior by subclassing from that base object. The derived class does not need to know or understand the internal workings of the base class.

Although object orientation opens the way to reuse, it also has been the topic of much debate. If object orientation is so wonderful, why then are so few high-level class libraries available? Reuse is examined more closely in Section 3.8. That section shows that reuse can be significantly improved by separating the objects to be reused from all database and user interface aspects.

An alternative but similar approach is to define an object as an abstraction of an entity, seen from a certain point of view [Hoffman95]. An object has the following characteristics: structure, behavior, identity, and state.

The *structure* of an object has to do with the internals of the object, while its *behavior* reflects how it reacts to external stimuli. Each object has an *identity,* which uniquely identifies it. Objects with the same structure and behavior are grouped in a class. A class thus can be regarded as a data type, while an object is an instance of that data type.

Each object resides in one of a number of *states,* each of which is consistent with the behavior of that object. The state of an object can be modified only by a number of predefined actions (methods). Any action can fail, in which case, it communicates the reason for failure. Methods should be the only means of access to an object. A method that changes the state of an object is responsible for ensuring the integrity of the new state. Even if an action fails, the object must never be left in an inconsistent state. Methods can be seen as transactions on objects.

3.5 Example: Student Administration

As an example, consider the student database of the University of Ghent. Several applications are working on this database, each having a limited view on the database. Figure 3.5

illustrates this. Two of these are the curriculum application, which deals with the academic issues of students (such as the courses they take and their exam results), and the administrative application, which maintains student administrative data, such as address, study program(s) enrolled in, and financial status.

Following is a short description of the administrative and academic applications [Hoffman95]. The text in italics represents changes that had to be made to the original applications because of a recent change in the law.

- **Administrative Application**

  A student is a person of a certain nationality. A person becomes a student by enrolling for one or more years in a study program. To enroll, the student has to present certain documents and fulfill certain requirements. The student also must pay a tuition fee, the amount of which depends on the student's social background and the chosen study program. A student normally repeats enrollment until all years of the chosen study program have been successfully completed. Reenrollment can be refused if a student repeatedly fails a year of study. Depending on the study program and the status of the student, *but also on whether that student finished the entire year of study, the university can receive a subsidy from the government for this student.*

- **Academic Application**

  A student follows a curriculum, which consists of a number of tasks. A task can be, for example, taking a certain course, writing a thesis, or practicing teaching. Certain tasks can be obligatory, while other tasks can be chosen by the student out of a number of possibilities. A student successfully finishes a year of study if he or she passes each exam and gets a certain overall result. Upon completion of all years of a study program, the student receives a diploma *and a diploma supplement that describes in detail each task the student has chosen.*

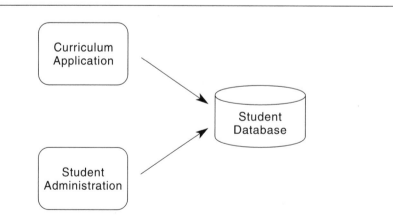

FIGURE 3.5 Student database. Several applications have to work on the same student database. Each application has only a limited view on the database.

3.5.1 Challenges

The changes in the business rules resulted in the original applications' having to be rewritten. The rewrite was required primarily because of two reasons:

1. The database schema and the user interface aspects were too tightly coupled to allow for further extensions to the application.
2. The business logic was scattered all over the application.

Avoiding such rewrites in the future required that the design of the new software system be able to cope with several potential problems, which were of both an organizational and technical nature:

- The business logic is rather complex and well understood by only a few people.
- This knowledge must be transferred every time the development team changes.
- If the business rules change, several applications must be modified.
- The database schema is complex and may require regular changes.
- Since users want to be able to employ the latest technologies, the application must be as open as possible to future technologies.
- The user interface technology or database system may change during the lifetime of the application.

A first step in meeting these challenges was to group all business logic in a separate business model. This model consisted of business processes and business objects, as explained next.

3.5.2 Business Processes and Business Objects

A **business process** is a (sub)action that implements an element of the application. The business processes of the administrative and academic applications include the following:

- Enrolling a student
- Specifying the individual curriculum of the student
- Determining whether the student passes his or her year of study
- Specifying all possible curricula
- Managing the student's financial aspects

Business processes are implemented by the **business model.** The business model defines the business objects. A **business object** is an abstraction of a participant in a business process. Examples of business objects in the student application are the following:

- Student
- Enrollment
- Curriculum
- Study program
- Course

In a good object-oriented design, these business processes and business objects are implemented independently of all user interface and database considerations. In other words, the business model reflects the way that the university works. Changes to the business rules stay confined to the business model and thus do not affect the applications working on it. This approach solves also the problem of managing and transferring the business knowledge, since all business rules are now implemented in one central model instead of being scattered all over the applications. Not only are the applications more maintainable; it also is easier to include new members in the development team. New team members can start out by working on the user interface aspects, for which very limited business knowledge is required. Once they become more acquainted with the software system, they can help maintain the business model.

3.6 Business Models and Supporting Multiple Applications

Section 3.2 warned against the dangers that arise when multiple applications have to work on the same database. In a business model-driven design, when a new application is added to the database, the business model likely will have to be extended to include functionality specific to that new application. Furthermore, just as in the RAD approach, the new application also may require changes to the database layout.

The changes in the database layout will require rewriting parts of the business model to accommodate these schema changes. However, since a fundamental property of the business model is that its public interface remains unchanged, modifications to this model will not affect the applications operating on it. Furthermore, because the business model is the only contact with the database, changes in the database layout will affect only the business model and will have no effect on the rest of the software (see Figure 3.6).

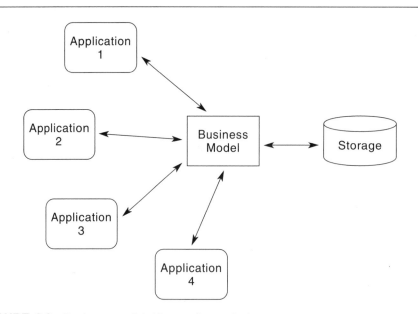

FIGURE 3.6 Business model-driven software design.

Although significant improvement in the extensibility of the software has already been obtained, adapting the business model to support the schema changes can still require a lot of effort. Thus a software architecture is needed that will make the business model largely independent of the database layout. A possible architecture to achieve this independence is presented in Part Two of this book.

3.7   C++, Java, or Smalltalk: The Ultimate Answer?

The problem sketched in the previous section is not limited to 4GL approaches. Many C++ and Smalltalk applications also suffer from it. The web architecture of Figure 3.2 has nothing to do with the choice of the programming language; rather, it concerns the overall view on software design. Figure 3.2 is the result of a view that is data-driven, while the approach advocated by object-oriented techniques is business model-driven.

Object orientation certainly has proven to be a very good marketing tool. Similar to the 1980s, when everything contained artificial intelligence, in the 1990s every self-respecting product has the label "object-oriented" attached to it. However, as the often-heard expression "I develop object-oriented because I program in C++" illustrates, many people still do not fully grasp the real meaning of object orientation. Programming in C++ does not guarantee that one is working in an object-oriented fashion. Many C programmers are now calling themselves C++ programmers, even though they have not changed their programming style. Even using C++ along with all of its latest additions (such as templates, exceptions, and the STL) is, in itself, not sufficient to guarantee a maintainable software architecture. True object-oriented client/server software is more than designing an object-oriented user interface that makes the necessary calls to the database. If you do not design your software using a business-model architecture, you will never get robust applications.

Object orientation is a philosophy. It is not limited to programming languages. Object-oriented languages such as Java, C++, and Smalltalk are just tools that are well suited to *implement* this philosophy. Whenever you develop a program, however, you must extend this philosophy over the borders of the programming language. Object orientation is a principle that has to be applied to the *entire* development process. It should include all aspects of program design, even those not directly supported by the programming language (such as the data storage). In other words, you always need to reason from an object-oriented point of view rather than from a language point of view.

3.7.1   Example: Functions in C++

Consider classes and objects in C++. Because classes are one of the key concepts of C++, there is a tendency among many programmers to implement just about everything by using classes. Where previously a function was used, now an object is used instead. Of course, many times this is indeed a legitimate thing to do. But consider a function that implements a program's main menu. In the old C days, this function might look as follows:

```
int dispatch_menu_choice(int n)
{
  switch(n)
    {
    case 1 : return work_with_customers();
    case 2 : return work_with_suppliers();
    case 3 : return enter_invoices();
    default: return 0;
    }
}
```

This function would typically be contained in a file *mainmenu.c,* while each of the functions called would be contained in their own files *customer.c, supplier.c,* and *invoice.c.* Each of these files might then contain a function of this form:

```
File customer.c:

int work_with_customers()
{
  Customer cust;
  cust.work_with();
}
```

However, in an object-oriented approach using C++, one might be tempted to write the following code:

```
File mainmenu.cpp:

int dispatch_menu_choice(int n)
{
  switch(n)
    {
    case 1:
      {
      Customer cust;
      return cust.work_with();
      }
```

```
case 2:
  {
  Supplier supp;
  return supp.work_with();
  }
case 3:
  {
  Invoice invoice;
  return invoice.enter();
  }
default: return 0;
  }
}
```

Although it may not look it, this second implementation is very different from the first one. More surprising, this is not object-oriented at all, even though from a C++ point of view it might be considered to be. On the contrary, it sins against one of the fundamentals of object orientation: information hiding and encapsulation. Here's how.

In the first implementation, the menu-dispatching function has no knowledge of the inner workings of the customer part of the program. When the file *mainmenu.c* is compiled, you do not even know that the function work_with_customers() actually exists. It is not until all compiled files are linked together that the link is made between dispatch_menu_choice() and work_with_customers() (thus between *customer.c* and *mainmenu.c*). Altering something on the data structures (classes) contained in *customer.c* has no influence on *mainmenu.c*.

The second (so-called object-oriented) implementation tells a completely different story. The dispatching function this time uses an instance of the Customer class, so it will need to include the class definition. The same goes for suppliers and invoices. This means *mainmenu.cpp* will start with something like this:

```
#include "customer.h"
#include "supplier.h"
#include "invoice.h"
```

However, changing the class definition of, say, the Customer class will now affect *mainmenu.cpp,* which will have to be recompiled. *Mainmenu.cpp* is directly dependent on the layout (and indirectly on the implementation) of Customer.

This interwoven file structure produces serious consequences. The need for recompilation might result in high compile times. It also will be more difficult to use dynamic link libraries (DLLs). It will not be possible to change just the customer DLL in order to add the new functionality, since the main file will also have to be recompiled. In essence, the binding mechanism has been transferred from link time to compile time.

The real problem is that we have *broken the rule of information hiding:* The definition of the `Customer` class is the private part *of the module* (which can consist of multiple files) dealing with customers. The menu-dispatching function does not have to deal with customers; it just has to execute the `Customer::work_with()` member function. This means it should do this through the public part of the customer module, which is the (global) function `work_with_customers()`.

As illustrated in this example, such an approach is no longer just a C++ view of object orientation. This example extends the principle of object orientation to include the compilation of C++ files themselves. A good discussion on *physical software design* is in [Lakos96].

3.8   Building Reusable Software

When people are asked about the benefits of object orientation, they often cite its reusability. Indeed, the concepts of inheritance and genericity (templates) allow developers to build specialized objects from generic ones. One would then also expect to find a wide range of available class libraries on the market—and indeed, every day new libraries appear. However, closer examination reveals that most of these focus mainly on two domains: user interface design and low-level classes such as containers, sets, and strings.

Although object orientation is perfectly suited for reusability, it is very hard to find a class `Customer`, `Invoice`, or `Employee`. However, it is just these kinds of classes that can greatly speed up the software development process and help to make programs more robust.

One reason that so few high-level classes are available is that classes such as `Invoice` need to contain much more knowledge than do simple classes such as `String`. However, it is not just the fact that these classes are more complicated that makes them harder to reuse. They are harder to reuse primarily because they are much more diverse and often depend on the database system and user interface.

The functionality of a class `String` is relatively straightforward. Strings are simple data types; they do not differ much from built-in types such as `int` and `double`. The same applies to container classes, sets, and even classes that represent currency. These could be regarded as low-level building blocks. These blocks are used to construct more-intelligent[1] classes (business objects) such as a customer, stock, or invoice.

A fundamental property of these higher-level classes is that the end user comes in direct contact with them. Customers can be entered, edited, and so on. A second important property is that the classes must be able to be stored in a database. Indeed, it would not make sense to spend a whole day entering invoices and at the end of the day to turn off the computer without saving them first.

It is just these user interface and database considerations that make the reuse of business objects so difficult. Strings, on the other hand, are mainly used for in-memory operations. Storing them to disk, if needed, is simple. Their functionality is restricted to the middle rectangle in Figure 3.7. As for user interface class libraries, these are just (often

---

1. *BEWARE:* "Intelligent" as used here does not mean that the low-level classes are easier to construct. Rather, it is used to express that the higher-level classes can be thought of as having a life of their own.

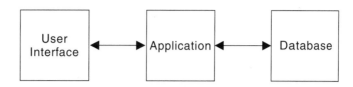

FIGURE 3.7 Applications consist of three main parts: the user interface, the actual application, and the data storage part.

intelligently designed) wrappers of the GUI-API. Their functionality restricts itself to the user interface aspects of a program and thus to the left rectangle in Figure 3.7.

Objects such as `Customer` or `Invoice`, on the other hand, play a part in each of the three parts of the application shown in Figure 3.7. Although customers play their main role in the application part, they also must be edited and displayed on the screen and must be written to and read from the database.

The choices in database and database technology can be very diverse. Possible choices for database technologies include network databases, relational systems, object databases, and flat-file systems. Within a single technology, you can choose from among many products. In a relational technology, for example, the choices include Oracle, Informix, DB2, Sybase, Ingres, and MS-Access. Each of these database technologies has its own specific approach, and each of the database systems within a technology has its own implementation of an API.

The same line of reasoning can be applied to user interface design. Here, too, you can choose from among many platforms, including Motif, OS/2, Windows, and DOS. Furthermore, for each platform several frameworks exist that can be used for developing the user interface.

Clearly, these considerations limit the design of reusable software. Where classes such as `String` have a huge market, a `Customer` class can be sold only to those people who share your database and user interface. And what if you use business objects from two different vendors? Although the objects may both be written for the same GUI platform, they might (and probably will) use different GUI libraries, thus complicating their otherwise easy integration in your application.

On the other hand, one could argue that a `Customer` object for a bank and a `Customer` object for a grocery shop are not fundamentally different, even though they will be stored into two very different databases. Both have an id, a name, an address, and so on. The application-specific attributes can easily be added by using inheritance or layering.

Some companies have implemented the concept of object orientation successfully and have developed reusable libraries of business objects. However, these libraries are almost always too business-specific to be distributed on a large scale and are thus used only in-house.

For business objects to succeed widely, a large enough market for them must first be created. This goal can be achieved only by making the business objects independent of both the storage mechanism and the user interface. As a rule, you should strive to limit the scope or functionality of all objects you want to reuse to only one of the three application parts depicted in Figure 3.7.

3.9   Toward Open Client/Server Applications

In classical mainframe architectures, the three parts of an application shown in Figure 3.7 are completely interwoven. The application runs on the mainframe. One machine does all of the processing, and each workstation acts as a dumb terminal whose only task is to display output from the mainframe. No use is made of the processing power of the workstation. In a client/server architecture, on the other hand, each of the three parts of an application is implemented as a separate entity.

A first step in this direction has already been made by the classical client/server architectures as presented by many 4GLs. These environments offer a first separation between the application and the database. This separation is mainly on the hardware level; that is, the program and its data can be on separate machines. The program does not know where its data resides. However, from a conceptual point of view, the three parts of the application are still interwoven.

In a true client/server architecture, the three parts of an application are implemented as logical, separate components. The user interface and the application logic may still be linked within the same executable file, but they must be designed separately on a programming level.

3.10   Object Orientation and Client/Server Design

The client/server philosophy and that of object orientation have many similarities. Both the units in a client/server environment and the objects in the object model have complete and unique control over their own internals. The object (server) controls all access to a certain resource in a well-defined way. How this resource is maintained and interpreted is the sole responsibility of that server and is totally invisible to the outside world (the client) (this is an example of encapsulation). The client can access these internals only by communicating with the object through a well-defined interface.

This observation suggests that the most natural way to implement a client/server design is through object orientation. Indeed, implementing all program units (objects on a high level of abstraction) of the architecture in an object-oriented way puts the client/server model into the deepest layers of the software, thereby resulting in a consistent and uniform structure throughout the entire system [Stroustrup91].

3.11   User Interfaces

User interaction is an important factor to consider when designing applications. A common notion of a user interface is that it is something that pops up dialog boxes on the screen to display messages and to accept information from the user. In this kind of user interface, the user is considered to be a human being. However, the task of a user interface is to offer a user certain access to an application, that is, to the information maintained by the application. This user might be a human sitting in front of a terminal; however, it might

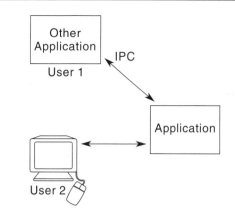

FIGURE 3.8   User interfaces. The most obvious kind of user of an application is a human sitting in front of a terminal. However, it could be another process using, for example, ActiveX, OLE, or an ORB to communicate with your application.

be another process (application) wanting to communicate with your application. Figure 3.8 illustrates this.

This kind of communication can be implemented through an interprocess communication (IPC) mechanism or with an ORB. Thus many different user interfaces (views) onto the same application are possible. This suggests that the user interface should not be an integral part of the application. Rather, it should be constructed to be as independent as possible from the application. From a client/server point of view, an application should have a client/server architecture, with the server being the application and the client being the user interface.

This line of reasoning immediately raises the question of what to put in the user interface part and what to put in the application part of the program. It is not always clear where exactly to draw the line. This topic is revisited in Chapter 12.

3.12   Analogy between User Interfaces and Databases

A significant analogy exists between user interfaces and databases. All that the database really does is what a normal user interface does: give information to the application and accept information from the application. The interface stores this information by putting it on the screen, while the database stores it to the disk. The interface gets its information by reading from the keyboard, while the database gets its from the disk.

Both the database and the user interface are projections of the information that is present in a system and in a certain format (the database schema, the various dialog boxes) that can be restored later. Other formats to represent this information are possible. Both the user interface and the database are thus views on the information stored in the business model.

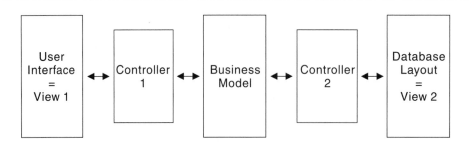

FIGURE 3.9 Analogy between user interface and database. Both the user interface and the database can be regarded as views on the business model. They both serve in presenting (storing) the information contained in the model.

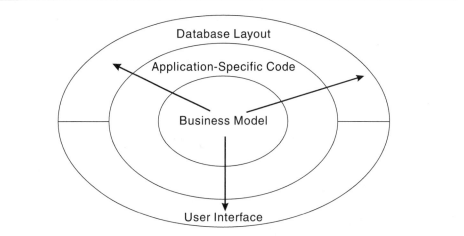

FIGURE 3.10 Designing applications "from the middle out." Object-oriented program development starts when you define an application-independent business model and use this model to build your application. You do this by writing application-specific code that maps the business model onto the user interface.

Because the database is a view onto the business model, the program should be independent from the database. It also must be independent from the database layout. Figure 3.9 illustrates this from the MVC perspective.

In applications designed using such an architecture, database layout and user interface become less dependent on one another. Furthermore, changes in either have only minor effects on the main portion of the program code, which is the business model. Thus, using this methodology, you start developing applications "from the middle out" (see Figure 3.10), where the middle is a stable and robust business model.

The MVC architecture and the analogy between user interfaces and storage suggest that what applies to the storage controller can also be applied to user interfaces. Chapter 11 presents an example of such a user interface controller.

3.13 Object-Oriented or Relational?

The choice between object databases and relational systems is much debated. In many articles, usually one of these options is portrayed as embodying all that is good and wholesome, while the other is portrayed as its evil twin. However, as most people in the software business can attest, life is seldom cut-and-dried. (By the way, the same discussion has been going on for years regarding 4GLs; that is, should we use them or not?)

The answer is simple: Use the best tool for the job at hand. Object-oriented databases offer some advantages over their relational counterparts. They are very efficient for storing complex objects, such as those encountered in CAD applications. Storing these objects in a relational database would require many joins between different tables and thus be very inefficient.

However, in a data-processing application, such as an accounting program, there is no reason not to use a relational approach. Doing so would enable you to take advantage of the hundreds of relational tools (for example, report writers and query tools). Furthermore, people feel more comfortable using a technology that has proven its merits than using a promising new technology with which few have had experience.

Saying that "object databases are more suited for *implementing* applications that . . ." gives the impression that it is the database that plays the central role in the design of an application. However, object-oriented databases must not be confused with object-oriented *access* to data. The database is merely a storage medium that is implemented according to a certain technology. How to access the database, however, concerns not so much the database technology as it does how we look at the concept of databases (or rather persistence) in general.

An important advantage that object databases offer to the application developer is the absence of the impedance mismatch between the application and the persistent storage. However, this is not so much a property of the ODBMS as such, but of the object-oriented view it offers on the database. In this regard, the object database could be considered to consist of two parts. The first is the database technology itself. This part is responsible for the physical storage of the data. It also is responsible for the performance gain that object databases offer when complex relationships are stored. The second part is an impedance mismatch resolver (IM resolver), which maps the transient objects onto the physical database. In most other storage technologies (including relational databases), only the first part is present [Heinckiens95]. So from the application developer's point of view, you should concentrate on developing IM resolvers regardless of the database technology underneath. As a result, applications will be able to use the full benefit that object orientation has to offer without having to be committed to a single database system, technology, or even layout.

From the programmer's point of view, the database system is merely a building block with a well-defined interface. You should be able to substitute it at any time with another block, whether the block's contents are object-oriented or relational, without affecting the programs depending on it. The database system is a mechanism for making objects persistent—nothing more, nothing less. This approach not only will accommodate future technologies, but also will allow companies to continue to use legacy systems, thus protecting a huge investment and allowing for a smooth transition to modern technologies.

3.14   Persistence from a Different Angle

We still tend to divide everything too much into separate categories. When talking about database systems, we speak of relational databases, of object-oriented database management systems, of distributed databases. We speak of ORBs and of a variety of other systems that all more or less serve the same purpose: They offer access to certain information. From an object-oriented viewpoint, it is no longer important where or how this data is obtained—whether it comes from a local disk, from a disk on the other side of the world, or through communication (through OLE, for example) with another application. All that counts is that we get the data from some information provider.

From a programming language point of view, two kinds of objects can be distinguished: transient and persistent. A **transient object** is an object that loses its value when the process terminates. Typical examples are automatic variables—when the variable goes out of scope, it is destroyed, and its value is lost forever. A **persistent object** is an object whose value can be restored after a process has terminated. In traditional software design, making something persistent means storing it in a database. From an object-oriented viewpoint, however, the word "persistent" has a much broader meaning. It means something that does not get lost. Persistent data can be retrieved from a hard disk, it can be recalculated every time it is needed, or it can be accessed in some other way, such as through the interrogation of a cooperating process. However, you must try to make all of this transparent to programmers. All they need to know is that they are working with persistent objects.

3.15   Persistence and Separation of Concerns

The principle of separation of concerns leads to an elegant view of persistence:

> The data in every process itself can be transient. However, toward *that* process, the data in all other processes should be considered as being persistent.

Of course, the data in each of those other processes can also be transient. However, to their clients, these processes must appear as if they contain only persistent data. Thus it becomes the task of each individual process to take care of all of its own persistence issues.

An example will clarify matters a bit. Imagine a director and her assistant. The director gets a phone call concerning the date for an important meeting. To remember this appointment, the director can do either of two things: Write the date in her calendar (make it persistent by writing it to her personal database) or call her assistant and ask him to remind her of the appointment (make it persistent by "storing" it in some other process). In the latter case, the director considers the appointment date is safely recorded and will not

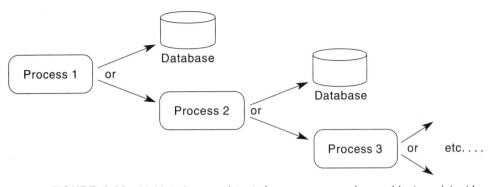

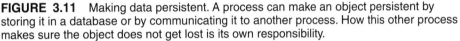

FIGURE 3.11 Making data persistent. A process can make an object persistent by storing it in a database or by communicating it to another process. How this other process makes sure the object does not get lost is its own responsibility.

be forgotten. How the assistant stores it is of no concern to her. The assistant, in turn, can choose to write the appointment down in a calendar or to ask someone else to remember it.

Of course, from a database point of view, the appointment is not persistent until it has actually been written to a database. As long as the information is given to some other process, it is still somewhere in transient memory. The point is that once the data has been given to another process, its storage becomes the responsibility of that other process. Hence, to the original process, the data has become persistent. Figure 3.11 illustrates how this works.

It is the responsibility of each process to make sure its data is made persistent. Such an approach considerably simplifies the job of data processing. Just as the director does not have to worry about the details of how her assistant does his job, programmers can deal with their own business without having to go into the details of data storage.

This principle can even be taken a step farther and be applied to individual objects:

> Although every object itself can be transient, toward that object, all other objects should be considered as being persistent. Each of these objects is responsible for its own persistence.

From this point of view, there is no longer any difference between transient and persistent objects. The difficulties imposed by the data storage problem are greatly reduced. Data storage has been encapsulated into the objects themselves and has become their responsibility alone.

When using objects, programmers no longer must be aware of which objects are attached to a database. It becomes as easy to use a `Customer` object (which is stored in a database) as it is to use an ordinary integer. When that object is assigned new information, it should take care of updating the database and handling all safety issues involved.

Thus transaction management is moved from the database domain to the programming language domain. As explained in Chapter 10, transaction management not only should work on the database tables, but because the database is reflected in memory objects, it also should cover those objects.

3.16   Safety Issues

Of course, the issues discussed in the previous section will immediately raise concerns about safety. How do you ensure the information is indeed stored correctly? This is the responsibility of the process accepting the data. Just as the director needs to be able to trust her assistant, you, too, should work only with processes (or objects) that you trust.

By encapsulating all of these safety issues into the objects, you get an additional advantage: Programmers do not need (and thus can never forget) to check safety requirements. Further, once you have tested an object enough to verify that it is safe, programmers never again have to worry about the tasks it performs. However, if you make the programmers using these objects responsible for persistence and safety issues, chances increase a lot that they will forget to check something or will introduce a programming error.

3.17   Summary

This chapter examined two main approaches to software design: data-centered and business model-centered. While data-centered design is situated in the application domain, business model-centered design is situated in the problem domain, thus leading to more stable software solutions.

Applications consist of three logical parts: the user interface, the business model, and the storage. The way to achieve truly open and reusable applications is to implement these as three independent entities that cooperate using a client/server architecture. The business model plays a central part in an object-oriented design. This model should be independent of all user interface and data storage considerations. It should contain the actual intelligence of the application.

There are different kinds of user interfaces. These include the normal user interfaces that interact with a human being (a GUI, for example), as well as the Common Gateway Interface (CGI), object linking and embedding (OLE), and IPC server facilities. To make your application as independent as possible from the user interface technology, you should try to obtain a conceptual separation between the two. The application has to act as a server to user interface requests.

There is a significant analogy between user interfaces and databases. In a MVC architecture, both the user interface and the database layout represent views on the model. The controller is responsible for providing the mapping of the view onto the model. This model should be independent of the views working on it. The independence between model and view also implies that the model (the actual application) should be independent of the database layout (and technology). This chapter showed that object persistence is the responsibility of the individual objects and that the concept of persistence must be viewed independently of persistence technology.

Object orientation is more than programming in C++ or Java. It is a philosophy that should be used in every aspect of the development process.

Part Two

An Architecture for Object Persistence

Chapter 4
Making Objects Persistent

This chapter gives an overview of the main issues involved in making objects persistent. It also looks at the basic requirements of an object-oriented persistence framework and examines some of the problems encountered when interfacing with a relational database.

4.1 Introduction

When using databases in programming languages, you can take either of two perspectives: database or programming language. With the database perspective, programmers commonly use embedded SQL in the programming language. This has a disadvantage, however, in that the programmer is, in fact, working in two different languages and will often have a lot of difficulty mapping them onto each other.

The more natural way to work is to take the programming language perspective and to consider the database system to be an extension of the programming language. With the programming language perspective, the programmer works with the *object* layout on the programming language level. Defining this layout is clearly the task of the programming team. The *database* layout, however, can be completely specified on the database level and can be designed by the database specialist, independent of the programming language. The database can, for example, be created using either SQL statements or specialized database design tools (starting from, for example, an entity-relationship, or E/R, diagram). The task of the persistence framework is to provide a mapping between those two layouts (or domains).

4.2   Basic Requirements of a Persistence Framework

The main goal of a persistence framework is to have a persistent storage mechanism that is independent of its environment and that is invisible to the application developer. When these goals are met, compatibility with existing systems will follow automatically.

To attain platform independence, you want to develop a universal interface with the outside world—that is, an abstract database class mapped onto the low-level database system that is used. This class will be the only link between the programmer and the database system and is illustrated in Figure 4.1.

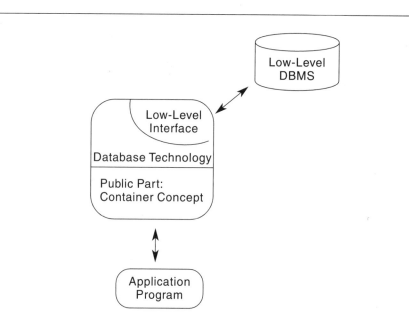

FIGURE 4.1   Hiding the database. An abstract database class hides the low-level DBMS from the application program.

4.3   Obtaining Scalability

Database systems range from simple and inexpensive to powerful and high-end. You want your applications to work with all of them, independently of the complexity of the underlying database management system.

One approach to accomplish this could be to adopt a least-common-divisor approach. That is, build a system that has only the capabilities that are common to all database systems. However, this would limit the capabilities of your system to those of the weakest system with which you want to be compatible. Fortunately, the database concept is hidden from programmers, so they cannot make any direct use of it. Hence, they need not bother about the strength of the database systems.

Alternatively, you could make the database abstraction layer responsible for making every implementation equally strong. This approach means that the implementation of the abstraction layer for a low-end system would be significantly more complex than for high-end systems. This is because the abstraction layer would have to implement all of the concepts that the big systems have but that the smaller systems lack.

On the other hand, it helps to be pragmatic. If a customer wants an application that needs to support hundreds of users at the same time and the customer has several strong requirements about fault tolerance and recovery, then you would not seriously consider using something like dBase or any other low-end product. Instead, you would go for some of the (much) more expensive products. Hence, it is of no use to include these advanced capabilities in the interface for low-end products, since they would not be used anyway. As long as all interfaces look the same, it is all right. In the low-end interfaces, the more advanced functions just contain some dummy functionality.

The important point is that the same class libraries can be used for both high- and low-end platforms. Thus the libraries you develop will be usable for a much larger market segment. This, in turn, will aid the availability of reusable business object libraries.

4.4   Interfacing with a Relational World: Problems to Conquer

A major use for a persistence layer is as an interface with relational databases. This section looks at some of the problems encountered when you are constructing an object-oriented interface that also must be compatible with relational systems.

If you want to apply the principles of object orientation to persistent data, keep the following characteristics in mind: inheritance, object identity, embedded objects, sets, and so on. And because you are dealing with a data storage system, you will need to address several topics from the relational database world: concurrency, transactions, queries, primary and foreign keys, and so on.

4.4.1   Mapping Relationships

In relational database design, four kinds of relationships can typically be distinguished: one-to-one, many-to-one, one-to-many, and many-to-many.

In *one-to-one* and *many-to-one* relationships, a column of a record points to a record (row) in another table or the same table. Figure 4.2 depicts this.

In relational terminology, table A is *joined* to table B. In object-oriented terminology, the same relationship is stated like this: An object of type A contains an object of type B. This latter relationship is depicted in Figure 4.3.

A join is implemented by storing in A the primary key of the corresponding row in B; that is, A contains a foreign key to B. From an object-oriented point of view, developers do

Table A

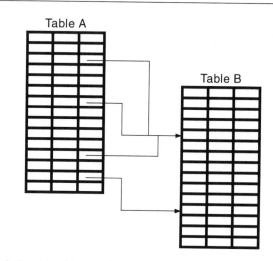

Table B

FIGURE 4.2   Relational implementation of the many-to-one relation. Multiple rows in table A (the "many" part) refer to the same row in table B (the "one" part).

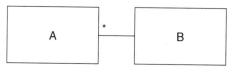

FIGURE 4.3   Many-to-one relationship in UML.

not worry about joins or about primary or foreign keys. An object of type A directly contains an object of type B. How this is physically implemented is the concern of the database system, not of the application developer.

This raises the question of referential integrity. That is, when a row in B that is referenced by A is removed, the database becomes inconsistent. Although many of the high-end database systems have automatic integrity support, you must not lose sight of integrity issues.

A third kind of relationship is *one-to-many,* illustrated in Figure 4.4. In this case, a column points to several rows in another (or the same) table, with each object in the other table referenced only once. This relationship is the reverse of the many-to-one relationship.

One way to implement this relationship is to have a column in the B table that contains the primary key of the record in A that references it. This is shown in Figure 4.5. Note that this table layout is the same as that in the many-to-one relationship, except that A and B are reversed. In object-oriented terminology, this relationship is phrased as "an object of type A contains a *set* of objects of type B." This kind of table layout is used to represent, for example, sets and lists.

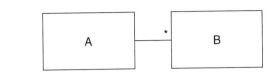

FIGURE 4.4 One-to-many relationship.

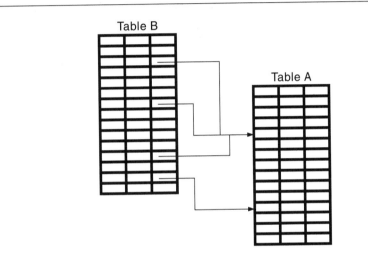

FIGURE 4.5 Relational implementation of the one-to-many relationship between table A and table B.

The fourth type of relationship is *many-to-many,* as shown in Figure 4.6. In this relationship, each row in A references multiple rows in B, while each row in B, in its turn, is referenced by multiple rows in A. A typical example of such a relationship is that between invoices and stock items. In this case, each invoice contains multiple items, while each stock item can be listed in several invoices.

This relationship is implemented by using a secondary table in which the links are maintained (see Figure 4.7). The link table InvoicedItems contains a column that points (a) to the row in the table Invoice that contains the set of invoiced stock items and (b) to the rows in Stock that are elements of the set in Invoice. It is important to note that from an object-oriented point of view, the tables Invoice and Stock differ from the table InvoicedItems. The tables Invoice and Stock could be regarded as representing objects of types Invoice and Stock. Table InvoicedItems, however, does not represent objects; rather, it represents a relationship between objects.

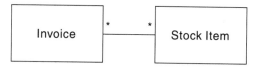

FIGURE 4.6   Many-to-many relationship.

INVOICE

InvoiceNumber	Customer	...
9512341	234	
9512342	434	
9512343	238	

INVOICED ITEMS

Invoice	StockItem
9512341	003
9512341	001
9512342	001
9512343	002

STOCK

ItemID	Name	...
001	Object Magazine	
002	C++ Report	
003	JOOP	

FIGURE 4.7   A many-to-many relationship is implemented in relational database systems using a secondary table (in this case, `InvoicedItems`) in which the links are maintained.

4.4.2   Mapping Inheritance

When you map objects to tables, you have to decide how to map an inheritance structure onto a relational database layout. This section describes three approaches for doing this.

One approach is to use one table for the base class and a separate table for each derived class that contains only the additional information needed to store this derived

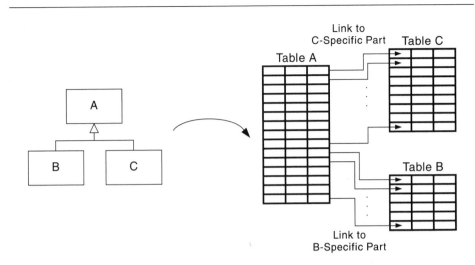

FIGURE 4.8   The most complete way to reflect an inheritance relation in a relational database is to construct a separate table for each class and then join them all together.

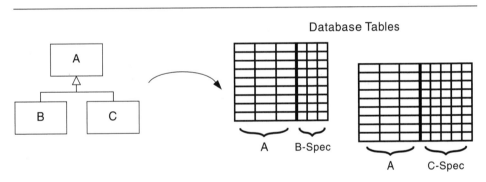
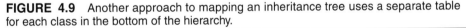

FIGURE 4.9   Another approach to mapping an inheritance tree uses a separate table for each class in the bottom of the hierarchy.

class (see Figure 4.8). This approach thus uses inheritance on both the programming language level and the database level. However, its drawback is that it introduces additional joins and can thus result in loss of efficiency.

A second approach is to use a single table for each class. This table contains all of the information for the class. This is illustrated in Figure 4.9. With this approach, you use inheritance only on the programming language level; on the database level, each object type (table) is considered to be unrelated. This implementation might present problems when polymorphism is needed on the database level (for end-user queries, for example), but it is useful when applying inheritance to allow reuse.

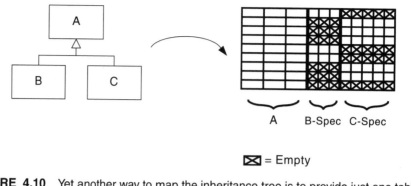

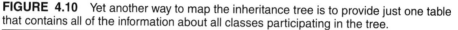

FIGURE 4.10   Yet another way to map the inheritance tree is to provide just one table that contains all of the information about all classes participating in the tree.

The third approach is to use only a single table that contains all of the information for all classes derived from the base class, as shown in Figure 4.10. The first series of columns contains all data corresponding to the base class. Each derived class has its own series of columns in the table. When a record is added to the table, the base class information and the columns corresponding to the derived class are filled in; all of the other columns are left blank. Although this approach is useful when polymorphism is needed on a database level, it uses space inefficiently. Furthermore, every time a new class is derived from the base class, the table must be modified.

Each of these methods is explored further in Chapter 8. There, you will see that the kind of mapping used depends on the reason for using inheritance. However, the mapping must be shielded from the application so that the program code is independent of this representation.

4.4.3   Concurrency Control and Transaction Management

Concurrency control and transaction management are two important topics in database design. They are not limited to purely database concepts. They can be applied throughout the entire development process, no matter whether you are dealing with transient or persistent objects.

An example is the GUI environment. Here, the user is largely in control of the navigation through the application. The user could decide to open multiple instances of the same dialog box. Or the user could start a certain transaction (by opening a corresponding dialog box), leave it half finished, and start another transaction that interferes with the first. To prevent complete chaos in such situations, you need to set up some kind of concurrency control. In a GUI, this control can be implemented by modal dialogs.

4.4.4 Performing Queries

Recall that a database can be looked at from two viewpoints: a programmer's and an end user's. When performing queries, the end user typically looks at the database from the second viewpoint, although this end user can also be the programmer designing a report. The main difference between programs and queries is that programs are created in advance and everything about them is known by the programmer, while queries are created and executed at runtime. Thus some kind of interpreter is needed to execute the query. Furthermore, when designing reports, the user not only needs the data; he or she also wants the report to be formatted nicely. Thus a report design tool becomes a complete application in itself. Indeed, there are many commercial reporting and querying tools available. Chapter 13 discusses how to incorporate these tools into your own applications.

4.5 Abstracting the Database

During application development, much time is spent discussing the database layout, since you have to determine the mapping of the data structures onto the native database fields. To do this mapping, you must consider several points, such as the data types of the database fields and their lengths, as well as how joins will be made between tables. Because the application will rely heavily on the decisions made in this phase, they are crucial for the rest of the design process.

This mapping problem is solved in object-oriented databases simply by extending the range of native database fields to include every object type one can create. The mapping is thus no longer your problem; instead; it is done automatically by the database system. In a relational system, this approach is not possible. A relational system supports only a fixed set of data types. Hence, this mapping must be implemented in the programming language domain.

One way for the programmer to abstract the relational technology is to use a preprocessor that maps the objects onto a relational structure. Most object-oriented databases built on top of a relational system use this approach. It has the advantage of being totally automatic. However, it also has some serious disadvantages. One is that it requires a preprocessor; this can lead to programs that are difficult to debug. Worse, however, it requires access to the source code. This requirement could pose difficulties if you want to be able to store third-party class libraries for which you do not have the source code.

Also, with automatic mapping, it often is difficult to use already existing database layouts, since doing so would force you to design the business model in such a way that the preprocessor maps it onto that specific database layout. You thus would have to reverse engineer the database layout to the business model. This approach seldom leads to optimal business models.

4.6   An Architecture for Object Persistence

The next few chapters examine some techniques for achieving object persistence. Those techniques are illustrated by looking at some of the concepts of Scoop. Scoop is a persistence architecture that is largely database-independent and database technology-independent. Here are the basic ideas behind it:

- Every object should be responsible for its own persistence capabilities.
- There should be no fundamental difference between persistent and transient objects.
- The impedance mismatch should not bother the object.
- Application programs should be independent of the persistence technology (relational, object-oriented, Web-based, CORBA, and so on).
- It should be possible to reuse third-party class libraries.
- Even when the database layout already exists, independently designing the business model should still be possible.

The main classes in Scoop are `PSet`, `DataSet`, and `IM_Resolver`. `PSet` offers object persistence; `DataSet` and `IM_Resolver` resolve the impedance mismatch.

4.6.1   Persistent Sets

A class `PSet` offers access to the database. It abstracts all operations that can be performed on databases. It is the only link between the application program and the underlying database management system. `PSet` can be considered a persistent container class. Its task is not only to abstract the database concept, but also to try to hide it altogether. A first step to achieving this goal is to let `PSet` take care of all routine tasks, such as selecting the right tables and selecting the right indexes.

4.6.2   Impedance Mismatch Resolvers

Recall that the mismatch between the representation of data in the programming language and data in the database is called the impedance mismatch. A closer examination of this mismatch shows that it exists on several levels. It thus might be more appropriate to speak of impedance mismatch*es*.

A comparison of objects and of records (rows) in a relational database reveals similarities. That is, an object corresponds to a record in a database table, while each of that object's attributes corresponds to a column of that database record. However, there is a fundamental difference between columns and attributes. Most relational database systems expect attributes to be one of a certain number of elementary data types (`string`, `numeric`, `boolean`, `date`, and so on). In contrast, in an object-oriented programming language, these attributes may be compound objects. It thus is not possible to have columns of, for example, type `picture`, `shape`, or `customer`.

Since you cannot directly store compound attributes in a database column, you have to map them onto columns of types that are supported by the database system. The memory objects thus must be disassembled into objects of native data types, using joins to other

Object Model   Database Layout

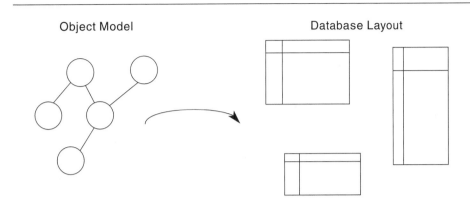
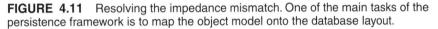

FIGURE 4.11   Resolving the impedance mismatch. One of the main tasks of the persistence framework is to map the object model onto the database layout.

tables if necessary (see Figure 4.11). This is the first impedance mismatch between the relational and the object model: the mismatch between *attributes* and *columns*.

The second impedance mismatch is the implementation difference between the object model and the database schema. This difference typically shows itself in inheritance relationships. For example, will you map a class and its parent class onto a single table or onto multiple tables? This mismatch is thus between *classes* and *tables*.

These impedance mismatches stand in sharp contrast with the prerequisite that it should be as easy to work with persistent objects as with transient ones. The mismatches can be resolved by using the classes IM_Resolver and DataSet.

The first impedance mismatch is resolved by attaching an IM_Resolver object to each of the object's attributes that specifies how that attribute must be mapped onto columns in the database. In other words, by using IM_Resolver objects, you can extend the number of available data types in the database. It is the associated IM_Resolver object that will contain all knowledge of how to store and retrieve objects of that data type. This is shown in Figure 4.12.

The class DataSet is used to resolve the mismatch between classes and tables. Each database table has a corresponding DataSet object. If an object is stored in multiple tables (as is often the case with inheritance relationships), this object will be connected to multiple instances of DataSet. By attaching the IM_Resolvers to the DataSet objects, you decide in which table(s) the attributes (columns) must be stored.

The interaction of the different DataSets and IM_Resolvers is coordinated by the class PSet, which appears to the outside world as a persistent container of objects. It thus allows the user to work with object sets instead of having to worry about tables, rows, and columns.

Thanks to the concept of IM resolvers, it is possible to *independently* design the object model and database layout and to make the application independent of the mapping of the one onto the other. This technique contrasts with many existing relational-based ODBMSs, which require the table layout to be generated from the object model. Although

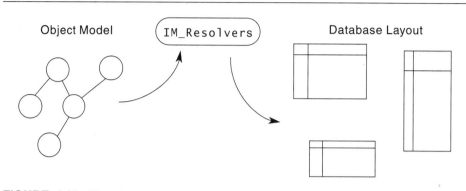

FIGURE 4.12   The class `IM_Resolver` is responsible for resolving the impedance mismatch between the object model and the table layout.

this approach most often leads to the optimal table layout, it is unusable in environments in which the database layout has already been designed and the application is thus required to use that database layout. Note that the current version of the ODMG standard also suffers from this problem.

4.7   Summary

This chapter used the Scoop architecture as an example of a controller that takes care of the mapping of the database layout onto the business model. This controller is responsible for resolving the impedance mismatch between the representation of objects in transient and persistent memories.

Scoop's main task is to abstract the database concept and provide database independence and scalability. The complete framework is designed around some closely cooperating classes. To the programmer, however, the entire system looks like a single class, `PSet`, which is a persistent container. Ordinary memory variables can be used to access the information contained in this persistent container. These variables are linked to the actual data through the use of objects derived from the `IM_Resolver` class.

The chapter gave special attention to some aspects of introducing object-oriented concepts in relational database systems. It also looked at the mapping of two kinds of relationships (associations and inheritance) onto relational database tables.

Chapter 5

Abstracting the Database

Chapter 4 outlined the basic requirements for a persistence framework. This chapter goes a step farther and examines some of the concepts involved in designing such a framework. It illustrates these concepts using Scoop. Its purpose is not to give a complete overview of the Scoop framework, but rather to use it to explain some techniques to achieve object persistence. The architecture introduced is largely technology-independent.

5.1 A Persistent Container Class

The central element of the persistence framework is the persistent container class PSet. PSet offers its clients a simple and consistent interface that is both platform- and database-independent. It encapsulates all calls to the database system, as well as the internals of the physical storage mechanism. Application developers who use the class become almost unaware that they are working with a database. The class takes care of all database operations transparently. It also handles all routine tasks such as allocating and deallocating SQL handles, opening and closing the database tables, selecting the right index tags, and so on. This class is now the only link between the programmers and the database (see Figure 5.1).

5.2 Basic Functionality of PSet

The services that PSet performs can be grouped into three categories:

1. Providing persistent container class services.
2. Assembling and disassembling the objects.
3. Hiding database concepts and automating routine tasks.

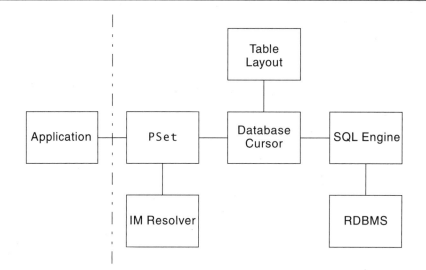

FIGURE 5.1   Hiding the database. Class PSet, which is a persistent container, is the only link between the programmer and the low-level database system. It abstracts both the database concept and technology. The PSet implementation sketched in this diagram uses a relational database technology.

The first task includes retrieving and storing objects, searching objects, deleting objects, and navigating through the container. The second task is to handle the impedance mismatch (IM). PSet has to make programs independent of how their data is stored in the database. In a relational system, this means that PSet hides all of the details concerning table layout, which has thus become the private part of the database. For the assembling and disassembling of the objects, PSet will rely on the IM resolvers DataSet and IM_Resolver. These are discussed further later in this chapter.

The third task is to automate the most routine tasks. These routine tasks often are what makes an application platform- and technology-dependent. Consider, for example, opening files or selecting indexes. In flat-file systems, these tasks are the responsibility of the programmer. In relational systems with an SQL interface, however, they are performed automatically. When the files must be opened explicitly, the open file limit must be taken into account; this limit may differ across platforms. Such issues tend to lead to applications that are platform- and technology-specific, thereby limiting both portability and scalability. By automating routine tasks, you go a long way toward hiding the database technology.

5.3 Implementing the Persistence Architecture

This section briefly describes an implementation of the persistence architecture on top of relational databases. In such an implementation, three layers can be distinguished, as shown in Table 5.1: low-level database, relational database, and object container.

5.3.1 Layer 1: Low-Level Database Layer

The low-level database layer consists of the API to the relational database. This API allows you to open and close databases , execute SQL statements, bind columns, open cursors, and so on. However, it is too low-level and too complicated to be used directly. It also is database-dependent. Further, as explained in Chapter 2, the choice of the interface heavily influences the application code that uses it.

Examples of such interfaces are ODBC, JDBC (Java), Sybase Open Client, and Informix CLI. Notice that although ODBC and JDBC are database system-independent, they still heavily influence programs that are written directly on top of them. For example, if the ODBC approach proved to be too slow and it thus became necessary to migrate the application code to the native database interface, practically the entire application would have to be rewritten.

TABLE 5.1 Layers of a Persistence Framework

	Layer 3: Object Container	*Layer 2: Relational Database*	*Layer 1: Low-Level Database*
Atoms	Objects	Rows and columns	Rows and columns
Classes	PSet IM_Resolver DataSet	DatabaseCursor Row Column Table SelectStatement InsertStatement UpdateStatement WhereClause	Low-level API SQL
Examples	Scoop	DBtools.h++	ODBC JDBC Sybase Open Client Informix CLI Codebase
Properties	Technology independent. Independent of database layout.	Dependent on relational technology. Dependent on database layout. Independent of relational database system.	Database system-dependent.

5.3.2   Layer 2: RDBMS Layer

The relational database layer consists of classes that encapsulate the low-level aspects of the relational technology. It is responsible for fetching records from the database and executing the necessary SQL statements. Among these classes is the class `Database-Cursor`, which abstracts the database table that contains the result set of an SQL select statement.

This layer contains functionality for updating, deleting, and inserting records in the database table. This functionality is implemented through classes `Table`, `Column`, `SelectStatement`, `UpdateStatement`, and so on. One can choose to build the classes of this layer oneself or to use one of the commercial relational database class libraries, for example RogueWave's DBtools.h++ [RogueWave96].

Layer 2 hides all low-level details and offers a relational database interface that is independent of the underlying relational database. This abstraction layer allows you to work with tables, rows, and columns.

However, this layer does not hide the relational technology or the database layout. Programs that are written directly on top of this layer are still too database-dependent. So it is important to have an additional layer that abstracts the database concepts and acts as a container of objects. It is this layer that the Scoop architecture offers.

5.3.3   Layer 3: Object Container Layer

A class `PSet` is responsible for resolving the impedance mismatch between the relational database tables and the memory objects. It does so by relying on the IM resolvers offered by the classes `DataSet` and `IM_Resolver`.

The object container layer offers to its users the notion of persistent sets. There is no longer an impedance mismatch between the persistent and transient objects. Furthermore, there is, to users, no fundamental difference between transient and persistent sets. The objects within a persistent set may come from the database. They also may come from the Web or from another process. The `PSet`s are thus independent of the persistence architecture.

A comparison of `PSet` with `DatabaseCursor` shows that `DatabaseCursor` operates on the record level, while `PSet` operates on the object level. Thus `DatabaseCursor` represents a relational database cursor, while `PSet` plays the role of an object cursor.

To store objects in the table, you must disassemble the objects within `PSet` to their equivalent representation in `DatabaseCursor`. So that you can assemble and disassemble aggregate objects, certain functions allow you to write and read elementary data types to and from database columns. These functions are members of `DatabaseCursor`, `Update-Statement`, and `SelectStatement` and are used by the IM resolvers.

A simplified version of the interface to class `PSet` is shown in Figure 5.2. The Appendix shows a sample implementation of this interface using the DBtools.h++ library.

```
class PSet {

  friend class DataSet;

protected:

  Container<DataSet*> setlist;

  Cursor cursor;
  SelectStatement selectstmt;
  Condition where_clause;

public:

  PSet();

  virtual int select();   // cursor points to first object
  virtual int read();     // resolve impedance mismatch
  virtual int next();
  virtual int append();
  virtual int write();
  virtual int erase();
  virtual int seek(Condition& crit);
  virtual void add_filter(Condition& crit);

  // etc...

};
```

FIGURE 5.2 Simplified class definition of PSet.

5.4 Resolving the Impedance Mismatch

A fundamental persistency issue is how to map the objects in the persistent set onto their equivalent representation in the database (see Figure 5.3). In a relational environment, for example, classes have to be mapped onto tables and class attributes onto columns.

You don't want to limit your system to a predefined set of attribute types, but you do want to be able to write any arbitrary object, so an ideal mapping is by no means obvious. Thus a default system that defines the mapping of each possible data class cannot be determined. The following sections offer various approaches to solving this mapping problem.

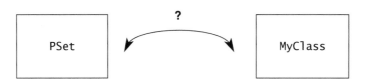

FIGURE 5.3   Storing objects in a persistent set. If you want to be able to store each arbitrary object in the set, you have to figure out a way to resolve the impedance mismatch between your own data types and the fixed set of data types supported by the underlying database system.

5.4.1   Letting Each Class Decide for Itself

One approach to the mapping problem is to let each class decide for itself how to serialize itself (that is, specify how it has to be written to or read from the database). This frequently used approach requires each class to provide a `read()` method and a `write()` method that implement the reading from and writing to disk (e.g., [Gorlen90]). This requirement can be enforced by deriving all classes from a single base class (the traditional `Object`), which implements virtual `read()` and `write()` functions (see Figure 5.4). Here is an example:

```
class Object {
  // ...
  virtual int read();
  virtual int write();
  // etc ...
};
```

If you now want to be able to store instances of a certain class in a database, you must derive it from class `Object` and override the `read()` and `write()` functions:

```
class Date: public Object {

  int d, m, y;

public :
  Date();
  Date(Date&);
  // ...
  virtual int read();
  virtual int write();
};
```

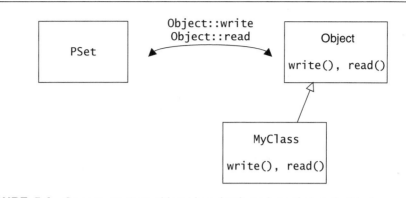

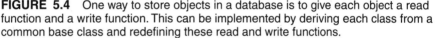

FIGURE 5.4   One way to store objects in a database is to give each object a read function and a write function. This can be implemented by deriving each class from a common base class and redefining these read and write functions.

This approach has some major drawbacks [Ellis93], in addition to the burden of having to provide read and write functions for all classes. For example, the standard C and C++ data types (`int`, `double`, and so on) have no read or write functions, so special provisions must be made to store these objects in the database. Further, if third-party libraries are used, the probability that these libraries share your common base object is small. Thus they, too, will have no read or write functions that can be accessed via polymorphism used on `Object`. Moreover, if the third-party library has also a common base object, name conflicts may occur.

It also can be argued that read and write functions have very little to do with the object itself. Consider classes such as `Date` and `Point`. Although storing dates or points in a database is often necessary, the classes themselves are not directly associated with databases. So it's not really their job to deal with reading and writing. Furthermore, the implementation of the storage of complex objects (such as images) is often a job for database specialists—and these are not necessarily the same people who develop the classes to be used in an application program.

5.4.2   Using IM Resolvers

An approach that conforms with the principle of separation of concerns is to associate a separate IM resolver class with each class whose instances must be stored in the database. This class specifies how the associated class must be read from or written to the database. In other words, it is this class that contains all intelligence about reading and writing objects to persistent memory. Note that this reading and writing is specified in a database-independent way. All IM resolver classes are derived from a common base class `IM_Resolver` (see Figure 5.5).

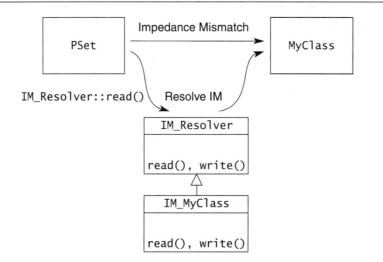

FIGURE 5.5   A dedicated class (IM_MyClass) derived from IM_Resolver contains all knowledge about the storage of a certain class (MyClass). Each time an object of that class needs to be stored or retrieved, the associated IM resolver is consulted.

A simplified version of the class IM_Resolver is presented here:

```
class IM_Resolver {

protected:
  Column *column;
  DataSet* iDs;
  PersistentSet* pset();

public:
  IM_Resolver(DataSet *base, const char *nme, FIELD_TYPE ftyp,
        int wdth, int dec=0);
  IM_Resolver(IM_Resolver& fld);
  ~IM_Resolver();

  virtual void to_select(SelectStatement& selectstmt)
    {
    selectstmt << *column;
    }
```

```
virtual void to_insert(Statement& insertstmt)
  {
  to_update(insertstmt);
  }

virtual void to_update(Statement& updatestmt)=0;
virtual read(Cursor& cursor)=0;

// etc...
};
```

The main properties of this class are the pure virtual read and write functions. These functions are responsible for mapping the associated object's data type onto the column data types supported by the relational database layer. It is here that the impedance mismatch is resolved. The persistent set's IM resolvers take care of assembling and disassembling the individual objects from and to their spare parts.

The write function itself comes in two variants: one for inserting an object and one for updating an object. Because the insert and update behaviors are almost always identical, the IM_Resolver::to_insert() function, by default, calls IM_Resolver::to_update(). Thus it is necessary to implement both functions only when the insert behavior differs from the update behavior.

For each of the relational column types, the operator << allows you to add an attribute of that type to a select, update, insert, or delete statement. It is also possible to read an attribute from a database column or write the attribute into that column using the operators >> and <<.

For each storable data type, you should derive a special class and override the member functions IM_Resolver::read() and IM_Resolver::to_update(). Consider, for example, an IM_char, which specifies how to write strings to a database column:

```
class IM_char : public IM_Resolver {

protected :
  char *str;

public :
  IM_char(char *txt, DataSet *base, const char *nme, int len)
      : IM_Resolver(base, nme, F_CHAR, len, 0),
    str(txt)
    {}

virtual void read(Cursor& cursor);
virtual void to_update(Statement& updateStmt);
};
```

The system learns how to store (retrieve) strings to (from) a DataSet by defining IM_char's member functions read() and to_update(). In this simple case, the to_update function is straightforward:

```
void IM_char::to_update(Statement& updateStmt);
{
  updateStmt[column->name()] << str; // Database independent!
}
```

All that IM_char::to_update does is to store the string str in the appropriate column of the relational database (see Figure 5.6). Because the same behavior can be applied to insert a string, the default to_insert function can be inherited. The read function is analogous. It reads the string directly from the corresponding database column:

```
void IM_char::read(Cursor& cursor)
  {
  cursor[column->name()] >> str;
  }
```

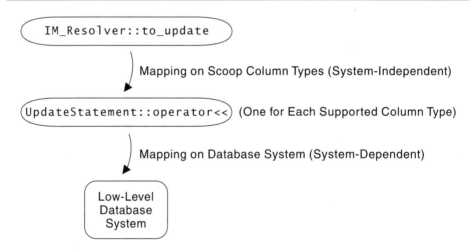

FIGURE 5.6 The write functions of the derived IM_Resolvers map the associated class onto the Scoop data types. For each Scoop column type, a Statement::operator<<() function performs the system-dependent mapping onto the low-level database system.

5.4.3 Using `DataSet`

You could choose to attach the IM resolvers directly to the `PSet` class. However, as shown in later chapters, in certain cases you will want to distribute an object over several tables. To allow for such a distribution, the IM resolvers are attached to a class `DataSet`, which specifies in which table the columns can be found. By attaching multiple `DataSets` to a single `PSet`, you can distribute a persistent object over multiple tables (or even databases). One reason you might want to do so is to implement inheritance relationships (see Chapter 8.)

Note, by the way, that the concepts of relational tables and columns must be viewed in a very broad sense. As discussed later in the chapter, they also can be used to communicate with another process through some IPC mechanism, in which case the columns are used to serialize the object. Or the table and columns might represent an Internet HTML form that has data fields that must be sent to some URL on the Web.

5.4.4 Advantages and Disadvantages of IM Resolvers

The use of IM resolvers has several advantages. One is that because the storage method is separated from the object itself, the objects no longer come in direct contact with the database. Thus there are no longer special requirements for these objects; it is sufficient to design an appropriate IM resolver for each class that will be used as an attribute. This technique also applies for the built-in data types and for classes found in third-party libraries, thus enhancing reuse.

Another advantage is that by grouping all of the storage methods in their own dedicated class hierarchy, you can extend these classes with other database-related functions (such as `seek()` and `say_as_string()`) without complicating the related object.

A disadvantage of using IM resolvers is that an IM resolver must be derived for each data type that will be stored in a database column. This may seem cumbersome. However, the implementation of these derived IM resolvers is almost always the same, so this problem can be easily overcome. For example, you could use template classes or inheritance, as shown in Chapter 7. Furthermore, the number of IM resolvers will be significantly smaller than the total number of classes. This is because you need IM resolvers for only those classes that will appear as attributes in other classes. Consider, for example, the classes `Customer`, `Invoice`, `Order`, `Shipment`, and `Repair`. Each of the last four classes will contain an attribute of type `Customer`. Thus you will need an `IM_Customer` derived from `IM_Resolver` that specifies how a customer must be stored in a column of the invoice, order, shipment, and repair tables. However, you will not need IM resolvers for invoices, orders, shipments, or repairs, since these objects do not appear as attributes of other objects.

5.5 Reading and Writing Objects

The reading and writing of objects is abstracted by the member functions `PSet::select()`, `PSet::read()`, `PSet::write()`, and `PSet::append()`. To see how this works, let's examine `PSet::read()`, which reads an object from a row in the database:

```
// read an object from a row in the relational cursor
PSet::read()
{
  for (int ok=setlist.go_top(); ok; ok=setlist.next())
    {
      setlist.current()->read(cursor);
    }
}
```

PSet tells each of its associated DataSets to read itself from its corresponding table in the database. This technique allows you to distribute an object over multiple database tables. Every DataSet instance, in turn, tells each of its IM_Resolvers to read its associated attribute from the corresponding column in that DataSet:

```
DataSet::read(Cursor& cursor)
{
  for (int i=0; i<n_fields; ++i)
    {
    resolver[i]->read(cursor); // polymorphism is used
    }
}
```

In short, the read (or write) process goes as following, which is also illustrated in Figure 5.7:

1. The application programmer sends a select message to an instance of PSet.
   In a relational implementation, this select function will build the appropriate
   SQL select statement. It does so by relying on the (possibly overridden)
   IM_Resolver::to_select() function. That select statement is sent to the
   database, and a relational cursor is returned that contains the result table of
   the select statement.
2. The programmer now can traverse the persistent set, for example by issuing a
   call to PSet::next(). This call invokes PSet::read(), which resolves the
   impedance mismatch between the relational table and the memory object. This
   read function sends a read message to each DataSet that is attached to the
   persistent set.
3. Every DataSet::read() sends a read message to each (derived) IM_Resolver
   that is attached to this DataSet object. All of these derived IM resolvers have their
   own overloaded read function that specifies how this object must be read from the
   corresponding database column(s).

The overloaded IM_Resolver::read() member functions can vary from extremely simple implementations (such as for an IM_char) to very sophisticated ones, in which links are made with several other DataSet or PSet objects. Examples of more sophisticated read functions are given in Chapter 6.

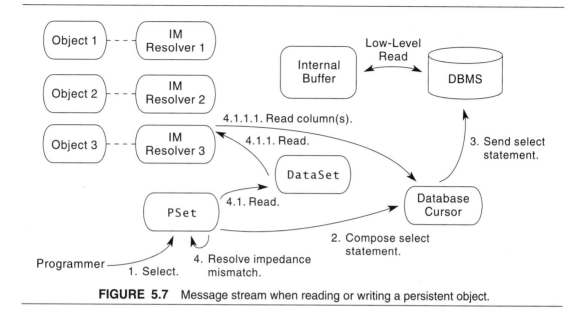

FIGURE 5.7   Message stream when reading or writing a persistent object.

5.6   Direct Instances of PSet

Now the PSet class can be used directly to access a database, as illustrated by the following example:

```
void test ()
{
    // the buffer variables; these will be used to communicate
    // with the database

    char name[31];
    char street[31];

    // the persistent set
    PSet set;

    // the DataSet (represents the table)
    DataSet ds(&set, "customer");

    // the IM Resolvers; these link the memory variables
    // to the DataSet
```

```
IM_char f_name (name, &ds, "NAME", 30);
IM_char f_street (street, &ds, "STREET", 30);

// list customers (no opening of database necessary)
int i=0;

for (int ok= set.go_top(); ok; ok=set.next())
  {
  // 'name' and 'street' get their values automatically
  cout << i << " : " << name << " " << street << endl;
  }

// remark: no closing of database or other clean-up code needed
// this is handled by PSet
}
```

Let's look at this example in more detail. We start by declaring the variables name and street that will be used to access the data in the database. Then we declare the PSet instance set, which abstracts our access to the database. The table itself is abstracted by the DataSet instance ds. The IM_char instances f_name and f_street link the memory variables to the DataSet instance (see Figure 5.8). Those two instances will make sure that name and street contain the right values at all times.

The first statement tells the system to go to the top of the persistent container. If this function returns successfully, both of the variables name and street contain the values corresponding to the top object in the container. Every time we call PSet::next(), we move to the next object in the set, and the corresponding values are automatically put in their variables.

Since the mapping onto the variables was done automatically, we were not confronted with the impedance mismatch. This mismatch was resolved by the IM resolvers. Nor did we have to worry about low-level details or about routine tasks such as selecting tables, opening files, or connecting to databases. We were able to work with the customer set as though it were an ordinary set kept in transient memory.

Notice also that nowhere in this example can we see which database system or technology is actually used. This technology can be flat-file, relational, object-oriented, or any similar technology.

This example has a drawback. Although we hid the implementation details of the database, up until now we were still confronted with the fact that we are working with a database. This is why no direct instances of this class should be created. Rather, the PSet class should be used as a base class for object-oriented database objects. Thus it becomes possible not only for these objects to hide the database concept, but also for us to apply inheritance to databases and to create persistent inheritance trees. This issue is further discussed in Chapter 6.

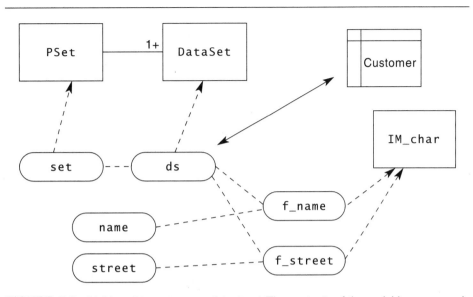

FIGURE 5.8   Linking objects to a persistent set. The contents of the variables name and street are linked to the database through the IM_char instances f_name and f_street. Through this mechanism, each navigation in the database will automatically update the corresponding variables.

5.7   Searching for Objects

The discussion so far has centered on how to read objects from persistent memory and how to write them to the database. However, often you want to read only those objects that conform to certain selection criteria. To allow for this functionality, PSet has a search mechanism implemented by its member function seek(), declared like this:

```
seek (Condition& condition);
```

The condition itself is specified by an IM resolver and the value of the object you are seeking.

5.7.1   Specifying the Search Strategy

When searching for objects, you can run into the same problem as when trying to read or write objects: *How* do you search for objects; that is, how do you specify the search criteria? Since the query condition can contain any arbitrary type of object, this knowledge about how to search cannot be preprogrammed.

The only thing that can be predefined is how to search the standard column data types (this functionality belongs to layer 2, discussed in Section 5.3). The search condition for arbitrary object types will thus have to be mapped onto the column types supported by

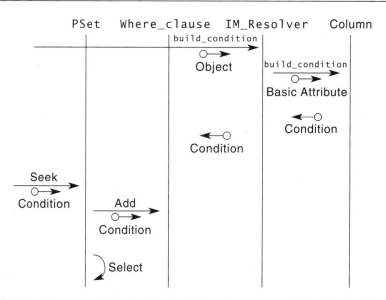

FIGURE 5.9 When searching for objects, PSet relies on a seek function that is attached to IM_Resolver to specify how the search request must be translated to the database layout.

layer 2. You can do so by using the same technique used for reading and writing objects. Thus you have to extend the appropriate IM resolver with a seek function that specifies the mapping of objects of that particular type onto layer 2 types.

When the search is performed, the following steps occur. These are also illustrated in Figure 5.9.

1. PSet::seek() is called with the search condition as parameter. This condition is composed of the IM resolver and the value of the sought object.
2. The IM resolver's search function maps the condition onto a conditional expression in terms of columns (or more generally, onto a layer 2 condition).
3. This layer 2 condition is added to the where clause that is connected to the select statement.
4. After the search is finished, a select command is issued to execute the corresponding SQL statement and retrieve the desired objects from the database into the persistent container. This container can now be traversed in the usual way.

5.7.2 Implementing a Search Mechanism

An example of implementing a search mechanism is the implementation of class IM_char. The implementation of IM_char::queryEqual() is straightforward because the C++ data type char* can be mapped directly onto a native DBMS (or rather, Scoop layer 2) data type:

```
class IM_char : public IM_Resolver {

protected :
  char *str;

public :
  IM_char(char *txt,DataSet *base, const char *nme, int len);
  virtual void read(Cursor& cursor);
  virtual void to_update(Statement& updateStmt);

  Condition queryEqual (const char* astr) const
    {
    return (column->queryEqual(astr));
    }
};
```

In this implementation, the class Column itself has a member function queryEqual()
connected to it for each of the built-in data types. These functions, which also return a
Condition object, define the search mechanism for the built-in column types. In an SQL
environment, they are responsible for building the appropriate where clause that must be
added to the SQL select statement. The difference between the search mechanism attached
to the IM resolvers and that attached to the Columns is that the first works on the object
level, while the latter works on the relational database level and is thus dependent on the
database layout and technology.

Building search conditions with longs, doubles, or dates should be equally straightforward as doing so for IM_char, since these data types, too, are supported as native
DBMS data types. In Chapter 7, however, you will encounter some queries that have more
complex criteria that specify, for example, customers or invoices. Searching these objects
will be independent of the database layout and will not differ in any way from searching
objects of built-in data types. This contrasts with traditional techniques whereby you must
know about primary and foreign keys in order to specify the search criteria.

5.7.3 Extensions and an Alternative Implementation

An elegant C++ implementation of the search mechanism is to define the operator==()
for the IM resolvers and let it return a Condition object [RogueWave96]:

```
Condition operator==(const IM_char& imr, const char* astr)
{
  return imr.queryEqual(astr);
}
```

You can specify conditions using other operators (such as greater than, >, or less than, <) by extending the IM resolver correspondingly. To allow testing for strings that are less than a certain value, for example, you could write the following code:

```
Condition IM_char::queryLess(const char* astr) const
{
  return column->queryLess(astr);
}
```

or alternatively:

```
Condition operator<(const IM_char& imr, const char* astr)
{
  return imr.queryLess(astr);
}
```

5.7.4 Searching by Multiple Criteria

To accommodate searching based on multiple criteria, PSet has a member function add_filter(). This function is analogous to PSet::seek(), except that it allows you to set the where clause without automatically performing the select afterwards. Thus by calling PSet::add_filter() multiple times, you can add multiple select criteria.

As an example, the following code searches the customers living in Texas who have the last name of "Jones":

```
void test ()
{
  // the buffer variables; these will be used to communicate
  // with the database

  char name[31];
  char street[31];
  char state[3];

  // the persistent set
  PSet set;

  // the DataSet
  DataSet ds(&set, "customer");

  IM_char f_name (name, &ds, "NAME", 30);
  IM_char f_street (street, &ds, "STREET", 30);
  IM_char f_state (state, &ds, "STATE", 2);
```

```
// add select criteria
set.add_filter(f_state == "TX");
set.add_filter(f_name == "Jones");

// traverse set
for (int ok=set.go_top(); ok; ok=set.next())
  {
  cout << name << " " << street << endl;
  }
}
```

An alternative would be to use the `PSet::seek()` function to specify the second search criterion and execute the select at the same time:

```
set.add_filter(f_state == "TX");

for (int ok=set.seek(f_name == "Jones"); ok; ok=set.next())
  {
  cout << name << " " << street << endl;
  }
```

5.8 Supporting Multiple Technologies

The previous examples illustrated that we are well shielded from the actual database system or technology used. The persistence architecture is not restricted to SQL-based systems. Thus far in this book, we have not come into direct contact with any relational technology.

5.8.1 File-Based Systems

It is possible to apply the persistence architecture to file-based systems (such as C-ISAM, dBase, or Btrieve). In this case, the level of abstraction provided by the `PSet` class has some far-reaching consequences. First, since programmers do not know they are using a database, they do not know that files might be opened and closed. A second important and useful consequence is that, as is the case with ordinary variables, several instances of the same `PSet` class can be created (and thus be active) at the same time—each, of course, with its own view on the underlying database. However, this also means that the programmer could be opening the same physical file several times simultaneously.

In file-oriented systems, additional bookkeeping must be done to ensure that files are opened and closed properly, that they are not opened twice, and so on. Further, most file-based systems allow only one record pointer; thus support is needed to allow multiple

PSet instances. This support can be provided through the use of the classes `Database-File` and `DatabaseManager` [Heinckiens92]. `DatabaseFile`, which abstracts all file management, opens and closes the files automatically.

Also, many operating systems limit the number of available resources (for example, the open file limit in DOS and the number of stream resources in UNIX). Since programmers no longer know which variables are linked to a database and since they certainly do not know how all of those database tables are linked together, they have no way to keep track of this number. You don't want to bother the application programmer with these limitations, so you need a central resource manager that is responsible for allocating and assigning resources. If the heap of available resources is nearly empty, it is the resource manager's responsibility to retrieve resources from other users in order to fulfill the needs of the new one. Those users who lose their resources may never experience any harm or discomfort from this (except perhaps a performance penalty). In fact, they must never know that they lost them. (They should not even know they had or needed those resources in the first place.) The class `DatabaseFile`, in cooperation with the class `DatabaseManager`, makes sure the open file limit is never exceeded, selects the right index tags, and so on. The actual details of this implementation are beyond the scope of this book.

5.8.2   Persistence through IPC

It is also possible to adapt the persistence mechanism to communicate with other processes instead of with a database. This is illustrated in Figure 5.10. It is sufficient to put IPC facilities in either `PSet::write()` and `PSet::read()` or in the table and column objects. In this case, the IM resolvers are responsible for serializing the object. Programs no longer need to know where they get their data; they only have to specify what they want to make persistent.

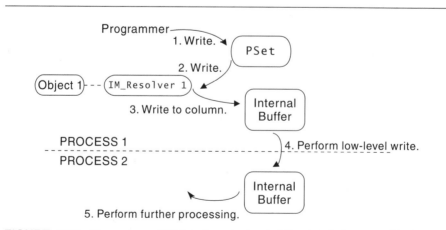

FIGURE 5.10   Scoop as an IPC interface. Instead of the data being stored in the database, it can be sent to another process.

5.9 Summary

Persistent containers hide all database-specific issues. They offer a mechanism for developing truly database-independent programs. Furthermore, they extend the definition of persistence so that persistence is no longer restricted to physical databases. It is possible to use the persistent container concept to support IPC, thus storing or retrieving information to or from other processes.

This chapter discussed the concept of IM resolvers, which resolve the impedance mismatch between the data structures used on the programming level and the basic data types supported by the database interface. Resolvers tell the corresponding PSet how to disassemble an object into its parts. By putting all storage intelligence in a separate class hierarchy, one can store objects for which source code is not available. Since the people implementing the IM resolvers do not necessarily have to be those designing the objects, a separation of concerns is achieved whereby each party involved can concentrate on his or her own domain of expertise.

The functionality offered by PSet provides not only an additional level of simplicity; it also helps to make programs more robust. Once the internal structure and functionality of class PSet have been validated and verified, the class's inherent reliability and simple interface ensure that developers can fully concentrate on the essence of their designs without having to care about routine operations or be burdened with handling them. Thus the software development process is hastened significantly, and the resulting software is more reliable.

Chapter 6
Encapsulating Data Access

Chapter 5 described an approach that hides the implementation details of the database. We were, however, still confronted with the database concept itself. This chapter goes a step farther by discussing how to hide the fact that we are working with databases. This is a first step to the development of so-called business objects.

6.1 Deriving from PSet

In Chapter 5, the database concept was visible because so far in this book, we have worked with direct instances of class PSet. In practice, however, no direct instances of this class should be created. Rather, it should be used as a base class for persistent objects. Thus it becomes possible not only for persistent objects to hide the database concept, but also for us to apply inheritance to databases and to create persistent inheritance trees.

When designing a storage mechanism for persistent objects, you have two alternatives. Figure 6.1 illustrates this.

1. Work with a separate container class. Thus the storage system is considered to be an object into which other objects can be inserted.
2. Inherit the objects directly from the storage class.

6.1.1 Working with a Separate Container Class

Consider, for example, a class Person. The first method would be to consider PSet to be a persistent container to which Persons must be added. This would give the situation pictured in Figure 6.2.

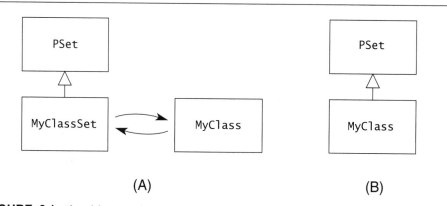

FIGURE 6.1   An object can be stored (made persistent) in two ways: (A) It can be put into a persistent container, or (B) it can be explicitly declared as being persistent by inheriting from a persistent base class.

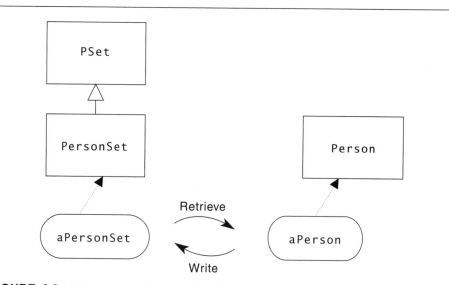

FIGURE 6.2   Using a persistent container. One approach to make Persons persistent is to explicitly add them to a persistent set. They can be retrieved by explicitly reading them from this set.

This set could then be used as follows:

```
void example1()
{
  PersonSet pset;
  Person *p;

  p = pset.seek_name("Jones");

  if (p==NULL)
    {
    p = new Person;
    p->name("Jones");
    p->address("Somewhere");
    pset.append(p);
    delete p;
    }

  pset.query ("STATE = TX");  // a query

  while ( (p=pset.current()) != NULL )
    {
    cout << p->name() << " " << p->address() << endl;
    pset.next();
    }

  // etc...
}
```

Although this approach is relatively easy to implement, it carries the overhead of having to work with both a class Person and a class PersonSet.

6.1.2 Directly Inheriting from the Storage Class

An alternative approach is to state explicitly that Person is a persistent object and thus to inherit Person directly from PSet. See Figure 6.3.

Person now has a double functionality. It represents both the actual person and the entire data set. The value of the Person instance is then the current object (record) pointed to in the data set. Person now plays the role of an object cursor. This situation is analogous to the cursor concept in relational database systems.

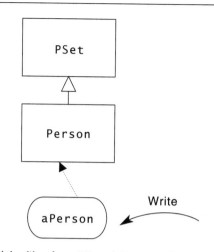

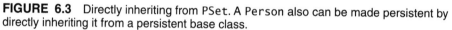

FIGURE 6.3 Directly inheriting from PSet. A Person also can be made persistent by directly inheriting it from a persistent base class.

The previous listing would now look like this:

```
void example2()
{
  Person p;

  if (p.seek_name("Jones")!=FOUND)
    {
    p.name("Jones");
    p.address("Somewhere");
    p.append();
    }

  p.query ("STATE = TX");

  do
    {
    cout  << p.name() << " " << p.address() << endl;
    }
  while (p.next());

  // etc...
}
```

In this approach, you can directly tell an object to make itself persistent and thus not need a separate container. This approach has the advantage of requiring less programming. A drawback, however, is that when working with multiple instances of Person, you get a slight memory overhead because each Person carries all PSet functionality and all IM resolvers. In the previous approach, the PSet functionality is kept only once (in the class PersonSet).

In the remainder of this book, primarily the first approach is used. However, all principles and ideas presented herein can be applied using either approach.

6.2 Example: Class `City`

This section develops the class City as an example of using persistent objects. It presents a transient version and a persistent version of this class. However, programmers will see no difference between the two.

6.2.1 Transient Version of `City`

A first implementation of this class might look as shown in Figure 6.4. Note that in this example, no databases are used.

This class can now be used in the same ways you use the built-in data types:

```
void city_test ()
{
  double number;
  char name[31];
  City city;
  cin >> number >> name >> city;
  cout << name << " lives in " << city.name();
}
```

Of course, this class also could be used to construct other classes, such as a class Person, as done here:

```
class Person {

  char iName[31];
  char iStreet[31];
  City iCity;

  friend istream& operator>>(istream& strm, Person& aPerson);

public :
  //...
  void set_city(const char *str);
};
```

```
void Person::set_city (const char *str)
{
  iCity.name(str);
}


istream& operator>>(istream& strm, Person& aPerson)
{
  strm >> aPerson.iName >> aPerson.iStreet >> aPerson.iCity;
  return strm;
}
```

```
class City {

  char iZip[11];
  char iName[31];

  friend istream& operator>>(istream& strm, City& acity);

public :

  City (const char *zp = 0, const char *cty = 0);
  const char* zip() const { return iZip; }
  const char* name() const { return iName;}
  void zip (const char* zp);
  void name (const char* str);
  City& operator=(City& other);
};

// set zip code

void City::zip (const char* zp)
{
  strncpy (iZip, zp, 10);
  iZip[10] = '\0';
}

// set city name
```

continued

```
                        void City::name (const char* str)
                        {
                          strncpy (iName, str, 30);
                          iName[30] = '\0';
                        }


                        // get city

                        istream& operator>>(istream& strm, City& acity)
                        {
                          strm >> acity.iZip >> acity.iName;
                          return strm;
                        }

                        City& City::operator=(const City& other)
                        {
                          if (this != other)
                            {
                            strcpy (iZip, other.iZip);
                            strcpy (iName, other.iName);
                            }
                          return *this;
                        }
```

FIGURE 6.4   Implementation of the business object City.

So far, nothing much spectacular has happened. This is just a very simple and basic
C++ program. It could be a solution to the simple design specification: "Design a class that
maintains a person's name, street, and city. The city itself consists of a zip code and the
city's name." You will see shortly, however, that although the specifications will gradually
become more complex, the program code will remain virtually unchanged. Furthermore,
regardless of how simple the city class may be, you already have a first object to add to
your library of reusable business objects.

6.2.2   Persistent Version of City

The City class is a rather naive implementation because it does not use the relation
between cities and zip codes. In a later stage, as your program grows more sophisticated,
you might decide that it should be sufficient for the user to enter either the city's name or
zip code and that the program should then retrieve the other automatically. This desired
functionality can be achieved by connecting the City class to a database that associates
each city with its zip code. So it will be sufficient to specify either the zip code or the city,
as the class retrieves the other automatically.

To implement this feature, you can design a class `CitySet` derived from `PSet`. `City-Set` now functions as a container of all known cities. This container will be used by `City` to match a zip code with a city name.

```
class CitySet : public PSet {

protected:

  friend class City;
  City *iCurrent;

  DataSet ds;
  IM_char f_zip;
  IM_char f_name;

public:

  CitySet()
    : iCurrent(new City),
      ds(this, "city"),
      f_zip(iCurrent->iZip, &ds, "ZIP", 10),
      f_name(iCurrent->iName, &ds, "CITY", 30)
    {}

  ~CitySet()
    {
    delete iCurrent;
    }

  City* current() { return iCurrent; }
};
```

This time, in contrast to the example in Section 5.6, the IM resolvers and the variables have become members of the derived `PSet` class. The buffer variables and the IM resolvers are hidden in the private part of the class.

It is important to note that you did not have to write select, read, insert, or update statements. These functions can be directly inherited from `PSet`, and they now perform by relying on the knowledge stored in the IM resolvers. This not only simplifies the development process significantly. It also makes the class largely independent of the database aspects and certainly of the database layout.

Class `City` can now use this container class to link zip codes and city names. The following code illustrates this:

```
static CitySet *allCities; // all known cities

class City {

  friend class CitySet;

  char iZip[11];
  char iName[31];

public :

  City (const char *zp = 0, const char *cty = 0);
  const char* zip() const { return iZip; }
  const char* name() const { return iName;}
  void zip (const char* zp);
  void name (const char* str);
  int setfrom_zip (const char* zp);
  int setfrom_name(const char* str);
  City& operator=(const City& other);
  City& operator=(const char* cityname);
};
```

An application using `City` does not see how this class gets its data. It does not even have to know that the class is connected to a database. To the users of `City`, there is no fundamental difference between the persistent and the transient `City` class. For example, to specify a city either by its zip code or by its name, special functions are provided. These by themselves are straightforward to implement. As the following code fragment demonstrates, a simple seek statement is sufficient to set all variables for a city:

```
// Specify a City by its zip code
int City::setfrom_zip (const char *zp)
{
  if (allCities->seek(allCities->f_zip == zp) != FOUND)
    return 0;
  *this = *allCities->current();
  return 1;
}
```

```
// Specify a city by its name
int City::setfrom_name (const char *str)
{
  if (allCities->seek(allCities->f_name == str) != FOUND)
    return 0;

  *this = *allCities->current();
  return 1;
}

istream& operator>>(istream& strm, City& acity)
{
  char tmp[81];

  strm >> tmp;

  if (tmp[0]!='%')
    {
    acity.zip(tmp);
    strm >> tmp;
    acity.name(tmp);
    }
  else
    {
    switch (tmp[1])
      {
      case 'C': acity.setfrom_name(tmp+2); break;
      case 'Z': acity.setfrom_zip(tmp+2); break;
      default: acity.name("INVALID"); break;
      }
    }

  return strm;
}
```

Note that the users of class CitySet do not see that this is actually a persistent set. All they know is that they are using a set of City's. This approach offers the advantage that the program is largely independent of the persistence technology.

6.3   Using Class `City`

Once persistent classes are implemented and validated for all objects relevant to the problem domain of the application, they can be used as easily as built-in data types. The following program fragment demonstrates that the programmer no longer sees any difference between an instance of a `City` and an ordinary data type, such as a `double`:

```
void city_test ()
{
  double number;
  char name[31];
  City city;
  cin >> number >> name >> city;

  cout << name << " lives in " << city.name();
}
```

This code fragment is identical to the listing in Section 6.2. When users execute this function this time, they still specify the city by entering its name and zip code. This is necessary in order to be able to reuse code that was written for the first implementation of `City`. However, it is now possible to enter only one of the city's attributes and to rely on the `City` class to fill in the other. Users do this by preceding the attribute with %C to indicate they are entering the city's name or with %Z to indicate they are entering the zip code. It is important to notice that this whole input process is hidden from the programmer. This is achieved by overloading the operator >> for `City`.

6.4   Member Objects

Of course, you also can use this new `City` class inside other classes. Consider, for example, the transient class `Person`:

```
class Person {

  char iName[31];
  char iStreet[31];
  City iCity;

  friend istream& operator>>(istream& strm, Person& aperson);
```

```
public :

  set_city(const char *str);
// etc...

};
```

This class, too, is identical to the one in Section 6.2. Notice that nowhere in this class can you determine that this time City is associated with a database. This also goes for all member functions of Person.

```
Person::set_city (const char *str)
{
  iCity.name(str);
}

istream& operator>>(istream& strm, Person& aperson)
{
  strm >> aperson.iName >> aperson.iStreet >> aperson.iCity;
  return strm;
}
```

This example illustrates the extent to which you have succeeded in abstracting the database concept. The persistence mechanism, and whether one is involved, has become just a private attribute of the object to which it corresponds (in this case, City). This object is now responsible for its own persistence capabilities. The outside world no longer sees any difference between persistent objects and transient objects. This approach differs fundamentally from many RAD approaches in which you would have had to radically change the way you were using Persons as soon as City became persistent. Instead of being able to continue to work with ordinary variables, you would have had to add select and update statements to your code in order to access the city table.

6.5 Derived IM Resolvers

As illustrated in the previous section, you can use the City object as a member in other objects, regardless of whether City is connected to a database. But what if you decide also to make your Person object persistent? In that case, you will need a PersonSet. You'll want this to be a persistent set, so you will have to derive it from PSet and add appropriate IM resolvers to this class, like this:

```
class Person {
  friend class PersonSet;
```

```
    protected:
      char iId[7];
      char iName[31];
      char iStreet[31];
      City iCity;

    public:
      char* id() {return iId;}
      char* name() { return iName; }
      char* street() { return iStreet; }
      int id(const char* str);
      int name(const char* str);
      int setby_id(const char* the_id);
      // etc...
    };

    class PersonSet : public PSet {
    protected:
      Person *iCurrent;

      DataSet ds_person;
      IM_char f_id;
      IM_char f_name;
      IM_char f_street;
      IM_city f_city;

    public :
      PersonSet() :
        iCurrent(new Person),
        ds_person (this, "person"),
        f_id(iCurrent->iId, &ds_person, "ID", 6),
        f_name (iCurrent->iName, &ds_person, "NAME", 30),
        f_street (iCurrent->iStreet, &ds_person, "STREET", 30),
        f_city (&iCurrent->iCity, &ds_person, "ZIP", "CITY")
      {}

      ~PersonSet();
    };
```

As far as iName, iId, and iStreet are concerned, there is no problem; ordinary IM_chars can be used here. For the member variable iCity, however, you have to derive the new IM resolver class IM_city. The implementation of IM_city can (but does not have to) depend on the version of City you are using. To the classes that use IM_city, however, this dependency, or not, should be totally transparent.

Let's first look at the IM_city class for the nonpersistent version of City (see Section 6.2.1). In this implementation, we write and read both the zip code and the city name:

```
class IM_city : public IM_Resolver {

  City *city;

  // the two names of the columns containing the city and zip values
  string cityColumnName;
  string zipColumnName;

public :

  IM_city(City *cty,DataSet *base,char *nmezp,char *nmecity)
      : IM_Resolver(base, NULL, F_CHAR, 30, 0)
      , city(cty),
      , cityColumnName(nmezp),
      , zipColumnName(nmecity)
    {};

  // write the city name and zip code to their columns

  void to_update(Statement& updateStmt)
    {
    updateStmt[cityColumnName] << city->name();
    updateStmt[zipColumnName]  << city->zip();
    }

  // read the city name and zip code from their columns

  void read(Cursor& cursor)
    {
    string buffer;
    cursor[cityColumnName] >> buffer;
    city->name(buffer);
    cursor[zipColumnName] >> buffer;
    city->zip(buffer);
    }
}
```

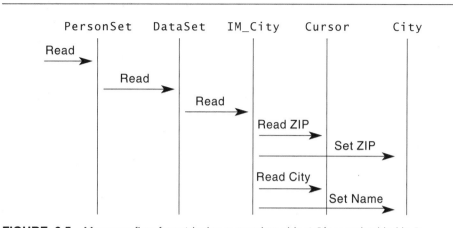

FIGURE 6.5   Message flow for retrieving a member object `City` embedded in `Person`.

The implementation of `IM_city::read()` shows that the city name first is read from the buffer and then is assigned to the `City` object. This is done by our calling the appropriate member function. Next, the zip code is read from the buffer. It, too, is assigned to the `City` object. Figure 6.5 shows how this works. Note also that `IM_city::read()` is independent of the database system used.

If you later decide to make `City` persistent, you have a choice. Either leave `IM_city` unchanged (and thereby introduce redundancy), or use a join to the city table, in which case you remove the redundancy and conform to the third normal form (in relational technology). In this case, `IM_city` becomes the following:

```
class IM_city : public IM_Resolver {

  City *city;

  // as we now use only one column, we can use the variable
  // provided by the IM_Resolver class for this.

public :

  // although for reasons of compatibility with code using
  // the previous IM_city implementation, the parameter
  // nmecity has been kept, it is no longer used.

  IM_city(City *cty, DataSet *base, char *nmezip, char *nmecity=NULL) :
      IM_Resolver(base, nmezip, F_CHAR, 10, 0), city(cty)
    {};
```

```
void to_update(Statement& updateStmt)
  {
  updateStmt[column->name()] << city->zip();
  }

void read(Cursor& cursor)
  {
  string buffer;
  cursor[column->name()] >> buffer);                                  (1)
  city->setfrom_zip(buffer);                                          (2)
  }

}
```

This time, to_update() restricts itself to just saving the zip code, which thus, in a relational terminology, will be the foreign key. The member function read() becomes slightly more complicated (see Figure 6.6). It has to first read the zip code and then call the zip assignment function of the City object. In other words, the link between the two objects is made through the city's zip code. By using the abstraction provided by the class PSet, we were able to make this implementation database-independent.

Note also that IM_city::read() makes no direct use of the fact that City is a persistent object. To specify a city, it uses only the knowledge that a zip code is sufficient. How the City object uses this information to retrieve its other attributes is of no concern to IM_city::read(). Indeed, according to the extended persistence philosophy of Section 3.15, how City implements its persistence should be the responsibility of only the class City.

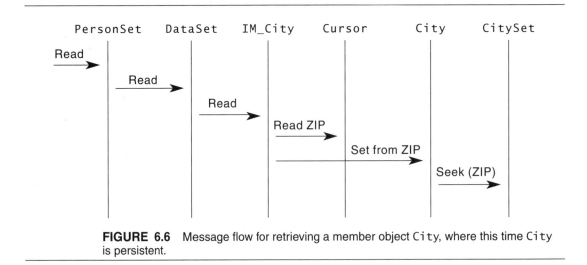

FIGURE 6.6 Message flow for retrieving a member object City, where this time City is persistent.

6.6 Class Extension

In Section 6.2.2, the `City` object relied on `allCities`, a global static instance of `City-Set`, in order to initialize itself by its zip code. This set represents the extent or class extension [Khoshafian93, Odell95]. The extension of a class is the set of all available instances of that class. In relational database technology, the city extent corresponds to the city table.

Since many business objects rely on their persistent set to achieve certain functionality, the extent plays an important role in database applications. In the ODMG standard, the extent is considered to be a fundamental property of the object model. It is common in object-database technology to specify the extent as part of the class definition [Cattell94]. This approach has the advantage of hiding the required persistency functionality within the business object itself.

In C++, you can use a static pointer to include the extent in the class definition. Since this pointer is static, it is common to all instances of the `City` class. `City` can thus be rewritten as follows:

```
class City {

    friend class CitySet;

    char iZip[11];
    char iName[31];

    static CitySet *iExtent;    // all known cities

public :
    City (const char *zp = 0, const char *cty = 0);
    const char* zip() const { return iZip; }
    const char* name() const { return iName;}
    void zip (const char* zp);
    void name (const char* str);
    int setfrom_zip (const char* zp);
    int setfrom_name(const char* str);
    City& operator=(const City& other);
    City& operator=(const char* cityname);
};
```

A difficulty with this implementation is the cyclic dependency between `City` and `CitySet`. However, since the extent is a static pointer, this problem is not hard to resolve. A possible solution is to make the first instance of an object responsible for allocating the extent:

```
CitySet* City::iExtent=0;

City::City(const char*zp, const char* cty)
{
  if (iExtent==0) {
    iExtent=(CitySet*)1; // Must be nonzero to avoid an infinite loop
    iExtent=new CitySet();
  }

  // rest of constructor code
}
```

The presence of the extent within City may seem to be a drawback because it introduces a coupling between the business object and the persistence framework. However, this coupling is very natural, since the extent was used to implement some specific functionality for the business object. The City needed its extent in order to initialize itself by zip code; a Customer object might use its extent to initialize itself by the customer's ID. In these cases, it is not the user of the business model who needs the set, but rather the business object itself that wants to use it. Thus it makes sense to hide the extent within the business object.

Furthermore, the business object expects only that its extent will be a set; it makes no assumptions on how this set should be implemented or whether it is transient or persistent. Thus by including this extent in the City class, you do not make this class dependent on the persistence architecture. You only give City access to a set of cities.

6.7 Compile-Time Decoupling

Although City and CitySet (and the rest of the application) are independent of the database from a logical point of view, there is still a compile-time coupling [Lakos96]. When you change the database system or technology, you must still recompile your application. Since the persistence aspects often are a major characteristic of the application (after all, you develop a database application) and since changes in database systems or technology happen only rarely, this coupling is normally not a problem. However, in some cases a decoupling might be needed. An example is when you are using a library of business objects that must be able to work on a variety of database systems. In this case, you must be able to change your database at runtime.

The coupling can be removed through the use of the *Bridge pattern* [Gamma94], also called *Cheshire Cat* [Carolan89]. This pattern, which allows you to decouple an abstraction from its implementation, offers you two advantages:

1. It is possible to select or switch the implementation at runtime.
2. Changes in the implementation of the abstraction have no impact on clients—their code does not have to be recompiled.

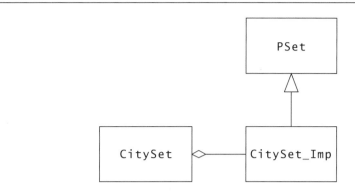

FIGURE 6.7   Bridge pattern applied to `CitySet`.

You can use the Bridge pattern on two levels:

1. `CitySet`
2. `PSet`

The following subsections briefly describe these options.

6.7.1   Applying the Bridge Pattern to `CitySet`

The design of Figure 6.7 is the most flexible in that `CitySet` is decoupled from both the database framework and the persistence architecture. Since `CitySet` contains only a pointer to its actual implementation, this implementation can be changed at runtime without affecting `CitySet`'s clients.

A sample implementation for `CitySet` and `CitySet_Imp` is given next:

```
// public interface file

class CitySet_Imp;

class CitySet {

  CitySet_Imp *imp;

protected:
  CitySet_Imp* getImp();

public:
  CitySet() {imp=0;}
  ~CitySet() {delete imp;}
```

```
    CitySet_Imp* getImp();
    City* current();
    next();
    // other functionality you want to give to CitySet
};


// private implementation file

class CitySet_Imp: public PSet {

protected:
    City *iCurrent;
    DataSet ds;
    IM_char f_zip;
    IM_char f_name;

public:
    CitySet_Imp()
        : iCurrent(new City),
          ds(this, "city"),
          f_zip(iCurrent->iZip, &ds, "ZIP", 10),
          f_name(iCurrent->iName, &ds, "CITY", 30)
        {}

   ~CitySet_Imp()
        {
        delete iCurrent;
        }

    City* current() { return iCurrent; }
};

CitySet_Imp*  CitySet::getImp()
{
    if (imp == 0)
        {
        imp = new CitySet_Imp;
        }
}
```

```
City* CitySet::current()
{
    return getImp()->current();
}

CitySet::next()
{
    return getImp()->next();
}
```

This implementation of the Bridge pattern is rather simple in that both CitySet and CitySet_Imp are implemented in a private file. Only the class definition of CitySet is public. There exists a whole set of alternative designs of the pattern, each offering a specific type of decoupling. You could, for example, use the Abstract Factory pattern or use an abstract base class to decouple the CitySet_Imp interface from its implementation. A discussion of these alternatives is in [Gamma94], [Lakos96], and [Dewhurst96].

6.7.2 Applying the Bridge Pattern to PSet

In the design of Figure 6.8, CitySet is independent of the database system and database technology but is still dependent on the persistence architecture (in this case, Scoop). This approach has the advantage, however, that the programmer does not come into contact

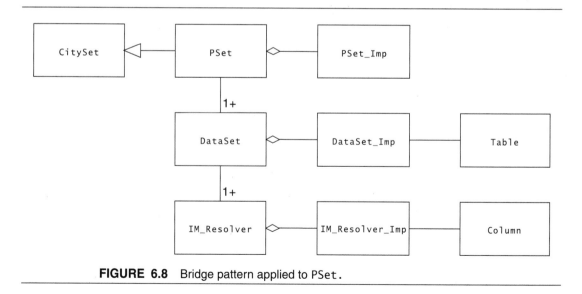

FIGURE 6.8 Bridge pattern applied to PSet.

with the Bridge aspects, since these are implemented within the persistence framework. CitySet can directly use the functionality offered by PSet without requiring a separate CitySet_Imp class. In this design of the persistence framework, it is best to use an Abstract Factory to create the implementation classes. More details are in [Gamma94].

6.8 Reuse and Migration to Other Technologies

The persistence architecture presented in this book is not restricted to relational SQL-based systems. So far we have not come into direct contact with any relational technology. Thanks to the technology independence of the persistence concept, reuse is significantly enhanced. Furthermore, migration to new technologies can be accomplished more gradually.

In this regard, a Scoop-based application was migrated from a file-driven dBase environment to an Informix database without the application code's having to be modified. Similarly, the same application was also migrated to a true object database without code modifications. Of course, had the application been written directly in the native language of the object database, it might have looked different and been more efficient. However, that is not the main issue. The important point is that you can reuse your library of business objects and can thus gradually migrate your existing applications to the new technology.

6.9 Summary

This chapter discussed how to hide the database concept further by inheriting from a persistent base class. Two approaches were presented: considering the objects themselves as being persistent (by inheriting them from PSet) or explicitly adding and retrieving the objects to and from a persistent container object.

As illustrated by the class City example, there is, to the outside world, no longer any real difference between persistent objects and transient objects, thanks to the object-oriented persistence mechanism. Objects become independent of the database schema. Furthermore, migrating to other database technologies does not require the programs to be modified.

Part Three
Implementing Business Models

Chapter 7

Designing Business Objects

Chapter 6 discussed how to design persistent objects. This chapter looks at some of the issues involved in designing robust business objects.

7.1 Developing a Simple Invoicing System

This section develops a simple invoicing class. At this stage, the purpose is not to design the best model for this program, but rather to use the model to explain some basic techniques.

7.1.1 Business Model

A simplified business model for this invoicing system might look like the one in Figure 7.1. Note that a significant amount of reuse can be achieved in the implementation of this model. The `Customer` object, for example, can be derived from the `Person` object that was designed in Chapter 6. Other reusable classes are the `Address` class, the `City` class, an account number class, and so on.

7.1.2 Class `Customer`

In this section, we design the class `Customer` by deriving it from the `Person` class of Section 6.5:

```
class Customer : public Person {

    Date iFirstVisit;
    Date iLatestVisit;
    Accountnumber iAccount;
```

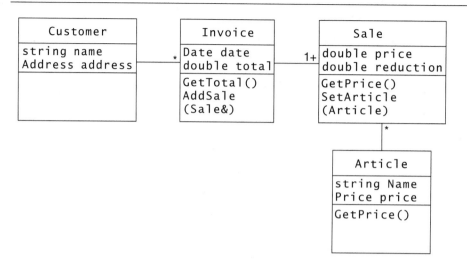

FIGURE 7.1　Business model for a simple invoicing system.

```
public:
  Customer();
  virtual ~Customer();
  // other customer-specific code
};
```

If you want to use this Customer class as a member object of other persistent objects, you have to design the IM_Customer class, which implements the way customers are stored in these other PSets:

```
class IM_Customer: public IM_Resolver {

  Customer *cust;

public :

  IM_Customer(Customer *var, DataSet *base, char *nme)
     : IM_Resolver(base, nme, F_LONG)
    {
    cust = var;
    }
```

```
        void to_update(Statement& stmt)
          {
          stmt[column->name()] << cust->id();
          }

        void read(Cursor& cursor);
          {
          long id;
          cursor[column->name()] >> id;           (1)
          cust->seek_id(id);                       (2)
          }
   };
```

The implementation of IM_Customer::read() shows that the link to the Customer object is made through the customer's ID. In (1), this ID is fetched from the internal record buffer, and in (2), the Customer object is initialized with this ID. Two important points must be noted. First, IM_Customer::read() is totally independent of the database system used. Second, the programmers do not know that any link with another persistent set is made; thus they certainly do not know that it is made through the ID. All they know is that the Invoice object contains a Customer object. They do not have to bother with how this customer is exactly stored in the invoice table.

Note that even IM_Customer does not know that a link to another table is made. It knows only that a customer can be identified through its customer ID; it does not know *how* this identifying is done. That is the task of class Customer.

7.1.3 The Relational Trap

An example of using Customer objects is a simple invoicing program that allows you to invoice certain articles to a customer. A first implementation of the business object Invoice might look as follows:

```
    class Invoice {

        long iNumber;
        Date iDate;
        long iCustomer;                            (3)
        double iTotal;
        // etc...

    public :
        Invoice();
        long customerId() const {return iCustomer;}
```

```
      void customerId(long custId) {iCustomer = custId;}
      long number() const {return iNumber;}
      double total() const {return iTotal;}
      // etc...
  };
```

From class `Invoice`, notice that in (3) the customer is specified by a variable of type `long`. This variable contains the ID (foreign key) of the corresponding `Customer` object. Although at first glance this approach may seem acceptable, it has serious drawbacks. It also breaks the principles of object-oriented software design in several ways.

1. The use of the ID is a direct result of how the data is stored in the relational database tables. Whenever the actual `Customer` object is needed, you have to make an explicit join and load that object from the database. Furthermore, the knowledge about this ID will appear throughout the entire program. It will be needed for searching and selecting invoices, for updating invoices, for inserting invoices, and so on.
2. Whenever the database technology—or even the database layout—changes, the object and all references to it must be changed.
3. If you ever decide to change the primary key of the customer table, all classes referring to `Customer` objects (your `Invoice` class, but also classes `Order`, `Delivery`, and so on) must be modified.

In class `Invoice`, you do not want the customer's ID; you want to work with the actual customer. You want to work with customers in the same way in which you work with dates, strings, and so on. This is often a source of confusion in client/server software. The fact that an object is stored in a separate table and referenced by a foreign key often leads one to believe that it should be treated differently than those objects that are directly stored in the column. This is what makes many client/server applications so difficult to maintain and only marginally reusable. It also makes any performance tuning difficult once the application is up and running.

7.1.4   Object-Oriented Version of Class `Invoice`

The following implementation of class `Invoice` works in the same way with customers as it does with built-in data types such as numbers or dates:

```
  class Invoice {

    long iNumber;
    Date iDate;
    Customer iCustomer;                                        (4)
    double iTotal;
    SaleSet iSaleSet;                                          (5)
```

```
        InvoiceSet *extent;

    public :

        Invoice();
        const Customer& customer() const;
        void customer(const Customer& cust);
        long number() const {return iNumber;}
        double total() const {return iTotal;}
        int addSale(Sale& item);
        // etc...
    };

    const Customer& Invoice::customer () const
    {
        return (iCustomer);                                          (6)
    }


    void Invoice::customer (const Customer &cust)
    {
        iCustomer = cust;                                            (7)
    }


    int Invoice::addSale (Sale& item)
    {
        item.invoiceNumber(number());
        if (iSaleSet.insert(item))                                   (8)
          {
          iTotal += item.total();
          return 1;
          }
        return 0;
    }
```

The most important thing to note is that in this whole business object, no mention is made of databases, foreign keys, or any other database-related aspects. By using Customer and SaleSet objects in (4) and (5), programmers use persistent objects and persistent sets without knowing it.

In (6), a Customer object is returned. This is a true object and not merely an identifier. In (7), a customer is assigned to the invoice. Note that once again, you are working with true objects and not with foreign keys. Although the customer is connected to a database, this aspect does not bother programmers. Persistent objects can be manipulated as easily as ordinary transient objects. In (8), a sale is inserted into SaleSet. Whether this is a transient or a persistent set is not seen.

7.1.5 Making Invoices Persistent

To make invoices persistent, we design a class `InvoiceSet`:

```
class InvoiceSet: public PSet {

    Invoice *iCurrent;

    DataSet ds;
    IM_long f_number;
    IM_Date f_date;
    IM_Customer f_customer;
    IM_double f_total;
    IM_SaleSet f_saleset;

public :

    InvoiceSet(Invoice *curr=NULL);
    List (Customer& cust);
    List (Date& date);
    // etc...
};

InvoiceSet::InvoiceSet(Invoice* curr) :
    iCurrent(curr==NULL? curr=new Invoice : curr),
    ds(this, "invoice"),
    f_number (&curr->number, this, "NUMBER"),
    f_date (&curr->date, this, "DATE"),
    f_customer (&curr->customer, this, "CUSTOMER"),         (9)
    // etc...
{}
```

In calling the constructor of `IM_Customer` in (9), we map the `Customer` object onto the customer column in the database. Note that we don't know that we are using a relational database; when initializing the derived `IM_Resolvers`, we cannot see which database or which database technology is actually used. Note also that although we may expect that there will be a join between the invoice table and the customer table (illustrated in Figure 7.2), this fact is not visible in (9), nor in the rest of the program.

To make an invoice persistent, we merely insert it into the invoice set. There is no need to specify exactly how it must be written to the database. This writing is done automatically, thanks to the use of the derived IM resolvers. To insert the invoice in the invoice

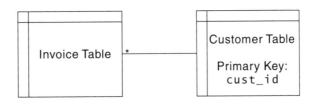

FIGURE 7.2   Example of relational table layout corresponding to the invoice example.

set, we have two options: either make it the programmer's task, or make it Invoice's task. In the latter case, Invoice gets a write function that inserts that invoice into the extent:

```
Invoice::write()
{
   extent->insert(*this);
}
```

7.1.6   Selecting Objects

The next code fragment shows two functions. The first lists all invoices sent on a certain date (the variable dte in the parameter list), and the other lists all of those sent to a certain customer (the parameter cust):

```
// list all invoices sent on a certain date

InvoiceSet::List(Date& dte);
{
   if (seek(f_date == dte)==FOUND)                                    (10)
      {
      cout << "Invoices sent on " << dte << endl;
      do
         {
         cout << iCurrent->number() << "; "
                  << iCurrent->customer().name() << "; "             (11)
                  << iCurrent->total() << endl;
         }
      while (next());
      }
}
```

```
// list all invoices sent to a certain customer

InvoiceSet::List(Customer& cust);
{
  if (seek(f_customer == cust)==FOUND)                      (10')
    {
    cout << "Invoices of " << cust.name() << endl;
    do
      {
      cout << iCurrent->number() << " : "
           << iCurrent->total() << endl;
      }
    while(next());
    }
}
```

A comparison of these two functions shows that they are almost exactly the same, both in functionality and in program code. Indeed, there is no fundamental difference between listing invoices sent on a certain date and listing those sent to a certain customer. However, in a low-level implementation, these functions are totally different.

Listing all invoices sent on a certain date is relatively straightforward. The date object is a pure transient object and also a primitive data type of many database systems. Consequently, the search in (10) is fairly simple, even in classical systems.

It becomes a completely different story, however, when we try to list all of the invoices sent to a certain customer. This time, the customer is no longer a basic data type of the low-level database. It also is no longer a purely transient object. Rather, it is stored in a PSet in its own right. When there is a relational database system underneath, Customer represents, in fact, a row in another database table. Figure 7.3 illustrates this.

In classical approaches, the search in (10') would not be at all straightforward. You would have to worry about the join and thus about foreign keys and so on. In less sophisticated file-oriented systems, you also would have to worry about opening and closing files, about selecting the right index tags, among other things. Furthermore, in classical systems,

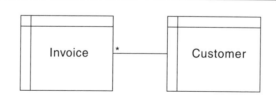

FIGURE 7.3 Using complex data types as class members. Although the programmer using class Invoice notices no fundamental difference between a date and a customer, in a relational system the Customer class represents a separate table.

you need to have (and use!) the knowledge of *how* the customer table is stored in (or rather joined to) the invoice table. But using this knowledge also means that your code depends on this join. This means that whenever you modify the join, you also must modify your code.

In the object-oriented approach, you do not have to specify any details about how to perform the search, no matter how complicated the search operation in (10') is. This is thanks to the complete abstraction of the database concept. Nor do you have to select the right index key.

Indeed, it makes no sense at all that, of two operations that perform exactly the same functionality, one should be simple and the other complicated. Object orientation means that the details (and thus the intelligence) about these operations should reside with the objects themselves. Further, to the user, those objects should all present the same interface and the same operations. All persistence aspects should be the responsibility of these objects only.

Note also that programs using `Customer` might still know that this class is associated with a database. However, in no way can they see that a second database is involved, namely, the one associated with `City`. In other words, the database has been totally abstracted, and there is no longer any difference between a persistent `City` class and a transient `City` class. `City` has indeed become responsible for its own persistence capabilities.

This also implies that a heavy responsibility is placed on the designers of `IM_City`. For example, if they decide to implement this `IM_City` to perform a join (in relational terminology) with the city table, they have to be aware of the consequences this will have. Every class that uses `Customer` (and thus performs a join with the customer table) will implicitly have another join with the city table. Of course, this join might result in a loss of efficiency. So it will be the task of the IM resolver designer to decide whether it is more appropriate to use a join or to store the object in its entirety. The latter might be the preferred choice in the city case.

One of the great strengths of the architecture described in this book is that if the designers of the `IM_resolver` class should find out they made the wrong choice for whatever reason, they can always change their strategy without the rest of the application ever being aware of it. In the case of the `City` class, the designer need only rewrite class `IM_City`; no classes using classes `City` or `IM_City` will need modification.

7.1.7   Comparison with Relational-Bound Techniques

This section looks at what would happen if you fell into the relational trap described in Section 7.1.3. There, `Invoice` contained only the customer's ID, and you would need to write something like the following instead of the code at (10'):

```
// search for rows in 'Invoice' where the relational
// column 'customerColumn' contains the customer's id

if (seek(customerColumn == cust.id())==FOUND)          (12)
   {
   // etc...
   }
```

In (12), you have to explicitly specify (shown in bold in the code fragment) how the customer is stored in the invoice table. Thus the database layout (and technology) also pops up, although it is somewhat disguised.

In (11) in Section 7.1.6, the customer's name was printed. When Invoice contained only the customer's ID, it would not have been possible to print the customer's name without first searching for that customer in the customer set (and thus manually performing the join between the invoice and customer table):

```
InvoiceSet::List(Date& dte);
{
  if (seek(f_date == dte)==FOUND)
    {
    Customer customer;

    cout << "Invoices sent on " << dte << endl;
    do
      {
      customer->seek_id(iCurrent->customerId());              (13)

      cout << iCurrent->number() << "; "
           << customer.name() << "; "
           << iCurrent->total() << endl;
      }
    while (next());
    }
}
```

This extra searching not only unnecessarily complicates the program, it also once again brings up the database layout. Furthermore, because the code to do table joining (shown in bold at (13)) is distributed all over the application, later performance optimizations to this code will be difficult (see Section 7.10.2). The use of the ID is a direct result of the relational database technology that is being used. Migration of this code to true object databases will be very difficult.

7.2 Searching Compound Objects

Chapter 5 examined a technique for searching objects in the database. The examples there implemented this searching for basic data types. This section examines this searching mechanism for the more complex data type Customer.

In Section 7.1.6, we searched the invoice table for those invoices that were sent to a certain customer. To do this, we used the following function call:

```
InvoiceSet::List(Customer& cust);
{
   if (seek(f_customer == cust)==FOUND)
      {
      // etc...
      }
}
```

To facilitate this searching, we have to define a search mechanism for IM_Customer:

```
Condition IM_Customer::queryEqual(Customer& cust)
{
   return column->queryEqual(cust.id());
}

Condition operator==(IM_Customer& imr, Customer& cust)
{
return imr.queryEqual(cust);
}
```

This time, we do not search the customer directly. However, we must search the pertinent table for the customer's ID, which is the field on which the join with the customer table is made (see Figure 7.4).

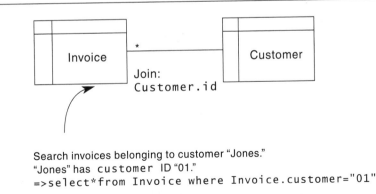

Search invoices belonging to customer "Jones."
"Jones" has customer ID "01."
=>select*from Invoice where Invoice.customer="01"

FIGURE 7.4   The search method of IM_Customer specifies how a customer must be searched in another table.

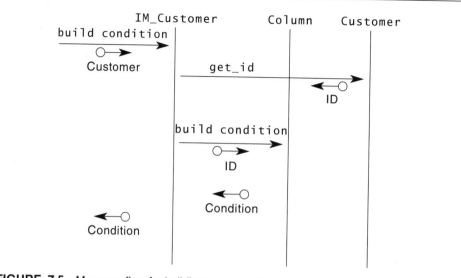

FIGURE 7.5 Message flow for building search criteria based on a `Customer` object.

Thus we can conveniently encapsulate all of this knowledge inside the `IM_Customer` class without having to burden the class `Customer` with it. Notice, too, that although in Figure 7.4 this search process was illustrated with a relational database system, `IM_Customer::queryEqual()` does not require the low-level DBMS to be relational. This function states only that the persistent set containing a customer (`Invoice` in this example) must be searched for a field containing a certain ID. Nowhere do we state that the customer itself is stored in a table or a persistent set. The message flow of this searching mechanism is presented in Figure 7.5.

7.3 Object ID versus Primary Key

In a programming language, an object is uniquely identified through a memory address that indicates where the object resides in the memory space. Hence, this address plays the role of the object identifier. Object databases extend this concept by giving all objects in the database a unique object ID (OID). Relational systems, on the other hand, do not have this concept and require the programmer to identify objects by using, for example, a unique primary key. In a relational environment, you could use this primary key to implement the OID.

There is a distinct difference, however, between OID and the way primary keys are mostly used in relational systems: The OID is assigned by the database system, while the primary key is under the control of the programmer. The most common way to define a database table's primary key is to assemble it from one or more columns of the table. This

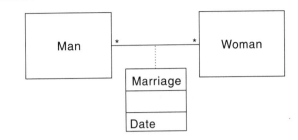

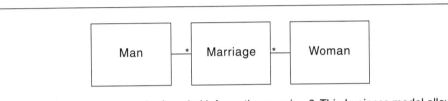

FIGURE 7.6   Keeping track of marital information: version 1. This business model allows people to have multiple marriages, but it does not allow people to remarry each other.

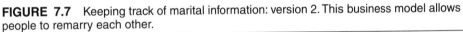

FIGURE 7.7   Keeping track of marital information: version 2. This business model allows people to remarry each other.

assembling must be done in such a way that the primary key is unique. The value of the primary key thus relies on the data it represents, as well as the meaning of that data. This contrasts with the concept of OID, since the OID is independent of the value or meaning of the data it represents.

   Making the primary key dependent on the value of the data stored in the record has some disadvantages. Consider, for example, a system that tracks the marital information of men and women. A first version of that system could be built around the business model shown in Figure 7.6. Following is one of the database tables resulting from this model:

MARRIAGE

Husband	Wife	Date	...

The primary key of this table is (shown in bold) the concatenation of the husband and wife columns. A closer examination of the business model for this system shows that although it allows people to remarry, it does not allow two people to divorce and then to remarry each other. This rule is also enforced in the database by the definition of the unique primary key. Indeed, if two people were to remarry each other, a duplicate primary key would result.

   Thus the primary key is defined not only by the values of the record, but also by the meaning of the data stored in the table. If, later, we alter the business model to allow people to remarry each other (shown in Figure 7.7), we have to alter the definition of the marriage table as follows:

MARRIAGE

Husband	Wife	Date	...

This time, the primary key consists of the columns Husband, Wife, and Date. An event in which two people remarry each other will no longer result in a duplicate primary key, provided, however, that they do not marry, divorce, and remarry all on the same day.

However, this change may have serious consequences on other tables stored in the database. Consider the following two tables:

PERSON

LastName	FirstName	CurrentMarriage	...

WEDDING CHAPEL RESERVATION

Chapel	Marriage	Time	...

Both tables have a foreign key to the marriage table. Changing the definition of the primary key of the marriage table thus requires updating all records stored in the person and wedding chapel reservation tables. These changes may result in a high maintenance cost of the database. In software systems designed using classical or RAD approaches, the situation is even worse. That is, the change in the definition of the primary key may result in having to modify all application programs that work on this database. Indeed, the code that calculates the foreign key values for all columns referencing the marriage table will have to be modified to include also the date of the marriage.

Making the primary key dependent on the value of the data thus breaches encapsulation: Other objects (tables in this case) are affected by changes in the implementation of the marriage table. A better approach is to add an additional column to the marriage table that represents the OID and to make this column the primary key:

MARRIAGE

OID	Husband	Wife	Date	...

The value of the column OID is independent of the value and meaning of the rest of the columns. You could further choose to make the database system itself responsible for assigning the value of this column. Certain database systems have default provisions for this functionality. Otherwise, you can implement it using, for example, stored procedures.

The rules used here to enforce the use of the primary key (such as the requirement that husbands and wives cannot remarry each other) can still be checked on the database level, for example by using triggers. Changes to these rules will no longer affect the other tables in the database.

7.4 Developing Generic IM Resolvers

One apparent drawback of the IM resolver mechanism is that for each new class that must serve as an attribute, an associated IM_Resolver class must be designed. This does not necessarily have to be true, however, if developers create careful class library designs.

There are two main ways to reduce the number of necessary IM_Resolver classes: using inheritance or using templates. Both rely on the OID concept.

7.4.1 Inheritance

An example of using inheritance to reduce the number of IM_resolver classes is the class Customer, designed in Section 7.1.2. To make instances of this class persistent, we created there the class IM_Customer. If we now also design a class Supplier, we will also have to create a class IM_Supplier, which does essentially the same thing as IM_Customer:

```
class IM_Supplier: public IM_Resolver {

    Supplier *suppl;

public :

    IM_Supplier(Supplier *var, DataSet *base, char *nme)
        : IM_Resolver(base, nme, F_LONG)
      {
      suppl = var;
      }

    void to_update(Statement& stmt)
      {
      stmt[column->name()] << suppl->id();
      }

    void read(Cursor& cursor);
      {
      long id;
      cursor[column->name()] >> id;
      suppl->seek_id(id);
      }
};
```

However, because both customers and suppliers are people, we could derive both Customer and Supplier from the common base class Person. This is shown in Figure 7.8. And because customers and suppliers are stored inside other objects very similarly, we do not

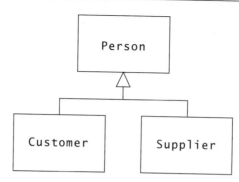

FIGURE 7.8 Applying inheritance. Because both customers and suppliers are in fact people, they can be derived from the common base class `Person`.

need IM resolvers for these objects. Instead, we can use the class `IM_Person` for storing both customers and suppliers:

```
class IM_Person: public IM_Resolver {

  Person *person;

public :

  IM_Person(Person *var, DataSet *base, char *nme)
    : IM_Resolver(base, nme, F_LONG)
   {
   person = var;
   }

  void to_update(Statement& stmt)
   {
   stmt[column->name()] << person->id();
   }

  void read(Cursor& cursor);
   {
   long id;
   cursor[column->name()] >> id;
   person->seek_id(id);
   }
};
```

We can take this line of reasoning even farther if we look at the way articles, shown in Figure 7.1, are stored:

```
class IM_Article : public IM_Resolver {

  Article *art;

public :
  IM_Article (Article *var, DataSet *base, char *nme)
     : IM_Resolver(base, nme, F_LONG)
    {
    art = var;
    }

  void to_update(Statement& stmt)
    {
    stmt[column->name()] << art->id ();
    }

  void read(Cursor& cursor);
    {
    long id;
    cursor[column->name()] >> id;
    art->seek_id(id);
    }
};
```

Here, too, the relationship between an article and another class is implemented by storing the item's ID. Indeed, there is not much difference between people and articles in that both have an ID and a name (or a description). An expression of this relationship is shown in Figure 7.9.

The base class IdObject might take the following form:

```
class IdObject {

  OID  iId;
  char iName[31];

public :
  IdObject();
  OID id() const {return iId;}
```

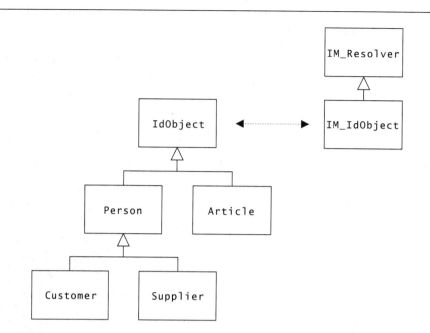

FIGURE 7.9 By using inheritance, we can significantly reduce the number of IM resolvers needed.

```
    void id(OID anid) {iId = anid;}
    virtual char *name() {return iName;}
    void virtual name(const char *str)
      {
      strncpy(iName, str, 30);
      iName[30]='\0';
      }
    virtual seek_id(OID anid) { return 0; }
    // etc...
  };
```

All that is needed now to store any of the classes derived from IdObject is a class IM_IdObject:

```
class IM_IdObject : public IM_Resolver {

  IdObject *obj;

public :
```

```
    IM_IdObject (IdObject *var, DataSet *base, char *nme)
       : IM_Resolver(base, nme, F_LONG)
    {
    obj = var;
    }

    void to_update(Statement& stmt)
    {
    stmt[column->name()] << obj->id ();
    }

    void read(Cursor& cursor);
    {
    long id;
    cursor[column->name()] >> id;
    obj->seek_id(id);
    }
};
```

In a relational philosophy, IM_IdObject represents a join between two database tables, that is, a one-to-one or a many-to-one relationship.

Using this IM resolver, we now can easily define the IM resolvers for customers and articles, which can be used by the persistent invoice set of Section 7.1:

```
typedef IM_IdObject IM_Customer;
typedef IM_IdObject IM_Article;
```

Note that it is better to use a typedef than to directly use IM_IdObject. This is because doing so allows for later changes in either IM_Customer or IM_Article without having to touch the code of the persistent sets.

7.4.2 Templates

Even if we didn't design a class hierarchy starting with a class IdObject, we can still make use of the analogy between classes. For example, we can define a template that specifies how to store a particular type of class. For the classes from Figure 7.9, this template would look like this:

```
template class <T>
class IM_IdObject: public IM_Resolver {

  T *obj;
```

```
public :

    IM_Idobject (T *var, DataSet *base, char *nme)
        : IM_Resolver(base, nme, F_LONG)
      {
      obj = var;
      }

    void to_update(Statement& stmt)
      {
      stmt[column->name()] << obj->id ();
      }

    void read(Cursor& cursor);
      {
      long id;
      cursor[column->name()] >> id;
      obj->seek_id(id);
      }
};
```

Again, we can easily define the IM resolvers that can be used by the `InvoiceSet`:

```
typedef IM_IdObject<Customer> IM_Customer;
typedef IM_IdObject<Article>  IM_Article;
```

As this example illustrates, the number of necessary `IM_resolver` classes has been significantly reduced. All references to other objects can be implemented using the `IM_IdObject` template as long as those objects have member functions `id()` and `seek_id()`.

7.5 An OID-Based Reference Class

In the previous section, we relied on the fact that all objects were identifiable by an OID in order to simplify storing them. The notation proposed in the ODMG standard [ODMG93] also relies on this fact. In ODMG, objects reference other objects by means of a reference template `Ref`. In this notation, the class `Invoice` would look like this:

```
class Invoice: {

    double total;
    long number;
```

```
    Date date;
    Ref<Customer> customer;
    Ref<Article> item[Max_items];

public:
  Invoice();
  Create();
  //etc...
};
```

Figure 7.10 shows a template that allows for a similar notation. When this template is used, the embedded object is no longer directly referenced; it is accessed through the overloaded operator->(). This template thus functions as a smart pointer to a persistent object. It is the ODMG alternative to using pointers. The advantage of using such a template is that it offers good control over how referenced objects are actually accessed. The corresponding IM resolver is presented in Figure 7.11.

The Ref template is implemented in such a way that when an aggregate object (e.g., Invoice) is read, the template retrieves only the OID from the master table (the invoice table). It uses this OID to retrieve the rest of the object (to perform the join) the first time this object is actually referenced. This technique can result in a significant efficiency improvement, especially for less frequently referenced objects.

```
template <class T>
class Ref {

  T* obj;
  int first_time;
  OID id;

public:

  Ref(OID anid = 0)
    {
    id = anid;
    obj = new T;
    first_time=1;
    }
```

continued

```
Ref(T& aT)
   {
   id = T.id();
   obj = new T;
   first_time=1;
   }

~Ref()
   {
   delete obj;
   }

T* operator->()
  {
  if (first_time)
    {
    obj->seek_id(id)
    first_time=0;
    }
  return obj;
  }

operator T*()
  {
  return this->obj;
  }

Ref<T>& operator=(OID anid)
   {
   if (id != anid)
     {
     id = anid;
     first_time=1;
     }
   return *this;
   }

Ref<T>& operator=(T& aT)
   {
   id = aT.id();
   *obj = aT;
   first_time=0;
   return *this;
   }
};
```

FIGURE 7.10 A template that allows for a notation similar to that proposed in the ODMG standard.

```
template <class T>
class IM_Ref: public IM_Resolver {

protected :

  Ref<T> *var;

public :

  IM_Ref(Ref<T> *obj, DataSet *base, const char *nme)
        : IM_Resolver(base, nme, F_LONG, 0, 0)
    {
    var=obj;
    }

  virtual void read(Cursor& cursor)
    {
    OID tmp;
    cursor >> tmp;
    *var = tmp;
    }

  virtual void to_update(Statement& stmt)
    {
    stmt[column->name()] << (*var)->id();
    }

  Condition queryEqual(Ref<T>& value)
    {
    return (*column == value->id());
    }

  Condition queryEqual(T& value)
    {
    return (*column == value.id());
    }
};
```

FIGURE 7.11   The IM resolver that goes with the Ref template.

7.6 Supporting Existing Database Layouts

One striking difference between the persistence architecture presented in Part Two of this book and that of the proposed ODMG standard is that the latter does not have (or seem to need) IM resolvers. This absence is normal, if one considers the function the IM resolvers perform for us: resolving the impedance mismatch between the programming language and the database system. Since ODMG is a standard for object-oriented databases—where the impedance mismatch, by definition, does not exist—there is no need for the IM resolver concept.

Certain ODMG-compliant ODBMS vendors offer products based on a relational architecture. Although the impedance mismatch does exist in these systems, it is handled by the ODBMS itself. Thus it is the ODBMS that is responsible for providing the mapping mechanism between the programming language and the table layout (the database schema). The table layout is directly derived from the business model. A precompiler is often used for generating the corresponding SQL code. As a result, once again the programmer does not come into contact with the impedance mismatch and so has no need for IM resolvers, at least as long as it is possible to derive the database schema directly from the business model.

The Scoop architecture, too, allows for such an approach. A code generator can easily be built that generates the persistent sets using predefined IM resolvers. By the programmer's using templates such as the Ref template given in the previous section, the program code takes the same form as described by ODMG. However, in the approach offered by the IM resolver concept, programmers retain control over the way their objects are eventually stored. This control is very important, especially in relational environments.

An example is the student administration of the University of Ghent. A relational database is used to store all administrative and academic data about the university students. Although this system has been in use for several years, it is continuously extended with new applications, all of which work on the same database. Some of these applications are written using object-oriented techniques, but the older ones were designed using classical approaches.

So we are in the situation mentioned in Chapter 2. That is, we often have to develop software that must use an already existing database. Thus we are no longer free to design the table layout ourselves; instead we have to map our business objects onto the existing database schema. In persistence systems that offer no control over the way objects are stored in the database, our only option is to design the object model so that it leads to the desired table layout. So we have to reverse engineer the database schema to obtain the business model. This means that, once again, our program is dictated by the table layout. This situation is highly undesirable and often leads to business models that are less robust and efficient. That is why one of the key requirements in a persistence architecture is to allow a total separation between the business model and the database layout.

In summary, the concept of IM resolvers brings together the best of two worlds. By using the standard IM resolvers, you get the same ease of working as with the ODMG approach. But because you can still explicitly design alternative IM resolvers, you maintain control over the way data is stored in the database. This control allows you to work with already existing database schemas and to optimize database schemas for maximum efficiency.

FIGURE 7.12 Historical versioning results in a linear version tree. An object is modified and results in exactly one new version of that object.

7.7 Versioning

A property frequently encountered in object-oriented database systems is *versioning*. Versioning allows you to maintain multiple versions of an object. It typically comes in either of two forms: historical and concurrent.

7.7.1 Historical Versioning

Historical versioning gives a linear version tree, as shown in Figure 7.12. It is used when you want to keep and be able to reference the old versions of an object that has been modified.

An example of when this might be necessary is an application that keeps track of a student's courses. Suppose that all students in the same discipline have to take the same courses. The following class definitions could be used:

```
class Student {

  char iName[31];
  //...
  Grade iGrade;

public :

    CourseList& courses()
    {
    return iGrade.courses();
    }
    // etc...
};


class Grade {

  char iName[61];
  //...
  CourseList iCourses;
```

```
public :

  CourseList& courses()
  {
  return iCourses;
  }
  // etc...
};
```

Note that the courses are not in the Student class, since it is a property of the Grade class. In a relational database system, the table layout might look as presented in Figure 7.13.

One problem with this approach is that whenever the faculty decides to change the courses of a Grade, the list of the courses of past students must not change. What actually occurs is that a new version of that particular Grade is created. This new version still has the same object ID, however. So you have not created a new object; you have just altered the old one. To maintain the integrity of the database, you also need to keep the previous versions of the Grade.

The alternative is to not use versioning and instead to keep a separate list of courses for each student, as discussed next.

Database Layout without Versioning

Rather than use historical versioning, you can construct a database layout that doesn't have versioning. In the example, you would maintain a separate list of courses for each student. The result is the database layout without versioning that is shown in Figure 7.14. However, because the same list must be stored for each student, this approach carries a much higher cost in disk space.

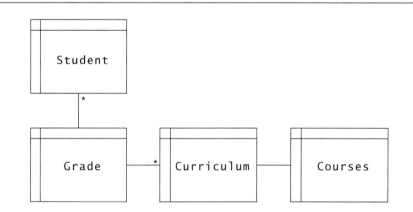

FIGURE 7.13 Student database. Because the list of courses is a property of Grade, there is a one-to-many relationship between the grade and the course list table.

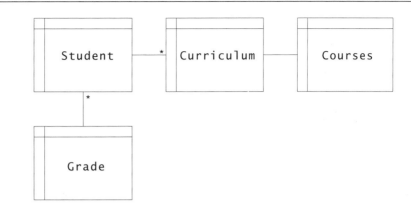

FIGURE 7.14 Student database without versioning. This time, each student can have his or her own specific set of courses, so the one-to-many relationship is now between the student and the curriculum table.

7.7.2 Concurrent Versioning

Concurrent versioning allows you to work with multiple versions of a certain object *at the same time*. Such versioning results in a branched version tree, as shown in Figure 7.15.

One occasion for using multiple, concurrent versions is when working with long transactions [Loomis95]. Such transactions often can last hours, even days, so we cannot always wait to start working on an object. Consider a partially finished document that needs to be revised by someone. The author cannot always wait for the reviser to hand it back so as to continue working on it. Thus each will work on his or her own copy of the document, and the two versions will be merged later.

Most object database systems allow this merging to be done semiautomatically. At the moment, much research is being done to fully automate it. One big obstacle to this, however, is that the database system does not have enough knowledge about the semantic meaning of the data to know whether the merging is meaningful. For example, suppose someone changed the color of the legs of a table object from brown to blue and someone

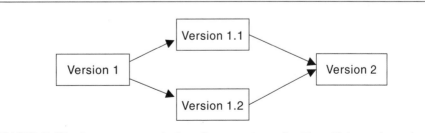

FIGURE 7.15 Concurrent versioning allows you to work with multiple versions of an object at the same time. Eventually, these objects are merged together.

else changed the color of its top to red. It is easy for the database system to merge these two versions. However, what if someone changed the legs to be paper and another person changed the tabletop to concrete? Although merging the two objects is still quite easy, how does the database system know whether this merging still makes sense? The tabletop might have become too heavy for the legs, for example.

7.7.3   Implementing Versioning in Relational Systems

In true object-oriented database systems, versioning is no problem, since most support it. Most other database technologies do not. A fairly simple method for using versioning in, for example, relational database systems is to add to each record a field that contains a version number. Whenever a new version of an object is created, the old record is duplicated, and a new version number is assigned to it. When referencing this record from other tables, you can automatically take the version into account by making the version number a part of the object's primary key. Thus the primary key will consist of the concatenation of the object identifier and the version number:

Primary key = OID + Version

7.8   Stability of Program Code against Schema Changes

The two database layouts presented in Section 7.7.1 (curriculum is part of Grade) and Section (curriculum is part of Student) differ significantly, from a database point of view. However, in a good object-oriented design, which one you use should have little effect on your program code.

For example, suppose a future regulation allows students to choose their individual curriculum, resulting in a different list for each student. Thus it now should become a direct member of class Student instead of class Grade.[1] The resulting database layout is shown in Figure 7.16. The class definitions now become the following:

```
class Student {

    Curriculum curric;
    Grade year;

    public :
```

----

1. Grade then could still contain an instance of Curriculum, this time specifying the possible courses from which the student can choose. For the sake of simplicity, this case is not considered here.

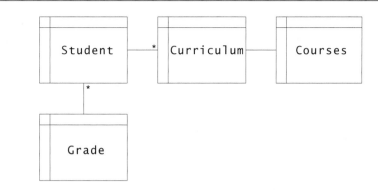

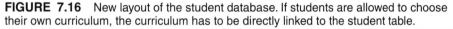

FIGURE 7.16   New layout of the student database. If students are allowed to choose their own curriculum, the curriculum has to be directly linked to the student table.

```
    Curriculum& curriculum();
    Grade& grade();
    // etc...
}
```

However, to the outside world, the student's curriculum can still be accessed in the same way: through the member function `Student::curriculum()`, which is now implemented as follows:

```
Curriculum& Student::curriculum()
{
    return curric;
}
```

Of course, the public interface to class `Student` will have to be extended with new member functions to implement the new functionality the program has to offer: entering a student's curriculum. However, this is clearly not the result of the database layout. As a rule, a class's public interface should change only to implement new functionality, never because of a change in the database layout.

7.9   Storing Multimedia Objects

Because the concept of IM resolvers totally abstracts the way objects are stored, it is well suited to storing multimedia objects. A multimedia object can be stored as easily as any other object. In systems supporting Blobs (binary large object blocks), these data types can be used to store the multimedia object; in other systems, they might be stored in a separate file.

As an example, say you want to design a class `Artist` that contains some general information about the performer, as well as a picture of the person and a sample audio track. The implementation would resemble this:

```
class Artist {

  OID id;
  char name[31];
  char street[31];
  City city;

  Picture photo;
  Music greatest_hit;

public :

  Artist();

  void PlayHit()
   {
   greatest_hit.Play();    // play the sound object
   }
  // etc...
};

class ArtistSet: public PSet {

  Artist *iCurrent;

  DataSet ds,
  IM_OID f_id;
  IM_char f_name;
  IM_char f_street;
  IM_City f_city;
  IM_Picture f_photo;
  IM_Music   f_greatest_hit;

public :

  ArtistSet(Artist *curr):
     ds(this, "Artist"),
     iCurrent(curr!=NULL? curr : curr = new Artist),
     f_id(&curr->id, &ds, "ID"),
```

```
        f_name(curr->name, &ds, "NAME", 30),
        f_street(curr->street, &ds, "STREET", 30),
        f_city(&curr->city, &ds, "ZIP", "CITY"),
        f_photo(&curr->photo, &ds, "PHOTO"),
        f_greatest_hit(&curr->greatest_hit, &ds, "HIT")
    {}
};
```

The corresponding classes `Picture` and `Music` could be part of some multimedia framework. Class `Picture` might look as follows:

```
class Picture {

  BYTE *_bitmap;
  //...

public :

  Picture();
  ~Picture();

  draw();
  name(const char *nme);
  store(const char *filename);
  read(const char *filename);

  BYTE* bitmap();
  bitmap(BYTE* map);
  // etc...
};
```

Although the multimedia framework might allow you to store pictures in a variety of formats (for example, JPEG or TIFF), the chances are very small that it will also contain functionality to store pictures in, for example, a relational database system. The same goes for class `Music`, of course.

To store the picture and music objects in the artist table, you must design the appropriate IM resolvers. An example is class `IM_Picture`:

```
class IM_Picture : public IM_Resolver {

protected :

  Picture *pict;
```

```
public :

  IM_Picture(Picture *p, DataSet *base, char *nme)
    : IM_Resolver (base, nme, F_CHAR)

  { pict = p;
  }

  void read(Cursor& cursor);
  void to_update(Statement& stmt);
};

IM_Picture::read(Cursor& cursor)
{
  string tmp;
  cursor[column->name()] >> tmp;
  pict->name(tmp); // picture takes care of its own persistence
}

IM_Picture::to_update(Statement& stmt)
{
  stmt[column->name()] << pict->name();
  pict->store(pict->name());
}
```

In this implementation, the picture is stored as a file, and the filename is kept in the database. IM_Picture is responsible for storing a picture in the database, and the class Picture knows about different picture file formats. This is indeed a valid approach when Picture is part of a third-party library that contains knowledge about saving pictures using different file formats.

However, it also could be argued that the principle of separation of concerns implies that IM_Picture should be responsible for these file formats. Especially if you were to develop the Picture class in-house, you might want to take this approach. The read function then becomes this:

```
IM_Picture::read(Cursor& cursor)
{
  char tmp[81];
  cursor[column->name()] >> tmp;
  BYTE* btmap = read_from_TIFF_file(tmp);
  pict->bitmap(btmap);
}
```

In an implementation in which you choose to store the picture in a Blob, the picture_field would look like this:

```
IM_Picture::read(Cursor& cursor)
{
  BYTE* btmap;
  cursor[column->name()] >> btmap;   // read BLOB
  pict->bitmap(btmap);
}
```

The same approach can be taken to store or read a music track, for example. You could opt to store the CD name and track number in the database and let the music object retrieve itself from the CD, like this:

```
IM_Music::read(Cursor& cursor)
{
  char tmp[81];
  cursor[column->name()] >> tmp;
  music->id(tmp);
}
```

Note that all of the information that the IM_Picture and IM_Music constructors need are the corresponding objects, the corresponding DataSets, and the symbolic names of the fields. The IM_Resolver classes themselves are intelligent enough to take care of the rest. Thus, as this example illustrates, it is no more difficult to store pictures and sound than it is to store an ordinary string.

7.10 Efficiency

An important consideration in software design is efficiency. One problem with optimizing efficiency is that many things that can affect efficiency don't happen until the program is actually up and running. To increase efficiency, one often must make serious modifications to the database layout or to the way the data is accessed, so it is important to be able to fine-tune an application without having to rewrite large parts of it.

Efficiency depends on several things, mainly the design of the database layout and the optimization of the database access. Optimizing the database access involves two actions: optimizing the network traffic and making no unnecessary calls to the database.

In the data-driven software design that most RAD approaches offer, the program depends heavily on the database layout and database access techniques. Modifications thus often have drastic consequences on the application program, possibly requiring large parts of the program to be rewritten.

However, in a design in which the business model is separated from the database, the problem translates to designing just a new (database layout) view for your model. This task can be done by the database specialist and, in principle, has nothing to do with your application. Next, you need to design a new controller that maps the new view on your model. In the Scoop approach, this controller consists of a collection of derived IM resolvers. Hence, to increase efficiency, it is sufficient to change the appropriate IM resolvers.

7.10.1   Reducing the Number of Joins

A first technique to increase efficiency is to reduce the number of joins between database tables. This can be done by storing the objects completely in a table instead of storing a reference to another table. This technique introduces a certain redundancy, but when it is used wisely, this redundancy should not give too much trouble.

As a rule, this technique should be used only when the redundancy you introduce remains relatively static. A typical candidate for this solution would be the City object. A City is a static object and rather small (only two fields), so it will not introduce much overhead when stored directly in the database. Furthermore, because it is static (the relations between the ZIP code and the city name rarely or never change), you do not have to worry much about getting an outdated version of the city. An example of this technique is given in the following customer table:

CUSTOMER

ID	Name	Street	ZIP	City	...
000001	Brown	Grampian Close	1000	Brussels	
etc...					

By using IM resolvers, you can delay the decision of how to store the City object for the containing objects. Start by having a join between the two tables. If this join becomes an efficiency problem, remove it and put the City object completely in the customer table. Both implementations of the corresponding IM_city were presented earlier in this chapter. It was shown that the rest of the program was independent of the implementation chosen.

An example of an object that is ill suited to be stored in its entirety into a referencing table, is Person. First, it is too big to be stored as a part of another record. Second, the data stored for a person does not stay constant over time. If you store the object in its entirety in each record that references the person, then each time one of the person's attributes changes, each of these records will have to be changed. Such an approach not only gives a significant performance penalty, but also opens a door to database inconsistencies.

You could, however, put part of the person's static data in the other table. This data could include perhaps the person's name, address, and the like. Of course, such decisions should be made very carefully and only if absolutely necessary. As a rule, you should use this technique only if all of the following conditions are met:

- The person's embedded data is needed every time you access the record. (Otherwise, a shallow read, discussed in the next subsection, might be more appropriate.)

- None of the unembedded data is needed every time. (Otherwise, you still have to make a join.)
- The embedded data remains relatively constant. (Otherwise, it is too difficult to keep the database consistent.)

Under no circumstances should any of these decisions affect the use of the business model. These table layout issues should be embedded in the corresponding object and should be totally invisible to all other objects.

7.10.2 Deep and Shallow Reads

In reading objects and joining tables, you can use either of two strategies: the shallow read or the deep read. In the **shallow read,** you read an object that is stored in another table only when you actually need to reference that object. This approach is also called a **read-on-request:** read only the master object. The objects embedded in this object are retrieved only when you actually reference them. The Ref template of Section 7.5 takes this approach.

In most cases, using a shallow read is the best strategy to follow, since tables often may become very deeply nested and only a small fraction of the data is actually needed. Consider an invoice table. This table will typically have joins to the customer and stock tables. The join to the stock table will be through an intermediate table that contains more detailed information about the articles sold (such as quantity and pricing). The stock table will probably have a link to the supplier table. The customer table, too, might have references to other tables (the city table, for example). Thus the invoice may have joins that are multiple levels deep. Reading all referenced objects each time a new row in the invoice table is fetched would be enormous overkill, as most of these objects would never be needed. Such an approach would dramatically impair efficiency. It is thus many times more efficient to fetch only the referenced objects and only when they are explicitly requested.

However, even when a referenced object is requested, it is still not always necessary to fetch it. For example, when you need such an object only to assign it to another object (in other words, to apply operator=), you really need only to pass the OID—and this ID is already known by the Ref template. Thus much will depend on how efficiently you design this template.

There are cases, however, in which you do know in advance that an object that is stored in another table will be needed. In these cases, it might be more efficient to explicitly state the join in the select statement. This might allow you to take advantage of the built-in join-optimization facilities that some of the more advanced relational SQL-based database systems have. Thus you'd want to perform a deep read.

Implementing a Deep Read

A **deep read** is a reading of the entire object at once, including all embedded objects. There are a number of ways to implement a deep read. One is to define appropriate views (and thus specify the necessary joins) on the database level. Alternatively, you could specify the join in the object itself. However, by doing this you explicitly put knowledge about the database schema in the business model.

In the Scoop architecture, it is possible to implement a deep read by redefining the appropriate IM resolver so that it retrieves both objects with a single select statement:

```
template <class T>
class IM_DeepRef: public IM_Ref<T> {

public :

   IM_DeepRef(Ref<T> *obj, DataSet *base, const char *nme)
       : IM_Ref<T>(obj, base, nme)
     {}

   virtual void to_select(SelectStatement& select)
     {
     // add the IM_Resolvers of the referenced object
     // to the select statement
     (**var).extent->buildSelect(select);
pset()->add_filter (*column == *(**var).extent->f_id.column);
     }

   virtual void read(Cursor& cursor)
     {
     // assemble the referenced object from the cursor
     // use dot instead of -> to avoid invoking the
     // overloaded Ref::operator->()
     (**var).extent->read(cursor);
     *var = (**var).extent->current();
     }
};
```

If you use this IM resolver in the invoice example, the data from the invoice table and that from the customer table will be returned in the same database cursor. This is shown in Figure 7.17. The invoice and customer objects can now assemble themselves from this cursor object.

The assembly procedure for class Invoice is the same as always. InvoiceSet's read function calls the read method of all IM resolvers attached to it. When the read method of IM_Customer is called, the associated customer object can directly assemble itself because the necessary customer record has already been fetched. This will result in an efficiency increase. Thus the low-level read function, which fetches the record from the database and puts it in the low-level (relational) buffer, can be skipped, and the read methods of the IM resolvers attached to Customer can be called directly. This saves you from having to make an additional access to the database.

A third approach is based on PrefetchHandlers and is described in [Cleal96].

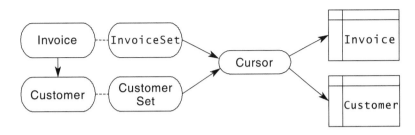

FIGURE 7.17   Increasing efficiency by using deep reading.

Dynamic Switching between Types of Reads

The advantage of using shallow and deep reads is that it allows for very flexible performance tuning. Initially, all relations can be specified using shallow reading. Afterward, when feedback from field tests comes in, those objects that can benefit from deep reading can be pinpointed and the IM resolvers changed from IM_Refs to IM_DeepRefs. When doing so, you do not need to change the rest of the program.

It is even possible to switch dynamically between deep and shallow reading. For example, the IM resolver could maintain a counter that keeps track of how often a referenced object is read. If this counter goes above a certain threshold, the IM resolver can switch from shallow to deep reading. This flexibility can never be achieved with traditional solutions whereby the business model directly accesses the database.

7.10.3   Reducing Network Traffic

Two possible ways to help reduce network traffic and thus help you realize a significant performance increase are

1. Optimizing the application partitioning over the client and server (especially effective in wide area networks (WANs)
2. Using object caching

Optimizing the Partitioning over the Client and Server

The most flexible approach for optimizing the network traffic is to put the business model partly on the server and partly on the client. This is illustrated in Figure 7.18. The business processes that are very database-intensive and do not require user interaction (such as initializing a set of records) can be run on the server. There are two main techniques for implementing this principle: remote procedure calls (RPCs) and object request brokers (ORBs). A complete discussion of ORBs is beyond the scope of this book. Further information can be found in [Otte96] or in [Siegel96]. In Java, remote method invocation (RMI) can be used instead of an ORB.

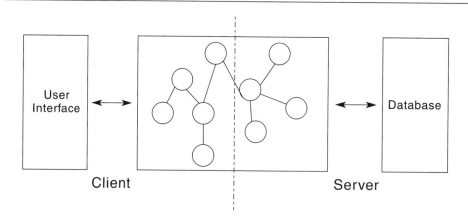

Client   Server

FIGURE 7.18   Application partitioning over the client and server.

Alternatively, you could implement application partitioning by using stored procedures in the database. This approach, however, has two drawbacks. First, it is not portable across database systems. Second, it requires the use of two different programming languages: (1) the database system's SQL dialect to implement the stored procedure and (2) C++ (or any other object-oriented language) to implement the business model.

Object Caching

A second approach that may significantly reduce database access and network traffic is object caching. If the principles described in this chapter are used consistently, object caching is easy to implement because the persistence framework has total control over all reading and writing.

An example of a project in which object caching proved its merits is the student administration of the University of Ghent. The initial application was designed with little regard for database efficiency. The basic premise was that not all of the efficiency aspects could be predicted, partly because they would depend on end-user behavior and partly because the database layout was expected to undergo some significant changes as the application evolved. After the application was introduced in the field, it worked fine for the first couple of months. But as the database grew, performance problems started to occur. These problems occurred mainly at the remote sites of the university that were not yet connected to the university's high-speed network (the university is spread over the city of Ghent). These sites had to connect through relatively slow Internet connections.

Because the user of the set objects sees no fundamental difference between transient and persistent sets, it is easy to introduce object caching in these sets. In the case of the student administration, all objects were derived from a base class `IdObject` with a corresponding persistent set `IdObjectSet`. Object caching was thus easily achieved by letting `IdObjectSet` maintain a transient list of cached objects. This caching mechanism enabled the application to realize an efficiency increase of over six times.

For this caching system to succeed, it was important to be able to cache objects instead of merely the relational data, since the caching algorithm depends on the behavior of the object. Since the algorithm knew why the objects were needed and which operations were performed on the objects, an optimal read and write behavior was achieved. The same level of caching could never have been achieved if the relational data had been accessed directly. As a matter of fact, in certain places in the initial program, the designer tried to make some performance optimizations by directly accessing the database. These were the places that presented problems when the programmers tried to introduce caching.

7.10.4 Paying a Performance Penalty for a Layered Approach

A business model-driven approach might seem less efficient than a two-tiered architecture because of the extra abstraction layer it uses. Although a layered approach does introduce some overhead, in practice this overhead is minimal to nonexistent. The introduction of the extra layer results, in the worst case, in an extra function call. However, the communication with the database (the parsing of the SQL statement, the network traffic, the disk access to fetch the data, and so on) is several orders of magnitude slower and is thus the dominating factor regarding efficiency.

Furthermore, the knowledge of the database layout must be put somewhere. The difference between traditional approaches and the use of a good persistence architecture is that in the latter case, this knowledge is put in a centralized place instead of being scattered all over the application. The overhead this might introduce is largely offset by the flexibility to do performance tuning.

7.11 Summary

This chapter has examined some of the issues involved in developing business objects. Through several examples, it demonstrated that a good persistence architecture makes working with persistent objects as easy as working with transient ones. It also showed that the database layout can be hidden to a fairly high degree and gave as an example the process of searching compound objects in a way that is independent of the database schema.

The chapter compared the object-oriented approach with the disguised relational approach used in many so-called three-tiered, client/server applications. It showed how easy it is to fall into the trap of putting relational knowledge into the business model. If this happens, the aspects of the database layout and database technology get scattered throughout the whole program, thereby making the program almost impossible to maintain.

The concept of object identity was discussed. The chapter showed that the way that primary keys are often used in relational database systems violates the principle of encapsulation. It also explained how generic IM resolvers can be designed based on object identity.

Storing multimedia objects becomes as easy as storing ordinary strings, thanks to the concept of IM resolvers. IM resolvers offer a lot of flexibility in the way in which objects are written to the database. It becomes possible to alter the reading and writing methods (to increase runtime efficiency, for example) without having to modify the rest of the program. The chapter also discussed ways to increase efficiency.

The concept of IM resolvers was compared with the approach offered by the ODMG standard. The chapter showed that it is possible to design a template that allows the same notation and ease as presented in the ODMG standard. However, the IM resolvers have the additional advantage that they completely separate the object model from the database layout. Thus it becomes possible to independently design both the object model and the database. This feature is very important if your application has to use an already existing database.

Chapter 8

Inheritance of Persistent Objects

A fundamental property of the object-oriented paradigm is the concept of *inheritance*. To extend this property to databases, one has to figure out how to apply inheritance also to persistent sets. Luckily, this is not difficult. These sets are nothing more than C++ classes, so it is perfectly possible to apply inheritance rules to PSets and thus design a persistent object hierarchy.

To map inheritance onto a database, you need to understand why inheritance is used in the first place. There are two main reasons to use inheritance: reusability and polymorphism. Depending on the underlying database technology used, choosing one or the other might somewhat influence the design of the actual (low-level) database layout. It is important to keep the application program code largely independent of this representation in the database.

8.1 Specialization: Using Inheritance for Reuse

Probably the most common reason for inheritance in traditional database applications is to achieve reusability. You start with some basic class library, and depending on the application you want to use it for, you derive a class and add some specific behavior to it. This class can be considered to be a specialization of the parent class. You will be working directly with the derived class, which means that you position yourself at the bottom of the inheritance tree.

Consider, for example, the development of an accounting program that concerns dealing with customers and suppliers. Both customers and suppliers are people, and both share functionality and attributes—that is, they both have a name, an address, and so on. Thus you could derive them from a common ancestor Person. Because you also want your people to be made persistent, you would derive a class PersonSet from PSet. This is shown in Figure 8.1.

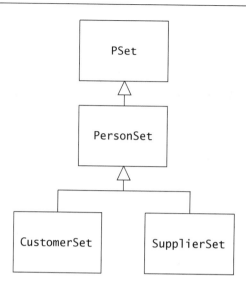

FIGURE 8.1 Inheritance for reuse. When using inheritance for reuse (in other words, to model a specialization), you position yourself at the bottom of the inheritance tree.

In a C++ implementation, the class `Person` might take the following form:

```
class Person {

protected :

  char iName[31];
  char iStreet[31];
  City iCity;

public :

  Person();
  char* Name() { return iName; }
  char* Street() { return iStreet; }

  // etc...

};
```

And the corresponding set class might be this:

```
class PersonSet : public PSet {

protected :

  Person *iCurrent;

  DataSet ds;
  IM_char f_name;
  IM_char f_street
  IM_City f_city;

public :

  PersonSet(Person* curr=NULL, char *setname="PERSON"):
    iCurrent(curr==NULL? curr=new Person : curr),
              ds(this, setname), f_name(curr->iName, &ds, "NAME", 30),
    f_street(curr->iStreet, &ds, "STREET", 30),
    f_city(&curr->iCity, &ds, "ZIP", "CITY")
    {}

  // etc...

};
```

You now can derive a standard class Customer from Person and have it contain all functionality that is common for all kinds of customers. This derived class Customer now has only to implement the customer-specific behavior:

```
class Customer : public Person {

protected :

  double iDebit;
  double iCredit;
  Date iFirstVisit;
  Date iLastVisit;

public :
```

```
    Customer();
    double Debit() const  {return iDebit;}
    double Credit() const {return iCredit;}

    // etc...
};
```

The corresponding set class decides for itself which of the customer attributes it wants to make persistent. The persistence aspects of the attributes that the customer inherited from Person have already been taken care of by PersonSet.

```
class CustomerSet : public PersonSet {

protected :

  IM_double f_debit;
  IM_double f_credit;
  IM_Date f_first_visit;
  IM_Date f_last_visit;

public :

  CustomerSet(Customer* curr=NULL, char *setname="CUSTOMER"):
    PersonSet(curr==NULL? curr=new Customer : curr, setname),
    f_debit(&curr->iDebit, &ds, "DEBIT"),
    f_credit(&curr->iCredit, &ds, "CREDIT"),
    f_first_visit(&curr->iFirstVisit, &ds, "FVISIT"),
    f_last_visit(&curr->iLastVisit, &ds, "LVISIT")
  {};

  Customer* current() { return dynamic_cast<Customer*> iCurrent; }
};
```

Such a Customer class could be developed generically. It has all of the properties that are common for all kinds of customers, whether it is a customer for a bank, a restaurant, or a hospital. This business object Customer can now be put in a generic class library and be made applicable to a wide range of applications.

If you now come into contact with a specific market (for example, banks, dentists, or restaurants) and wish to develop a dedicated program for it, you can derive special-purpose customers from your base class. For example, in a program for dentists, your customer might take the following form:

```
class DentistPatient : public Customer {

  Teeth iTeeth;
  Date iBirth;

public :

   // functionality specific for a DentistPatient.
};
```

And the corresponding set class would look like this:

```
class DentistPatientSet : public CustomerSet {

  IM_Teeth  f_teeth;
  IM_Date   f_birth;

public :

  DentistPatientSet(DentistPatient* curr=NULL,
                    char* setname="PATIENT") :
    CustomerSet(curr==NULL?
                  curr=new DentistPatient: curr, setname),
    f_teeth(&curr->iTeeth, &ds, "TEETH"),
    f_birth(&curr->iBirth, &ds, "BIRTH")
    {}

  DentistPatient* current()
    {
    return dynamic_cast<DentistPatient*> iCurrent;
    }
};
```

Thus you have actually created a persistent class hierarchy, which is shown in Figure 8.2. By careful design of a class library, you not only can cut development time. You also can, as desired, reuse the library in future projects and even distribute it (or sell it) to other developers.

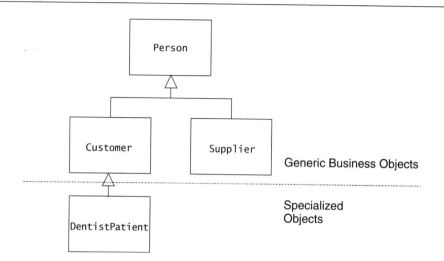

FIGURE 8.2 A persistent inheritance tree. A well-designed framework of persistent business objects not only cuts development time, but also enhances reusability and further hides database-specific issues.

8.2 Generalization: Using Inheritance for Polymorphism

The second reason to use inheritance is to take advantage of *polymorphism*. As an example, consider a sales program in which you want to sell two kinds of things: articles (such as a television or a computer) and services (such as advice or labor). Both things serve the same purpose and share a lot of functionality; specifically, they both represent something that can be sold. However, articles have a supplier and a purchase price, and there is a certain number of them in stock. Services do not have these properties. Thus you could define a common base class Product as follows:

```
class Product {

protected :

  OID iId;
  char iDescription[31];
  int iType;
  double iPrice;
  long iAmountSold;
```

```
public :

    Product();
    virtual ~Product();

    OID id() { return iId;}
    char* description() { return iDescription; }

    int seek_id(OID id_);

    long amount_sold() { return iAmountSold;}
    void update_amount_sold(int n);
    double price() {return iPrice;}
    virtual long in_stock() const;
    virtual double profit() const;

    int type() {return iType;}
};
```

Product could be regarded as a generalization. This time you position yourself on top of the inheritance tree; it is Product with which you want to work. Depending on the particular case, it might take a different form, either Service or Article (see Figure 8.3).

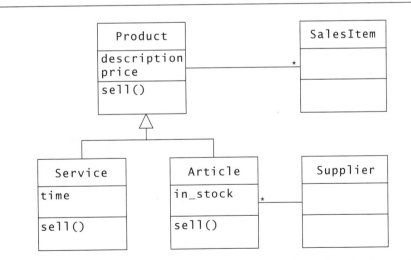

FIGURE 8.3 Both kinds of sales items are derived from a base class Product, which can be regarded as a generalization. It is this base class that you actually want to use.

Each derived class might now look like this:

```
class Service : public Product {

   int iTimeUnits;
   // etc...

public :

   Service();
   long in_stock() const; // returns dummy value
   double profit() const;
   int time_units() const;
};


class Article : public Product {

    double iPriceBuy;
    long   iCurrStock;

public :

    Article();
    long in_stock() const {return iCurrStock;}
    double profit() const {return iPrice - iPriceBuy;}

};
```

Figure 8.4 gives the corresponding sets. Suppose you want to sell an item.[1] You could implement the corresponding function as shown on pages 156–157.

---

1. In this and all other examples, error checking is omitted for simplicity's sake. Furthermore, all user interaction is implemented directly in the code. This, too, is done for simplicity. In real applications, these user interface concepts (the view) should be separated as much as possible from the code.

```
class ProductSet : public PSet {

protected :

  Product* iCurrent;
  DataSet   ds;
  IM_OID    f_id;
  IM_char   f_description;
  IM_long   f_amount_sold;
  IM_double f_price;

public :

  ProductSet(Product* curr=NULL, char* setname = "PRODUCT") :
     iCurrent(curr==NULL? curr=new Product : curr),
             ds(this, setname),
     f_id(&curr->iId, &ds, "ID"),
     f_description(&curr->iDescription, &ds, "DESCRIPTION", 30),
     f_amount_sold(&curr->iAmountSold, &ds, "N_SOLD"),
     f_price(&curr->iPrice, &ds, "PRICE")
     {}

  virtual ~ProductSet();
};

class ServiceSet : public ProductSet {

  IM_int f_time_units;

public :

  ServiceSet(Service* curr=NULL, char* setname = "SERVICE") :
    ProductSet(curr==NULL? curr=new Service : curr, setname),
    f_time_units(&curr->iTimeUnits, &ds, "TIME_UNITS")
    {}

Service* current()
    {
    return dynamic_cast<Service*> iCurrent;
    }
};
```

continued

```
class ArticleSet : public ProductSet {

    IM_long    f_curr_stock;
    IM_double  f_price_buy;

  public :

    ArticleSet(Article* curr=NULL, char* setname = "ARTICLE") :
      ProductSet(curr==NULL? curr=new Article : curr, setname),
      f_curr_stock(&curr->iCurrStock, &ds, "STOCK"),
      f_price_buy(&curr->iPriceBuy, &ds, "PRICE_IN")
      {}

    Article* current()
      {
      return dynamic_cast<Article*> iCurrent;
      }
};
```

FIGURE 8.4 The persistent sets corresponding with `Product`, `Service`, and `Article`.

```
void sell_item()
{
  Product *item;
  int n;

  switch (get_type())
    {
    case SERVICE : item = new Service;
                   break;
    case ARTICLE : item = new Article;
                   break;
    }

  if(item->get())
    {
    n = get_amount();
    if (n > item->in_stock())
      {
      cout << "Not enough in stock";
      }
```

```
    else
      {
      item->update_amount_sold(n);
      cout << "Profit on "<< item->description() << " is "
             << item->profit();  // polymorphic function
      }
    }

  delete item;
}
```

Note that this code is independent of the underlying database layout. Whether services and articles are stored in the same or in different tables, for example, has no influence on this code.

A drawback of the function sell_item() is that the switch statement was needed in order to create the appropriate Product, either Service or Article. A better approach is to use a function New() that takes as arguments the product type and a pointer to the product to be created, as follows:

```
void New(int type, Product** obj)
{
  if (*obj)
    {
    if ((*obj)->type() == type)
      return;   // object is of same type, thus no creation
                // needed
    else
      delete *obj;
    }

  switch (type)
    {
    case SERVICE : *obj = new Service;
                   break;
    case ARTICLE : *obj = new Article;
                   break;
    default      : *obj = NULL;
    }
}
```

This New() function first deletes the old product and then creates a new, derived product, depending on the type parameter. The function sell_item() now becomes the following:

```
void sell_item()
{
  Product *item=NULL;
  int n;

  int type = get_type();
  New(type, &item);

  if(item->get())
    {
    n = get_amount();
    if (n > item->in_stock())
      {
      cout << "Not enough in stock";
      }
    else
      {
      item->update_amount_sold(n);
      cout << "Profit on "<< item->description() << " is "
           << item->profit();  // polymorphic function
      }
    }
  delete item;
}
```

8.3 Using Generalizations as Member Objects

Consider the following class SalesItem, which contains a Product, the number of products sold, and the price of the product:

```
class SalesItem {

private:

  PolymorphicRef<Product> product;
  double amount;
  double price;

  // etc...
}
```

To make this class persistent, you need to address the issue of reassembling it when it is read back from the database. The problem in doing this is that the product attribute will actually be an instance of one of the derived Product classes: Article or Service. So you cannot use the normal Ref and IM_Ref templates. Instead, you have to use templates that take into account this polymorphic behavior.

```
class SalesItemSet : public PSet {

protected:

  SalesItem *iCurrent;

  IM_PolymorphicRef f_product;
  IM_double f_amount;
  IM_double f_price;

  // etc...
}
```

Such a reference can be implemented generically by using the following PolymorphicRef template. This template expects there to be a New() function that creates an object of the specified type.

```
template <class T>
void New(int type, T** obj);

template <class T>
class PolymorphicRef {

  T* obj;
  int type;
  int first_time;
  OID id;

public:

  PolymorphicRef(OID anid = 0, int atype=0)
    {
    set(anid, atype);
    }
```

```
PolymorphicRef(T& aT)
  {
  set(aT.id(), aT.type());
  }

virtual ~PolymorphicRef()
  {
  delete obj;
  }

void set(OID anid, int atype)
  {
  id = anid;
  type = atype;
  first_time = 1;
  }

T* operator->()
  {
  if (first_time)
    {
    New(type, &obj);
    if (obj)
      obj->seek_id(id);
    first_time=0;
    }
  return obj;
  }

// etc...
}
```

This template is largely analogous to the Ref template of Section 7.5. Before the object is fetched from the-database, it first is created via a call to the New() function. This is necessary because after each read, the object can be of a different type. The corresponding IM resolver also is fairly straightforward. The main difference with IM_Ref is that this time, you also store the object type to the database.

```
template <class T>
class IM_PolyRef: public IM_Resolver {
```

```
protected :

  PolymorphicRef<T> *var;
  Column *typeCol;

public :

  IM_PolyRef(PolymorphicRef<T> *obj, DataSet *base,
             const char *nme, const char* nmetype)
     : IM_Resolver(base, nme, F_LONG),
    {
    var=obj;
    // define a second column to maintain the object's type
    typeCol = new Column(base->Table()[nmetype]);
    }

  virtual ~IM_PolyRef()
    {
    delete typeCol;
    }

  virtual void read(Cursor& cursor)
    {
    OID id;
    int type;
    cursor[typeCol->name()] >> type;
    cursor[column->name()] >> id;
    var->set(id, type);
    }

  virtual void to_update(Statement& stmt)
    {
    stmt[column->name()] << (*var)->id();
    stmt[typeCol->name()] << (*var)->type();
    }

  Condition queryEqual(Ref<T>& value)
    {
    return ((*column == value->id()) &&
            (*typeCol == value->type()));
    }
```

```
Condition queryEqual(T& value)
  {
  return ((*column == value.id()) &&
          (*typeCol == value.type()));
  }
};
```

8.4 Inheritance in Relational Database Systems

As stipulated in Chapter 4, there are several ways in which you can map an inheritance relation onto a relational database. Which you choose depends on why you are using inheritance, that is, whether for reuse or polymorphism. Note that the `PolymorphicRef` template does not need to know the representation of the inheritance relationship in the database.

8.4.1 Using Inheritance for Reuse

The mapping of inheritance for reuse onto a relational database table is relatively straightforward. In this case, you do not really need to access other, similar tables. Each class can be considered as a separate, independent entity that has no relationship with any other class that shares the same parent. Thus you use inheritance only on a programming language level, not on a database level. You would not use it in the first place so as to exploit similar behavior between classes. Rather, you rely on those similarities to speed the software development process and to make the software more robust via the use of previously developed modules.

As a result, when translating the object model to a database layout, you do not need to model this dependency. It is perfectly possible to construct a table that contains the fields of both the parent and the descendant classes. In this way, you get for each (nonabstract) class exactly one table that contains all of the information about that (and only that) class. This is illustrated in Figure 8.5. The customer and supplier tables thus look like the following:

CUSTOMER

ID	Name	Street	ZIP	City	Phone	Fax	Debit	Credit	FVisit	LVisit
...										

SUPPLIER

ID	Name	Street	ZIP	City	Phone	Fax	AccountNr	Debit	Credit
...									

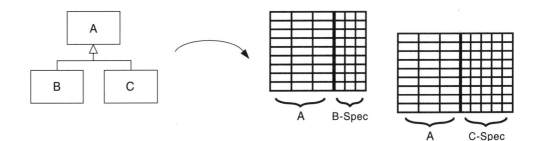

FIGURE 8.5   Mapping specialization. The most common way to map inheritance for reuse (a specialization) is to provide a separate table for each specialization, with each table containing both the parent class data and the specialization-specific data.

8.4.2   Using Inheritance for Polymorphism

When you use inheritance for polymorphism, your table layout will depend on the level at which you want to use the polymorphism. If you want to use the generalization just on the programming level, you will use a different layout than if you want to use it also on the database level (for example, to perform runtime queries).

Using a Single Table

The choice of the table layout also depends on the ways in which the objects differ. If they differ only in functionality and have more or less the same attributes, you can safely put them in the same table. This is shown in Figure 8.6.

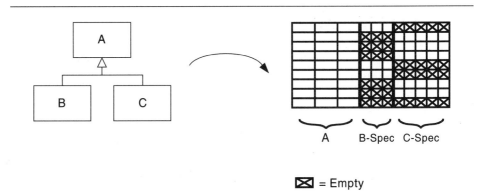

= Empty

FIGURE 8.6   Modeling inheritance. If all objects have more or less the same attributes, a possible way to model inheritance in the database is to place all information about all classes in the same table.

Consider, for example, an employee database. In many countries, the regulations for employing blue-collar workers and white-collar workers differ. So it could be useful to have two different classes, `BlueCollarEmployee` and `WhiteCollarEmployee`, both derived from the base class `Employee`. However, although those two objects will have different behaviors, their table layouts will be nearly the same. Hence, specifying whether a given employee is a white-collar worker or a blue-collar worker can be implemented by a simple type attribute in the database, as shown in the following table:[2]

EMPLOYEE

ID	Name	Class	Function	...
1	Jones	WC	Accountant	
2	Smith	BC	Mechanic	

Using Separate Tables

When the attributes of two objects differ considerably, however, the previous approach can lead to a serious waste of disk space. Consider the example of the services and articles. Putting both types of products in the same table would not only be highly inefficient. It also would cause problems when you want to introduce a third kind of product (such as a menu, which consists of services). This is because you would have to extend your table again, thereby leading to even greater inefficiencies. In this case, you have the option of using the same technique used for specialization and thus put the different types of products in two completely separate tables (see Figure 8.5).

The third alternative is to use one table to represent the common attributes of the derived products, placing the specific attributes in two dedicated tables, as shown in Figure 8.7. Which alternative you choose depends on what you want to use the polymorphism for. If you want to use it just on individual objects (for example, to edit items, sell items, and so on), you can safely put them in separate tables (as illustrated in Figure 8.4). This approach will give you the advantage of having one join less, thereby increasing the runtime efficiency.

SERVICE

ID	Description	Price	Time_units	N_Sold
1	Labor	25	1	67
4	Installation	32	2	72
5	Adjustment	42	4	14

---

2. It could even be argued that the use of inheritance for such a small difference is excessive to start with. However, for the sake of argument, suppose that the two types of objects have behaviors that are different enough that it is worth putting them in separate classes.

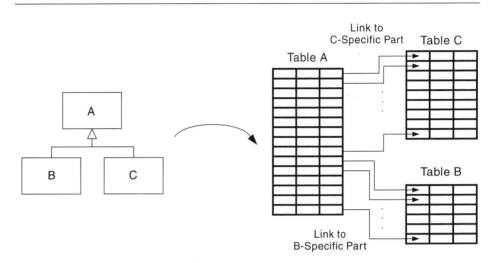

FIGURE 8.7 The third way to model inheritance in the database is to use a separate table for each class.

ARTICLE

ID	Description	Supplier	Price	In_stock	Price_buy	N_Sold
2	Television	Nokia	1000	6	700	17
3	Video	Sony	699	7	500	16

However, if you want also to be able to work on collections of Product objects, it is better to put them in tables that share a common ancestor. An example of an operation that works on a collection of products is sorting the products based on the number sold. Sorting by using separate tables would require a constant switching between the two tables. Even worse, it would not allow you to use the built-in indexing capabilities of the low-level database system.

You can avoid this situation by creating a separate table for each class: one for the parent class and one for each of its children. The children tables contain pointers to the corresponding record in the parent table. By putting all common attributes in the parent table, then if you want to draw statistics on these attributes, you have to query only a single table. All attributes that are unique to a derived class are, of course, put in the table dedicated to that particular class.

PRODUCT

ID	Description	Price	N_Sold	Type
1	Labor	25	67	1
2	Television	1000	17	2
3	Video	699	16	2
4	Installation	32	72	1
5	Adjustment	42	14	1

SERVICE

Parent	Time_units	. . .
1	1	
4	2	
5	4	

ARTICLE

Parent	Supplier	In_stock	Price_buy
2	Nokia	6	700
3	Sony	7	500

8.4.3 Implementing Multitable Inheritance

As explained in previous chapters, each DataSet instance corresponds with a database table. Thus to implement the multitable inheritance of Figure 8.7, you need an additional DataSet instance to represent the table that contains the attributes of the derived class. Every IM resolver now can be attached to the Dataset that corresponds with the table into which the column(s) must be stored. Figure 8.8 shows how this is done.

   The implementation of the multitable versions of the persistent sets ServiceSet and ArticleSet is shown in Figure 8.8. Notice how little these classes have been changed from their single-table versions. The only changes needed were the adding of another DataSet and another IM resolver, IM_Inherit, which is used to join the two tables together. The task of IM_Inherit is to add the appropriate where clause to the select and update statements. It also must set the foreign key with the OID of the parent object in the insert statement.

```
class ProductSet : public PSet {

protected :

  Product* iCurrent;

  DataSet    ds;
  IM_OID     f_id;
  IM_char    f_description;
  IM_long    f_amount_sold;
  IM_double  f_price;

public :

  ProductSet(Product* curr=NULL, char* setname = "PRODUCT") :
     iCurrent(curr==NULL? curr=new Product : curr),
              ds(this, setname), f_id(&curr->iId, &ds, "ID"),
     f_description(&curr->iDescription, &ds, "DESCRIPTION", 30),
     f_amount_sold(&curr->iAmountSold, &ds, "N_SOLD"),
     f_price(&curr->iPrice, &ds, "PRICE")
     {}

  virtual ~ProductSet();
};

class ServiceSet : public ProductSet {

DataSet ds_Service;
  IM_int f_time_units;
  IM_inherit f_inherit;

public :
```

continued

```
       ServiceSet(Service* curr=NULL, char* setname = "SERVICE") :
           ProductSet(curr==NULL? curr=new Service : curr),
                      ds_Service(this, setname),
                      f_time_units(&curr->iTimeUnits,
                      &ds_Service, "TIME_UNITS"),
              f_inherit(&f_id, &ds_Service, "PARENT")
       {}

       Service* current()
       {
       return dynamic_cast<Service*> iCurrent;
       }
};


class ArticleSet : public ProductSet {

    DataSet ds_Article;
    IM_long    f_curr_stock;
    IM_double f_price_buy;
    IM_inherit f_inherit;

public :

   ArticleSet(Article* curr=NULL, char* setname = "ARTICLE") :
      ProductSet(curr==NULL? curr=new Article : curr),
                 ds_Article(this, setname),
                 f_curr_stock(&curr->iCurrStock, &ds_Article, "STOCK"),
      f_price_buy(&curr->iPriceBuy, &ds_Article, "PRICE_IN"),
      f_inherit(&f_id, &ds_Article, "PARENT")
      {}

   Article* current()
      {
      return dynamic_cast<Article*> iCurrent;
      }
};
```

FIGURE 8.8 The persistent sets corresponding with Product, Service, and Article
implemented using three separate tables.

For example, the generated SQL code for selecting and updating a service must become the following:

```
// select a service:
select Product.ID, Product.DESCRIPTION, Product.N_SOLD,
Product.PRICE, Service.TIME_UNITS from Product, Service where
Service.ID = Product.ID

// update a service

// first update the product table
update Product set DESCRIPTION = <service->description()>, N_SOLD
= <service->amount_sold()>, PRICE = <service->price()>

// next update the service table
update Service set TIME_UNITS = <service->time_units()> where
Service.ID = <service->id()>
```

The IM resolver that performs this functionality is given next:

```
/*
    IM_OID *fld:     the IM resolver in the top class that
                     represents the primary key of the base table
    DataSet *base:   the DataSet to which this IM resolver is attached
    char* nme :      the name of the column containing the foreign
                     key to the base table
*/

class IM_Inherit : public IM_Resolver {

protected :

  OID foreign_key;
  IM_OID *f_id;       // the id column of the top class

public :

  IM_Inherit(IM_OID *fld, DataSet *base, const char *nme)
        : IM_Resolver(base, nme, F_CHAR)
    {
    f_id = fld;
    }

  virtual void to_select(SelectStatement& selectstmt)
    {
    pset()->add_filter(*column == *f_id->column);
    }
```

```
virtual void read(Cursor& cursor)
  {
  // do nothing
  }

virtual void to_insert(InsertStatement& insertstmt)
  {
  foreign_key = *f_id->obj;
  insertstmt[column->name()] << foreign_key;
  }

virtual void to_update(UpdateStatement& updatestmt)
  {
  pset()->add_filter(*column == *f_id->obj);
  }
};
```

This resolver takes as arguments an IM_OID, a DataSet, and a column name. The first argument is the IM resolver that is connected with the objects OID (which is thus an attribute of the base class and is stored in the Product table). The second argument is the DataSet instance that represents the service table. The last argument is the name of the column in the service table that contains the reference to the product table.

The easy transition achieved between the different kinds of inheritance implementation is a very important characteristic. This is because the mapping of the object model onto the table model is something that can change significantly over time. For example, you could start out with one table per class. However, due to performance considerations you later have to group several classes of the inheritance hierarchy into a single table. If you had written your code directly on top of the RDBMS layer, you would have to change every update, insert, select, and delete statement, as well as all search criteria. In medium-to-large-sized applications, such changes may require several weeks of work.

8.5 Designing Reusable Software Components

This section looks at some of the issues involved in designing reusable software components. You will see that an important consideration in this regard is the domain of usability.

8.5.1 Develop Independent Designs

As shown with the previous examples in this chapter, inheritance allows you to design software components that can be reused in a wide range of applications. When designing a library of reusable components, you must take into account a number of considerations.

You should always try to develop classes that are as independent from each other as possible. Classes should depend on each other only if they have to work together to accomplish a common goal. Such a collection of classes is called a *framework*. It's very frustrating to come across a class that is perfectly well suited for a certain application and then have to reject it just because, to use it, you would have to include in your application a whole library of other, unneeded classes. For example, how many extremely smart string classes have turned out to be unusable because they depend on a whole set of other classes (very often starting with a base class Object) that you never want to use and that sometimes even give name conflicts with other frameworks you are using?

   This design principle, as shown later in the chapter, also influences how you implement relationships.

8.5.2   Determine the Domain of Usability

One of the first things you have to decide when designing a class library is the range, or domain, of applications for which you want the classes to be useful. Of course, the larger this domain, the better. It is important to realize that every time you inherit a class from a certain parent, the domain of the child is a subset of that of the parent class (see Figure 8.9):

$$A \text{ is parent of } B \Rightarrow \text{dom } B \subseteq \text{dom } A$$

   Thus, by using inheritance, you limit the application domain of a class. However, you can extend the application domain of a certain amount of code by introducing a base class.

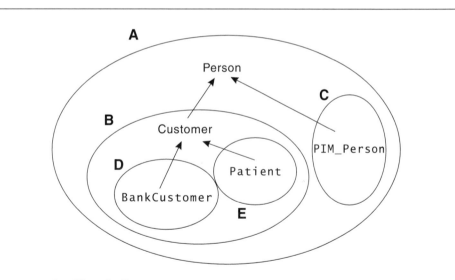

A = All applications
B = Business applications
C = Personal information managers
D = Banking applications
E = Medical applications

FIGURE 8.9   Domain of usability. Using inheritance, you can specialize a generic object for a certain application domain.

So it can be very useful to introduce certain base classes even if you do not need them right away, as doing this can significantly enlarge the reusability of your software.

Consider the development of a banking application. You could directly construct a class BankCustomer that contains all of the customer's properties (see Figure 8.10). However, you then would have a class that is usable only in banking applications. So it's wiser to design your class as pictured in Figure 8.11. In this case, a separate class is created for each possible subdomain, thus leading to a class BankCustomer that will be reusable in banking applications, a class Customer reusable in all kinds of business applications, and a class Person reusable in an even wider range of applications.

For example, class Customer could be reused to develop an application for dentists or for bookstores. Person could be reused to develop a class Supplier (which has the same

FIGURE 8.10   A class BankCustomer. By putting all information in the same class, you limit the application range to banking applications only.

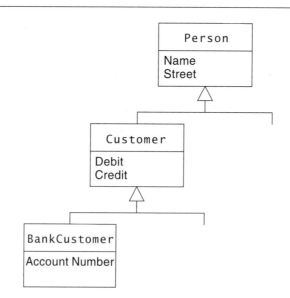

FIGURE 8.11   Reusable design. By dividing BankCustomer over several classes, you enlarge the domain of applications in which you can reuse portions of the inheritance tree.

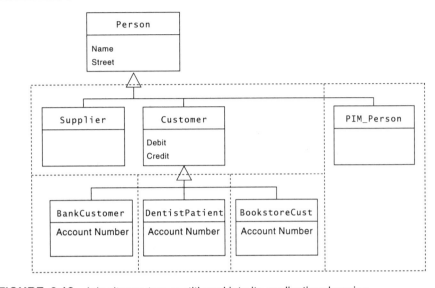

FIGURE 8.12 Inheritance tree partitioned into its application domains.

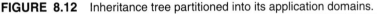

application domain as Customer). However, it also could be used in a PIM (personal information manager) to maintain an address and phone list. These possibilities are depicted in Figure 8.12. As you can see, a clever use of inheritance allows you to construct inheritance trees that are reusable in a wide range of applications.

8.6 Summary

This chapter discussed the two main reasons to use inheritance—reusability and polymorphism—and showed how a reusable persistent inheritance tree can be built.

It also discussed the construction of reusable software components and introduced the notion of the domain of usability. Further, it showed that by careful use of inheritance, you can develop a framework of business objects that can be reused in a very wide range of applications.

The chapter also presented some methods of mapping the inheritance tree onto a relational database table layout. You can choose from among three methods: putting each class in a separate table, putting all classes in the same table, or designing one table per class, in which only the properties specific to that class are placed. The choice among these methods depends largely on why inheritance is used.

Chapter 9

Associations

Chapter 7 discussed a first type of association: making an object a member of another object. Chapter 9 looks in greater detail at modeling and implementing associations. In light of the importance of relational databases, it also discusses the mapping of associations onto a relational database layout. It is important to note that it discusses the mapping of the object model onto the relational database layout, not the other way around. Your object model, and thus also your program, will be largely independent of this mapping and of the relational technology.

9.1 Many-to-One Relationships

In previous chapters, when we were embedding a persistent object into another, we actually were implementing a one-to-one or a many-to-one relationship. Here's a review of the Person-City relationship:

```
class Person {

private :
  long iId;
  char iName[31];
  char iStreet[31];
  City iCity;

public:
  // etc...
};
```

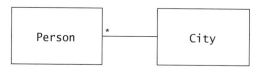

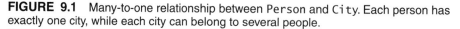

FIGURE 9.1 Many-to-one relationship between `Person` and `City`. Each person has exactly one city, while each city can belong to several people.

Graphically, this relationship could be represented as in Figure 9.1.

Thus one can conclude that by making a persistent object a member of another persistent object (a "has-a" relation), a many-to-one relationship is implicitly implemented. Important here is the ease and the naturalness with which this is done. You do not have to worry about foreign keys, or joins, or anything similar. You can work as easily as if you were working with transient objects. Furthermore, the way in which this relationship is mapped onto the database can be altered at any time without affecting the rest of your program.

9.2 Attributes versus Associations

Traditional database design methodologies (for example, those using entity-relationship (E/R) modeling) consider a significant difference between attributes and associations. This difference is one reason why E/R diagrams are often many times more complex than object-oriented business models. When the question is asked, "What is the distinction between an attribute and an association?" the answer often is that an attribute is an elementary data type, while an association is made to a compound data type.

When looking at, for example, an invoicing class, you could say that the invoice number is an attribute, whereas the relationship with `Customer` is an association (see Figure 9.2). This is indeed correct, as the invoice number is merely a long integer, and thus a basic data type, whereas the customer is a class on its own and thus worth some extra attention. However, don't confuse elementary data types with the built-in data types of, for example, the RDBMS or the programming language. With relational databases, an attribute is often considered to be of a built-in data type. When the related object is stored in another database table, reference is to an association.

Although it is correct to regard the built-in data types as being elementary data types, a class (or a table in an RDBMS) can also be regarded as being elementary. Whether A is an attribute or an association of class B depends on whether the two data types A and B are situated on the same level of abstraction. In this section's example, `Invoice` and `Customer` are on the same level of abstraction. However, an examination of some of class `Customer`'s attributes shows that many of them might be classes themselves, as shown in the following table:

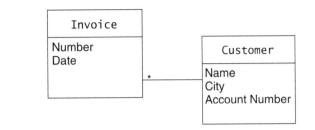

FIGURE 9.2 Customer-Invoice relationship.

Built-in Data Types	Compound Data Types
Name (string)	City (class City)
Street (string)	Account (class BankAccount)

Not only is class City a class, but, as illustrated in the previous paragraph, it is even connected to a database table. However, when Customer is modeled, this connection to a database table is completely beside the point; because City resides on a lower level of abstraction, it can be considered an attribute. The same line of reasoning goes for class BankAccount.

Another example is the modeling of the classes Invoice and Article. The relationship between Article and Invoice is an association. A closer look at Article shows that every article has a name, and each article belongs to a certain category. This category, although a class of its own (and very likely connected to a database table), can easily be considered an attribute of Article. This is shown in Figure 9.3.

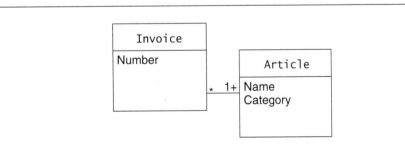

FIGURE 9.3 Invoice-Article relationship. Whether a relationship is called an attribute or an association depends on how important that relationship is in the model being designed.

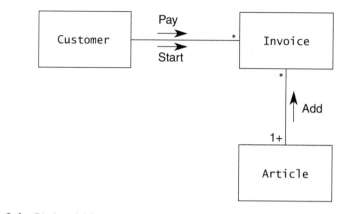

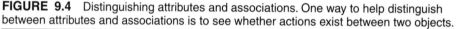

FIGURE 9.4 Distinguishing attributes and associations. One way to help distinguish between attributes and associations is to see whether actions exist between two objects.

From an object-oriented point of view, the distinction between an attribute and an association is, strictly speaking, purely artificial. Whether something is called an attribute or an association depends on how important that object is to the model being designed. An association usually takes place between objects on the same level of abstraction. Both objects can exist independently in the object model. An attribute usually resides on a lower level of abstraction and is less meaningful when considered on its own. Also, the object containing the attribute is missing something when the attribute is removed.

One way to distinguish between attributes and associations is to determine whether actions exist between the two objects. For example, from an examination of Invoice and number one can say only that an invoice has a number; no real actions exist between the two objects. Only the attribute's value is of importance. In contrast, in reviewing Invoice and Customer, one can distinguish several actions. That is, the customer starts an invoice, the customer pays the invoice, and so on. The same reasoning goes for the relationship between Invoice and Article: You can add items to the invoice, and you can subtract them, as shown in Figure 9.4.

Note, by the way, that this model differs from an E/R representation, in which the City and Category would also be included. This is shown in Figure 9.5.

9.3 Collections: One-to-Many Relationships

The modeling of Invoice and Customer allowed each invoice to have only one customer. However, a fresh look at the relationship between Customer and Invoice shows that each customer can have *several* invoices, that is, Customer can have a collection of Invoices.

A collection, or container, is a common data structure in programming. It exists in many different implementations: sets, bags, lists, and so on. It is characterized primarily

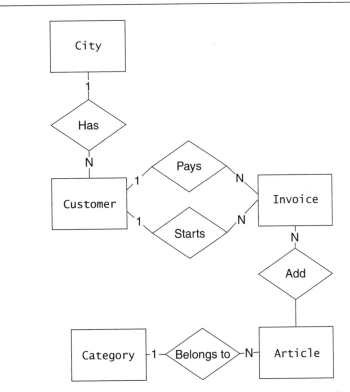

FIGURE 9.5   In an E/R diagram, the `City` and `Category` objects are also modeled, even though these are situated on a lower level of abstraction.

by its ability to contain an unspecified number of objects. This contrasts with an array, for which the dimensions have to be known in advance.

Containers correspond to a one-to-many relationship. In a relational model, they are implemented using a separate table, while arrays are implemented using a fixed number of fields in the table that contains the array.

9.3.1   Example: Department-Employee-Project Relationship

An example is a department that hires employees and accepts projects. It assigns to each project only one employee; however, an employee can be assigned to several projects at the same time.

The relationship between `Employee` and `Project` is a one-to-many: Each project belongs to one employee, and each employee can have several projects. This is shown in Figure 9.6.

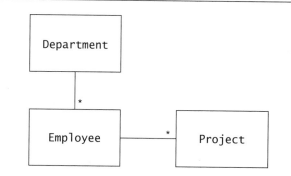

FIGURE 9.6 Department-Employee-Project relationship. Three one-to-many relations can be distinguished in this example. One is between Department and Employee, and another is between Employee and Project. The third is between Department and Project, but this relationship is not considered here.

In a C++ implementation, this model might result in a class Employee that contains, among other things, a Department and a list of Projects:

```
class Employee {
   String iName;
   Ref <Department> iDepartment;
   List <Project> iProjects;// one-to-many
   // etc...
};
```

The relationship between Employee and Department is a "has-a" and was discussed in the previous section. Next, we look at the relationship between Employee and Project.

In the relationship between Employee and Project, Employee does not contain a single project, but rather a list or a set of them. Notice, however, that from the viewpoint of Project, the relationship between Project and Employee is "has-a," which might be implemented in the usual way, as follows:

```
class Project {
   String iName;
   Ref<Employee> iEmployee;
   // etc...
};
```

9.3.2 ODMG Notation

To express the bidirectional path of the previous association, the ODMG standard introduced the keyword inverse. Using the notation of this standard, you get the following class definitions:

```
class Employee: Persistent_Object {
  String iName;
  Ref<Department> iDepartment;
  List<Project> iProjects inverse Project::iEmployee;
  // etc...
};

class Project: Persistent_Object {
  String iName;
  Ref<Employee> iEmployee inverse Employee::projects;
  // etc...
};
```

Among other things, the inverse keyword allows the database to automatically check referential integrity. Furthermore, it automatically ensures that if you set Project::iEmployee to a certain value, the corresponding Employee member also references that particular project.

However, by implementing the association in this way, you make the classes Project and Employee dependent on each other. Whether this dependency is acceptable depends on the application you are designing, the importance of the relationship, and the domain of usability of each object. This problem is tackled later in the chapter.

9.3.3 An ODMG-like List Class

Following is a List template that offers a similar notation to that found in the ODMG standard. It expects the owner of the list to be an object that is identifiable and derived from the class IdObject designed in Section 7.4.

```
template <class T>
class List: public PSet {

  IdObject* iOwner;
  Ref<T> iCursor;

  DataSet ds;
  IM_Ref<T> f_cursor;
  long iOwnerId;
  IM_long f_owner;

public:
  List (IdObject* owner, char* setname,
        char *ownrnme, char *manysidenme);
```

```
    IdObject* GetOwner (void);
    const Ref<T>& Current (void);
    void SetOwner (IdObject* owner);
    void SetCurrent (const T& curr);

    int FirstElement (void);
    int NextElement (void);
};

template <class T>
List<T>::List(IdObject* owner, char* setname,
                char *ownrnme, char *manysidenme)
    : ds(this, setname),
      f_owner (&iOwnerId, &ds, ownrnme),
      f_cursor (&iCursor, &ds, manysidenme)
{
    SetOwner (owner);
}
```

In this approach, it becomes the responsibility of the member function FirstElement()
to allow only those objects that are referenced by owner:

```
template <class T>
int List<T>::FirstElement(void)
{
    return (seek (f_owner == iOwner->id())==FOUND);
}
```

The implementation of the other member functions is straightforward:

```
template <class T>
int List<T>::NextElement(void)
{
    return (next());
}

template <class T>
IdObject* List<T>::GetOwner (void)
{
    return (iOwner);
}
```

```
template <class T>
const Ref<T>& List<T>::Current (void)
{
  return (iCursor);
}

template <class T>
void List<T>::SetOwner (IdObject* ownr)
{
  iOwner = ownr;
}

template <class T>
void List<T>::SetCurrent (const T& curr)
{
  iCursor=curr;
}
```

An example is the `Employee-Project` relationship implemented with this `List` class. The definition of class `Employee` now looks like this:

```
class Employee {
  String iName;
  Ref<Department> iDepartment;
  List<Project> iProjects;

public:
  String& name();
  List<Project>& projects();
  // etc...
};

Employee::Employee() :
    iProjects (this, "ProjList", "EMP", "PROJECT"),
    // etc...
{}
```

In a relational database system, this relationship would be implemented using the table layout on the next page.

EMPLOYEE

ID	Name	FirstName
1	Van Damme	Philippe
2	Van Hollebeke	Michelle
3	Carron	Kris
4	Tromp	Herman

PROJECT LIST

Employee	Project
1	1
1	2
2	2
3	1
4	3

PROJECT

ID	Name	...
1	VerySecretMission	...
2	EvenMoreSecretMission	...
3	MostSecretMissionEver	...

This example illustrates that once more, the business model and the implementation of the business classes are in no way connected to the actual database layout. The following code uses the List template to list all projects assigned to a certain employee:

```
ListProjects(Employee& emp)
{
    cout << "Projects for employee " << emp.name() << endl;
    List<Project>& projects = emp.projects();

    if (projects.FirstElement())
      {
      do
        {
        cout << projects.Current()->name() << endl;
        }
      while (projects.NextElement());
      }
}
```

9.3.4 An Alternative Approach

An alternative way to implement the association between `Employee` and `Project` is to let class `Project` take care of it. (Section 9.7.2 covers this in more detail.) In this case, you get a many-to-one relationship and can thus work with the ordinary embedding relationship explained in the previous section.

Say you want to assign a new project to an employee. You could say either that you assign the project to the employee or that you assign the employee to the project. And since the project can have only one employee assigned to it, this is an ordinary embedding relationship. The simplest way to implement this is as follows:

```
class Employee {
  String iName;
  Ref<Department> iDepartment;
  // note: no mention of Project


public :
  void assign_project(Project& project);
  // etc...
}

Employee::assign_project(Project& project)
{
  project.employee(*this);
}
```

The `Project` class and its corresponding set class are presented here:

```
class Project {
  String iName;
  Ref<Employee> iEmployee;
public:
  void employee(const Employee& emp) {iEmployee=emp;}
  // etc...
};

class ProjectSet: public PSet {

  Project* iCurrent;
  DataSet ds;

public:
  IM_String f_name;
```

```
    IM_Ref<Employee> f_employee;
    Project* current() {return iCurrent;}
    // etc...
  };
```

If you want a function that lists all projects assigned to a certain employee, you could implement it as follows:

```
    ListProjects(Employee& emp)
    {
      ProjectSet projects;
      cout << "Projects for employee " << emp.name() << endl;
      if (projects.seek(project.f_employee == emp))
      {
      do
        {
        cout << projects.current()->name() << endl;
        }
      while (projects.next());
      }
    }
```

In this approach, you do not have to maintain a member `ProjectList` or an associated `IM_ProjectList` in the class definition of `Employee`. This approach not only simplifies development, but also allows you to design `Employee` independently of `Project`.

9.4 Associations and Reuse

When you are designing with an eye for reuse, it is always a good idea to construct classes (or groups of closely cooperating classes) that are as independent from each other as possible. In this way, you won't have to carry too much unnecessary weight when using them in other projects.

In the design process, don't worry too much about the attributes, as they have only a secondary role and have a domain of usability that spans that of the classes using them. (This is normal, since the attributes reside on a lower level of abstraction and are thus used to build higher-level objects. This could be compared with using nuts and bolts to construct an engine. The domain of usability of the nuts and bolts is clearly larger than that of the engine.) When using an association, however, you must ensure you do not make associations with classes that are part of a subdomain of the class under construction. Doing that would limit the usability of the newly constructed class to that subdomain.

Let's once again consider the invoicing example and look at the relationship between `Invoice` and `Customer` (see Figure 9.7).

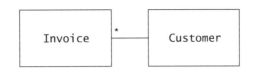

FIGURE 9.7 Many-to-one relationship between Invoice and Customer.

When this model is translated into C++ classes, class Invoice will get a member object of type Customer:

```
class Invoice {
  //...
  Ref<Customer> customer;
  //etc.
};
```

No problem so far. However, when implementing the class Customer, you might opt to include a reference to the invoices connected to that customer (whether it is wise to do so is left undecided for now):

```
class Customer {
  String name;
  Address address;
  List<Invoice> invoices;
  //etc...
};
```

Notice from the domains of Customer and Invoice that the range of applications that can use customers is significantly larger than the range of applications that use invoices. Invoices are restricted mainly to applications in the retail sector, whereas customers can be used in many other applications, for example, a banking application.

The association between Invoice and Customer (making Customer a member of Invoice) presents no problem, since no invoice can exist without a customer. Customers, however, can exist without invoices. But by embedding an Invoice object in the Customer class, you automatically restrict the domain of that class to retail applications as well. A better solution is to create a base class Customer and to put the association in a derived class, as shown next and in Figure 9.8:

```
class Customer {
  String name;
  Address address;
```

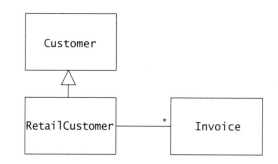

FIGURE 9.8 You can increase reusability by putting the association between `Customer` and `Invoice` in a derived `Customer` class, thereby increasing the reusability of the base `Customer` class.

```
    // no references to Invoice.
    // etc...
};

class RetailCustomer: public Customer {
    // ...
    List<Invoice> invoices;
    // etc...
};
```

9.5 Many-to-Many Relationships

The many-to-many relationship is often encountered. Consider the following business model: A department hires employees and accepts projects. It assigns to each project a number of employees. An employee can be assigned to several projects at the same time.

The relationship between `Employee` and `Project` clearly is many-to-many: Each employee can be assigned to several projects, and each project can be worked on by several employees. This is depicted in Figure 9.9.

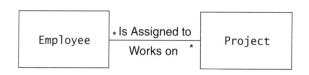

FIGURE 9.9 A many-to-many relationship between `Project` and `Employee`.

This is implemented in an ODMG-conforming notation as follows:

```
class Employee : Persistent_Object {

   String name;
   Ref<Department> department;
   List<Project> projects inverse Project::employees;

   // etc...
};

class Project : Persistent_Object {

   String name;
   List<Employee> employees inverse Employee::projects;

   // etc...
};
```

9.6   A Closer Look at Associations

A `List` template could be designed that allows for an ODMG-like implementation of many-to-many associations. However, first, a closer look at what associations really are is in order. The following question must be answered: "Why do you want to model the association between `Employee` and `Project`?" The most likely answer is "to do something with it."

One thing you might want to do with the association is keep track of the time that an employee spends on each project. However, there is no place to put attributes such as `time_spent_on`. These attributes belong to neither `Employee` nor `Project`, but they are uniquely connected to the corresponding relationship instance. This immediately suggests you should introduce an additional object that implements the association and that contains all attributes connected with the association [Rumbaugh91] (see Figure 9.10).

An alternative way to model this is the one presented in Figure 9.11. From the multiplicity of the resulting relationships, you likely can see that from the viewpoint of the newly introduced object `ProjAssign`, you get two many-to-one relationships. Indeed, each instance of `ProjAssign` corresponds with exactly one employee and one project.

Note that class `ProjAssign` is different from classes such as `Employee` or `Project`. The class `ProjAssign` is the result of an action performed between two classes: `Employee` and `Project` [Kristen93]. It represents the association between an employee and that employee's projects.

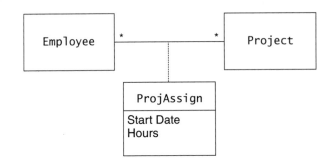

FIGURE 9.10 The association between `Employee` and `Project` is modeled by introducing an additional object that contains all attributes connected with this association.

FIGURE 9.11 Alternative modeling of the `Employee-Project` association.

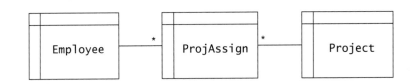

FIGURE 9.12 Relational implementation of the many-to-many relationship. In a relational database, the `Employee-Project` relationship is implemented using an intermediate mapping table. Thus the relationship is split into two one-to-many relationships.

Notice also that this approach is similar to that taken in a relational model, where this relationship would be mapped using an intermediate mapping table (see Figure 9.12). Thus the relationship is split into two one-to-many relationships.

EMPLOYEE

ID	Name	Address	...

PROJECT

ID	Name	. . .

PROJECT ASSIGNMENT

EmployeeID	*ProjectID*	Time Worked	. . .

So unless you want merely to store a series of bidirectional pointers, there is not much point in using the notation of Section 9.5. A more flexible approach is to use a separate class to model the relationship, as follows:

```
class ProjectAssignment {

    Ref<Employee> employee;
    Ref<Project> project;
    Date start_date;
    double hours;

    // etc...
};
```

This class contains an instance of both `Employee` and `Project`, both using a "has-a" relationship. A comparison of this with the relational model shows that table-`ProjAssign`, which is the intermediate mapping table, represents a relationship that is an association (or, according to [Kristen93], even an action), whereas the employee table and the project table represent entities (objects).

9.7   Associations as Independent Entities

Section 9.4 suggested deriving a dedicated customer class if you want to embed the association with the invoice objects. However, in the light of the previous section, you might ask whether the association should have been modeled this way from the beginning.

9.7.1   A Dedicated Association Object

Many authors (for example, [Tanzer95]) suggest that most associations should be modeled using a separate class. This applies not only for the many-to-many relationship, for which it is the only way, but also for the one-to-one relationship. Modeling associations in this way significantly enhances reusability and extensibility. For example, if you want to alter a relationship from a one-to-many to a many-to-many, you will not have to change a thing in the object model.

An example of such a one-to-one relationship is a person and his or her spouse. One way to model this is to embed the associated class in the class that references it. Thus the class `Person` would take the following form:

```
class Person {
  String name;
  Sex sex;
  Ref<Person> partner;
};
```

However, if you want to enhance reusability and choose to model the association as an independent entity, you get the object model of Figure 9.13.

The model of this figure results in the following classes:

```
class Person {
  String name,
  Date birth;
  Sex sex;
};

class Marriage {
  Ref<Person> husband;
  Ref<Person> wife;
  Date weddingday;
  // ...
};
```

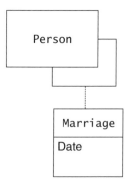

FIGURE 9.13 Modeling relationships. By modeling the marriage relationship as an independent class, you can enhance extensibility and reusability.

Because associations might appear at several places in the business model implementation, it can be a good idea to design a generic association object, like this:

```
template <class T, class U>
class Association: public PSet {

  Ref<T> left;
  Ref<U> right;

  DataSet ds;
  IM_Ref<T> f_left;
  IM_Ref<U> f_right;
  // etc...
};
```

Following this template, class `Marriage` looks as follows:

```
class Marriage: public Association<Person, Person> {
  Date weddingday;
  // ...
};
```

Class `Association` could be implemented to contain a mechanism to perform integrity checking. However, the question remains whether this is the right place to do integrity checking. This question is tackled later in this chapter.

The choice of representation method depends on the importance of the association and the domain of usability of the associated objects. One could say that if the association is a fundamental property of the associated objects and if it carries only a few specific attributes, it is all right to embed it in these objects. Otherwise, you had better design a separate class for it.

9.7.2 The Employee-Project Relationship Revisited

Let's look again at the `Employee-Project` relationship presented in Section 9.3.4. In that section, it was suggested that you allow class `Project` to take care of implementing the one-to-many relationship. This section reconsiders this relationship in light of the previously presented method, which suggests implementing such a relationship by modeling the association as an independent entity, as shown in Figure 9.14.

When these classes are implemented, neither `Employee` nor `Project` any longer contains a reference to the other; only a specialized class `ProjAssign` knows of those references. This becomes very clear from the alternative model presented in Figure 9.15.

In a C++ implementation, this model would lead to the following class layout:

```
class Employee {
  String name;
  Ref<Department> department;
  // note: no reference to 'Project'
```

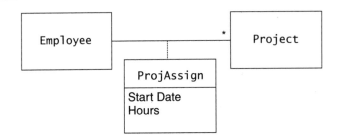

FIGURE 9.14 The Employee-Project relationship revisited. The assignment of an employee to a certain project is best modeled as an independent class.

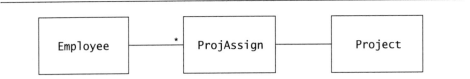

FIGURE 9.15 By modeling the relationship between Employee and Project as a class of its own, you can have both classes be implemented independently of each other.

```
public:
  void list_projects();
  // etc...
};

class Project {
  String name;
  // note: no reference to 'Employee'
  // etc...
};

class ProjAssign {
  Ref<Employee> employee;
  Ref<Project> project;
  Date start_date;
  double hours;
  // etc...
};
```

Or if the `Association` template is used, class `ProjAssign` becomes this:

```
class ProjAssign: public Association<Employee, Project> {
  Date start_date;
  double hours;
  // etc...
};
```

The result is a class layout in which `ProjAssign`, as the association, has references to both `Project` and `Employee`, but not the other way around; that is, classes have no references to their associations. Note that `ProjAssign` is the same class used to model the many-to-many relationship in Section 9.6.

Modeling associations as separate entities has several advantages. First, it increases flexibility and extensibility. If you ever want to make the relationship between `Employee` and `Project` many-to-many, you can use the same model. Second, reusability is improved because `Project` and `Employee` are now independent of one another.

The relationship between `ProjAssign` and `Project` is one-to-one. If the `Association` class has only a few association attributes, you could choose to merge this class with the project class. However, this class would then get a double functionality: It would represent both the actual project and the relationship expressed by the former class, `ProjAssign`. This approach would lead to a class implementation in which `Project` references `Employee`, but `Employee` has no reference to `Project`:

```
/*
    Project now has a double functionality: It represents
    the actual project, as well as the association
*/

class Project {
  String name;
  Ref<Employee> employee;
  // etc...
};
```

In other words, class `Project` is allowed to take care of the relationship discussed in Section 9.3.4 because of its dual functionality.

9.7.3 Customer-Invoice Relationship

In the `Customer-Invoice` relationship, too, you could map the association as an independent class, as shown in Figure 9.16.

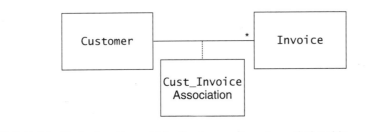

FIGURE 9.16 First attempt model for `Customer-Invoice` relationship.

However, let's look at what the business really does. The business involved is not about invoicing people, but rather about selling things to people. Thus, when modeling this business, you start not by creating an `Invoice` object, but by expressing that the business is about selling things to people. This is depicted in Figure 9.17.

The `Customer-Item` relationship is many-to-many, thus the logical thing to do is to model it as a separate class `Sale` that contains two attributes: the item's purchase price and the number of items bought (see Figure 9.18).

The relationship between `Customer` and `Sale` can have a number of attributes. For example, the collection of sales can have a grand total, and the sales can have a reduction

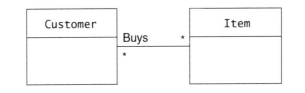

FIGURE 9.17 A business model must express what a company really does. In the text example, the business sells things to customers.

FIGURE 9.18 Once again, the association can be modeled as a separate object.

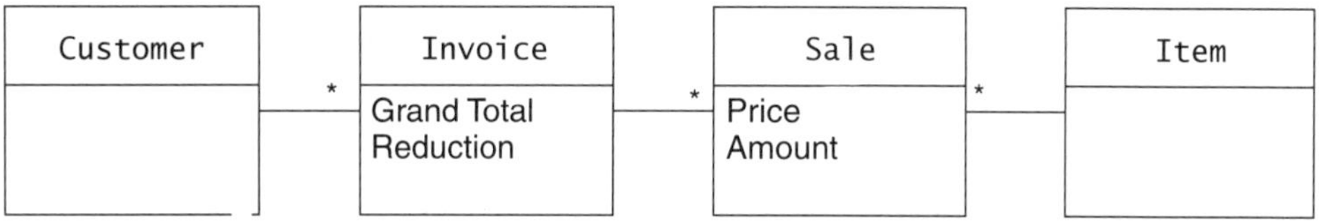

Customer		Invoice		Sale		Item
	*	Grand Total Reduction	*	Price Amount	*	

FIGURE 9.19 Because the relationship between `Customer` and `Sale` has a number of attributes, it is modeled as a separate object. The perfect name for this relationship is `Invoice`.

percentage. This is illustrated in Figure 9.19. An ideal name for this relationship is `Invoice`. It represents the relationship between customers and their–purchases. This is why `Invoice` has a reference to `Customer`, while `Customer` has no reference to `Invoice`. The following code implements this model:

```
class Invoice {
    long number;
    Ref<Customer> customer;
    // etc...
};

class Customer {
    String name;
    Address address;
    // note: no reference to Invoice !
    // etc...
};
```

9.8 Referential Integrity

In the employee-project example, deleting an employee that still has projects would make the database inconsistent. To prevent such an inconsistency, you need to implement some kind of referential integrity checking. Two main types of referential integrity constraints exist: those on the database level and those on the business-model level.

Integrity constraints on the database level are concerned only with maintaining the correctness of the data stored in the database. These constraints will, for example, ensure that a record never gets deleted as long as it is still referenced by another record.

As the business model contains not only data but also behavior, the semantic content of this model is richer than that of the database. Thus an additional level of integrity checking is necessary: business-model integrity. Business-model integrity is concerned with maintaining the *consistency of the information* stored in the business model.

9.8.1   Checking Referential Integrity in the Application

A first way to maintain referential integrity is to redefine the function PSet::erase() in the derived PSet classes and have it check the integrity constraints before it deletes an object. In the employee example of Figure 9.6, this would take the following form:

```
EmployeeSet::erase()
{
    // if no projects exist for this employee
    ProjectSet projects;
    if (!projects.seek(projects.f_employee==*this))
        {
        return PSet::erase();
        }
    else
        return FALSE;
}
```

One problem with this approach, however, is that a class does not always know by which other classes-it is used. Class Employee, for example, could be used not only in Project, but also in a variety of other classes such as Department and Contract.

It also could be argued that this checking violates the information-hiding principle. So far in this book, we have gone to great lengths to hide the database layout (and even the fact we are using a database at all). And if the database layout has to be hidden from the application program, this program does not have enough knowledge about the database to check its integrity. Now is hardly the time to start violating this encapsulation. Thus, for clarity, ensuring data integrity is largely the responsibility of the database administrator (or the designer of the database layout).

However, the program can check, for example, the requirement that no customer be deleted as long as there are still invoices unpaid for that customer. But that is not really a requirement of database integrity, but rather of the business model. Even then, you cannot be completely sure the customer can be safely deleted. In a relational system, for example, other tables might still be referencing it. Even if you made it the responsibility of the application program to check this referencing, the situation would still not be completely safe. Indeed, the application has only a limited view of the database; it references only those tables in which it is interested. However, other applications might be working on the same database, although using other tables. Both applications might use a different table referencing the customer table, as depicted in Figure 9.20. Thus for a customer record to be safely deleted, neither application can be referencing it anymore. Because none of the applications are supposed to have knowledge about the others, the only way that integrity can be guaranteed is by letting the database system take care of it.

So this prevention is the task of the database manager; consequently, the referential integrity must be checked on the database level (for example, by using stored procedures

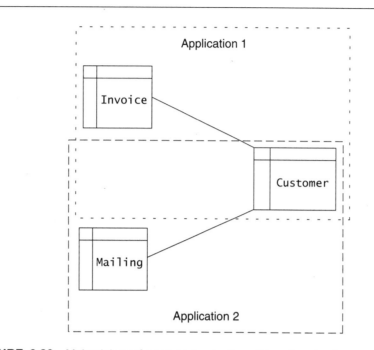

FIGURE 9.20 Maintaining referential integrity. Two different applications use the same customer table. However, each application has only a limited view on the other tables referencing this customer.

and triggers). However, note that such an approach might limit the portability of the application because there is no standardized way to support this kind of integrity checking.

9.8.2 Cascaded Delete

An alternative to the previous method (refusing to delete an object if it is still referenced) is to also delete all referenced objects. This is called a **cascaded delete.** Consider a class Person, which has a Note attribute:

```
class Person {
  String iLastname, iFirstname;
  Note iNote;
public:
  Person();
  virtual ~Person();
  String& lastname (void);
  // etc...
};
```

```
class PersonSet: public PSet {
  Person* iCurrent;
  DataSet ds;
  IM_String f_lastname, f_firstname;
  IM_Note f_note;
public:
  PersonSet();
  virtual ~PersonSet();
  // etc...
};

class Note {
  char *iText;
  static NoteSet* extent;
public:
  Note();
  char* getText (void);
  void setText (const char* text);
  void initialise (void);
  int erase();
};
```

Suppose you want to store the note in a separate table in order to save space (the note for most people turns out to be empty anyway) (see Figure 9.21).

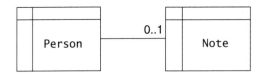

FIGURE 9.21   Person-Note relationship. To save space in the database, this relationship is implemented using two separate tables and a one-to-one or one-to-zero relationship.

Now if a person is deleted, the corresponding note should be deleted, too. Although it is still preferable to implement this kind of integrity rule on the database level, this time it is possible to implement it in the business model. A first implementation could be to redefine PSet::erase():

```
PersonSet::erase()
{
  if (iCurrent->note.erase())
    return PSet::erase();
  else
    return FALSE;
}
```

However, one could rightfully argue that it should not be PersonSet's task to delete that note. Indeed, as far as PersonSet is concerned, there is no fundamental difference between, for example, the note and the person's name, so they should not be treated differently.

This difficulty can be resolved by extending class IM_Resolver with a virtual member function erase(). This function is called by PSet::erase() whenever an IM_Resolver is erased. Usually, the default implementation of this member function, which returns true (meaning "go ahead"), will be enough. However, in the case of the IM_Note, this member could be redefined and implemented in such a way that it also deletes the corresponding note (if it exists):

```
virtual int IM_Resolver::erase()
{
  return 1;
}


class IM_Note: public IM_Resolver {

    Note* note;

  public:
    IM_Note(Note* var, DataSet* base, const char* nme=NULL);
    void read (Cursor& cursor);
    void to_update(Statement& stmt);
    int erase()
      {
      return note->erase();
      }
};
```

9.9 Summary

This chapter discussed the modeling of relationships. It distinguished two kinds of relationships between objects: attributes and associations. These differ mainly in that an association takes place between objects on the same level of abstraction, while an attribute relies on a lower level of abstraction than the object to which it belongs.

It also talked about the implementation of different kinds of associations (many-to-one, one-to-many, and many-to-many) and discussed two alternatives for dealing with associations. That is, you can either put the association within the classes that take part in it or design a separate class for the association. The latter approach will usually lead to programs that are more easily maintained.

The discussion showed that an association should be embedded in an object only if it is made within the same domain of usability or a domain that spans the application domain. However, if a relationship is made with a class that has a domain of usability that spans the domain of the wrapper class, often the relationship no longer is an association, but the object becomes an attribute.

Also discussed was maintaining referential integrity. The conclusion was that this is mainly the task of database administrators, since they are the only ones who have a complete view of the entire database.

Chapter 10

Transaction Management and Concurrency Control

So far, all of the examples in this book have been developed under the supposition that a single-user system was being used. However, a fundamental property of almost every database system is its ability to serve multiple users at the same time. Of course, this ability requires that certain precautions be taken to prevent users from interfering with one another's data. This chapter looks more closely at concurrency concerns.

10.1 The Transaction

An important concept in maintaining data consistency is the concept of a transaction. A **transaction** can be defined as a collection of operations that form a logical unit of work. Consider, for example, a money transfer from one bank account to another. The money is debited from the first account and then credited to the second. While these operations are being executed, the database resides in an inconsistent state. This process is depicted in Figure 10.1. Only when all operations are completed is the database in a consistent state again. You must always ensure that the database is never left in an inconsistent state, no matter what happens. This means that either all operations should be executed successfully or none should be executed.

10.2 The ACID Test

For a transaction to be considered a transaction, it must pass the ACID test; that is, it must satisfy four properties:

- <u>A</u>tomicity
- <u>C</u>onsistency
- <u>I</u>solated execution
- <u>D</u>urability

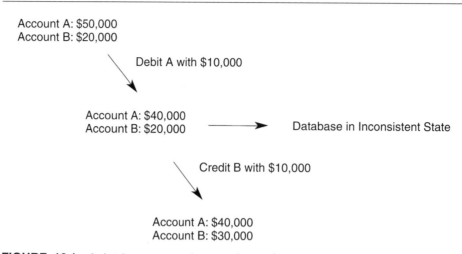

FIGURE 10.1   A database transaction transferring $10,000 from account A to account B.

10.2.1   Atomicity

Atomicity means a transaction is an all-or-nothing process. A transaction can never be performed only partially. It is always either of the following:

- **Committed:** All operations and modifications to the database are completed successfully and made persistent.
- **Rolled back:** The transaction is canceled, all operations and modifications are undone, and the database is restored to the state it was in before the transaction was started.

10.2.2   Consistency

A transaction is supposed to bring the database from one consistent state into another consistent state. Although within a transaction, the database may reside in an inconsistent state, before and after the transaction, the database must be consistent.

In a multiuser environment, no other user than the transaction owner sees any of the changes that the owner makes to the database until the transaction commits. Hence, all other users always see the database in a consistent (although maybe outdated) state.

10.2.3   Isolated Execution

A transaction should be executed in isolation from the effects of any other concurrently running transaction. A commonly used criterion here is the serializability property of a transaction. Serializable transactions are transactions that, when executed concurrently, have the same effect as when executed in a serial order. A technique used to ensure serializability is *locking,* which is examined later in the chapter.

10.2.4   Durability

Durability implies that once a transaction commits, you are guaranteed that all changes made to the DBMS are never lost, even if a hardware or other failure occurs. Once a transaction is committed, it can never be undone.

The ACID properties teach us that transactions provide for two main facilities: concurrency control and data recovery. They protect us from the influence of hardware and other failures. Whenever a failure occurs, the database should be restored to the last consistent state before the failure.

10.3   Transaction Management Exceeds the Database Level

It is important to note that a transaction is application-defined. Indeed, because it is the application that defines the consistency rules, the DBMS cannot determine the logical boundaries of a transaction. Thus it is the application that is responsible for determining what constitutes a logical unit of work. This implies that all transaction management belongs to the application level and thus the programming language level. Of course, you do still need transaction support on the database level, but that support must be considered in a larger context.

Reference to "programming language level" includes not only databases, but also program constructs in which transient objects can take part. You thus must consider what must be done with those transient objects when a transaction is rolled back.

Traditional database systems make a distinct separation between programming language and database topics and consider transaction management to apply only on the database level. However, from an object-oriented point of view, attempts are made to abstract the database concept as much as possible—that is, to remove the distinction between persistent objects and transient objects. This uniform treatment of objects implies that transaction management should be considered as a part of the programming level rather than of the database level. It should not be directly related to database processing, but rather to programming in general. Other observations support that conclusion. A few examples follow.

10.3.1   Transactions and Object Orientation

A special form of (implicit) transaction handling is also found in the object model. An object consists of two main parts: member variables and member functions (methods). Each member function can be seen as an implicit transaction on the object of which it is a part. Indeed, when the member function is entered, the object is in a consistent state. No matter what happens inside the member function, when it has finished, it is supposed to leave the object in a consistent state.

10.3.2   Graphical User Interfaces

Consider a GUI in which you work with a dialog box. Most dialog boxes have, in addition to data entry fields, two buttons: OK and Cancel. This, too, can be considered as some kind of transaction management: The user either clicks OK and the transaction commits or clicks Cancel and the transaction aborts. Such transaction management, however, does not happen on the database level, but on the user-interface level. Concurrency control is enforced here by making the dialog box modal; that is, the user is allowed no access outside of the dialog box.

In many RAD environments, this transaction management is confused with database transaction management. This, too, is because there is a direct coupling between the user interface and the database. All data processing code is directly integrated in the dialog boxes of the user interface. Closing the dialog box then corresponds to closing the database transaction. In other words, you could say that each database transaction is directly mapped onto a dialog box.

In contrast, in an object-oriented approach, the user interface communicates with the business model. Thus closing a dialog box means either that all data entered in the data entry fields is sent to the business model (the user clicked OK) or that no data is sent (the user clicked Cancel). In other words, this transaction mechanism does not work on the database, but on the business model.

10.3.3 Transactions and Exception Handling

As shown, transactions serve two main purposes: controlling concurrency and ensuring database integrity. Another mechanism to help ensure integrity is exception handling.

An exception try block (in C++) marks out a logical unit of work. If something goes wrong within a try block, an exception is raised, and a catch routine is invoked. This routine handles the effects of the exception.

When this mechanism is compared with transaction management, the try block could be compared with the transaction, while the exception handler is responsible for restoring things to a consistent state when something goes wrong. It could be considered an abort function.

However, the reverse is also true. That is, transactions and exceptions are analogous in that database transactions could be considered a special case of exception handling. Here, transaction boundaries are defined in the try block, while the catch block is responsible for bringing the database back to a consistent state—that is, performing a rollback.

10.4 Concurrency Control: Locking

Although a transaction guards against inconsistencies that can occur when something goes wrong within itself, it can guarantee the database consistency of only a single thread of execution. Whenever two or more transactions access the database at the same time, there is still a danger of leaving behind inconsistencies, since the two transactions might be interfering with each other and be modifying the same data. Some kind of concurrency control is necessary. One technique for controlling concurrency is *locking*. The next sections discuss locking in more detail.

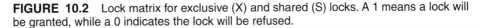

FIGURE 10.2 Lock matrix for exclusive (X) and shared (S) locks. A 1 means a lock will be granted, while a 0 indicates the lock will be refused.

10.4.1 Read and Write Locks

To guard against database inconsistencies, both traditional and object-oriented database systems support the concept of locking. By locking an object (or a record in a relational system), you prevent other users from modifying that object for the duration of the lock.

There are several types of locks, the most important being read locks and write locks. A **read lock,** also called a **shared lock,** allows several users to simultaneously read an object but not modify it. To modify an object, a user must request a **write lock** (also called an **exclusive lock**). A write lock can be obtained only if the object has no other locks pending. This applies regardless of whether these pending locks are read locks or write locks. This locking rule is expressed in the lock matrix of Figure 10.2.

Read locks have the advantage of enabling greater concurrency while still ensuring that the owner of the lock never works with outdated data (because no write lock on the locked object will be granted).

Under certain conditions, users can be allowed to bypass the locking system and to read an object that has been write locked by another user. This is called a **dirty read,** and it can increase concurrency. It is the application's responsibility to determine when a dirty read is appropriate. This depends entirely on the business logic, so the database system has no way of knowing it.

10.4.2 Preventing Inconsistencies

Whenever two users access or modify the same data at the same time, there is always the danger of leaving behind an inconsistent database. There are typically three kinds of potential database inconsistencies:

- Lost update
- Assumed update
- Inconsistent analysis

These can be avoided using adequate concurrency control in the form of locking [Date95].

Lost Update

Suppose user A fetches a `Person` object from the database and user B reads the same object. Then suppose that user A changes the person's attire by adding sunglasses, while user B gives the person a hat. First user A writes the object back to the database, and then

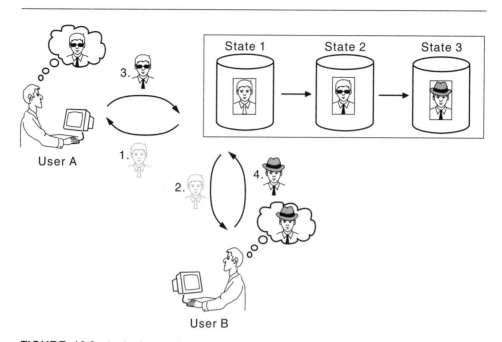

FIGURE 10.3 In the lost update scenario, when user B sends modifications to the database, user A's changes are lost.

user B writes his or her version to the database. When B does this, all modifications made by user A will be lost. This scenario is depicted in Figure 10.3.

This kind of inconsistency can be prevented by locking the object while it is being modified. Indeed, if user A locks the object, user B will not be able to access it until user A is finished making his or her modifications.

Assumed Update

Consider again user A fetching a person from the database. User A gives the person sunglasses and writes the new version of the object back to the database. Next, user B reads this object, gives the person a hat, and writes the person to the database. If user A then decides to roll back its modifications, the database will be brought back to the state it was in prior to user A's transaction. However, doing this will undo all modifications made by user B—without user B's knowledge. Figure 10.4 illustrates this scenario.

This kind of inconsistency can be avoided by keeping all locks until the end of the transaction. In this way, user B won't be able to make any modifications until it is certain that user A's transaction will never be undone.

Inconsistent Analysis

Consider two transactions in a banking application, as shown in Figure 10.5. The first transaction calculates the total amount someone has, totaled over all of the person's

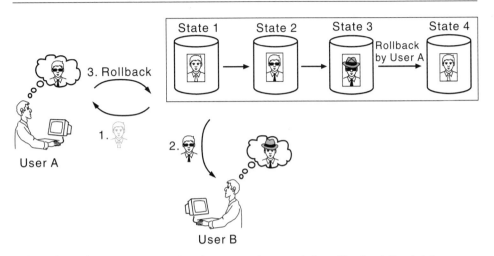

FIGURE 10.4   In the assumed update scenario, user A, by rolling back the database, also undoes user B's modifications.

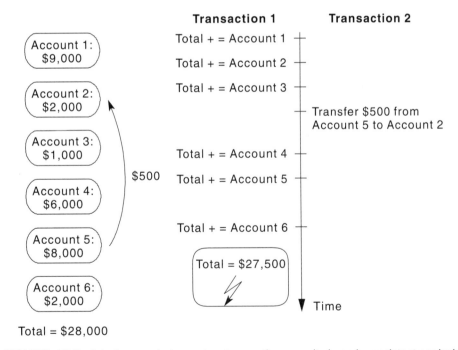

Total = $28,000

FIGURE 10.5   Interference between two transactions results in an inconsistent analysis.

accounts. The second transaction transfers $500 from account 5 to account 2. This transfer happens when the first transaction is finished summing only the first three accounts. This means that when that transaction reaches account 5, its balance will be only $7,500, while the balance of account 2 will be $2,500. As a result, this $500 will never be seen by transaction 1, and the total calculated by this transaction will be $500 short of the real total.

You could try to avoid this type of inconsistency by using the technique of the previous subsection (keeping all locks until the end of the transaction). Indeed, as transaction 2 debits $500 from account 5, it will lock this Account object. However, crediting this amount to account 2 will be impossible because transaction 1 will already have accessed and locked the first three accounts. Transaction 2 will thus have to wait until transaction 1 terminates. However, this termination will never happen because transaction 1 has to access account 5, which has been locked by transaction 2. Each transaction will thus indefinitely wait for the other to complete. A deadlock situation has occurred.

A way to prevent this deadlock situation is to have transaction 1 lock in advance all objects it will need and to make it keep these locks until the end of the transaction. In the example here, transaction 2 will have to wait on the completion of transaction 1 before it can access account 5.

10.4.3   Shallow Locking and Deep Locking

When locking an object, you must determine how deep you want to go. You can either lock only the object itself, called **shallow locking,** or lock that object as well as all subobjects contained in that object, called **deep locking.** Consider, for example, an instance of a persistent class Invoice:

```
class Invoice {

    long number;
    Ref<Customer> customer;
    // etc...
};
```

Invoice has, among other things, a member object, customer, that is a persistent object itself. In a relational environment, customer could be stored in a separate table. If you lock the Invoice object, do you want also to lock customer? A shallow locking situation is pictured in Figure 10.6.

Suppose the Invoice instance *a* references the same customer as process 2's customer instance *c*. If only shallow locking is used, both processes will be able to modify the customer instance, and process 1 will undo process 2's changes. If you intend to make changes to customer, deep locking is required. However, if you want to modify only other attributes of the invoice, deep locking is not necessary. Thus concurrency is significantly increased.

An approach that will usually be adequate is to lock the aggregated object only when you actually reference it. This is the default behavior of most database systems. With this

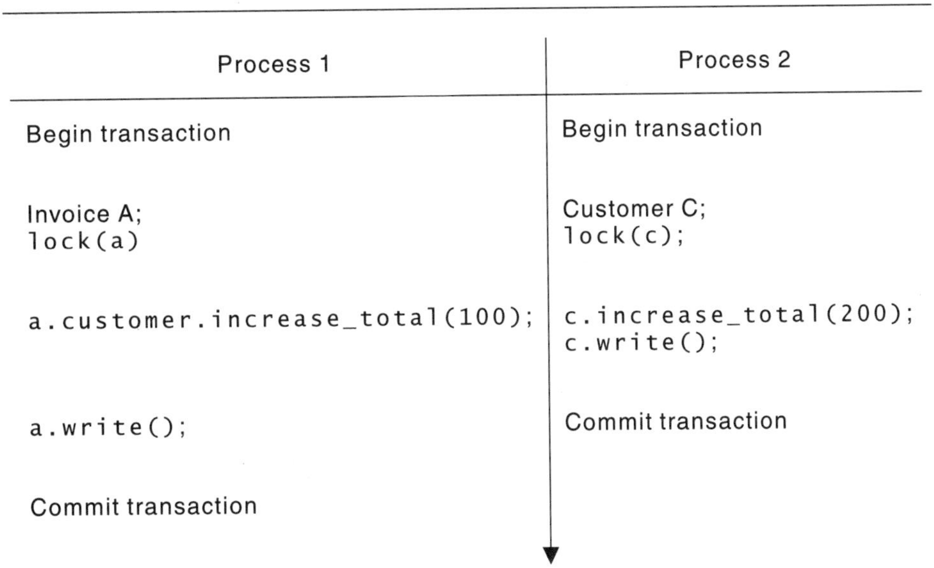

Process 1	Process 2
Begin transaction	Begin transaction
Invoice A; `lock(a)`	Customer C; `lock(c);`
`a.customer.increase_total(100);`	`c.increase_total(200);` `c.write();`
`a.write();`	Commit transaction
Commit transaction	

FIGURE 10.6   Shallow locking.

approach, shallow reading (which can be implemented, for example, with the Ref template of Chapter 7) will result in shallow locking, while deep reading will result in deep locking.

If explicit locking is needed, this functionality can be implemented easily by giving the persistent base class PSet a member function lock() that calls the appropriate locking function of the database system.

10.5   Example: A Transaction Class

This section examines an example of a technique to implement transactions, specifically the Transaction class defined in the ODMG standard [ODMG93]. The current ODMG standard supports transaction management only of persistent objects. Aborting a transaction does not yet restore the state of modified transient objects.

The ODMG C++ binding gives the following definition for the Transaction class:

```
class Transaction {

public :
  Transaction();
  ~Transaction();
  void Begin();
  void Commit();
  void Abort();
  void Checkpoint();
};
```

A transaction must be explicitly started by a call to the member function begin(). It is ended by a call to either commit() or abort(). When commit() is called, all modifications made to persistent objects are sent to the database. When abort() is called, all changes to the database are aborted. Calling either of the two functions releases all locks.

The member checkpoint() commits all changes made to the database since the last call to checkpoint(). All locks are retained, and all pointers and references are left unchanged. The destructor is implemented in such a way that if an active transaction object goes out of scope, it is automatically aborted.

Locking is normally done automatically by the transaction mechanism. However, the ODMG standard allows implementations to have explicit locking facilities. The default locking model supported by ODMG is **pessimistic concurrency control**. This means that a read lock is acquired before an object is read and that before an object can be modified, a write lock must be obtained.

ODMG requires all access, creation, modification, and deletion of persistent objects to be done within a transaction. All locks normally stay in effect until the completion or abortion of the transaction. When the transaction is ended, all locks are released and the state of all references (Refs) from persistent objects to other objects becomes undefined.

10.6 Transactions in Relational Database Systems

Implementing a Transaction class on top of a relational database system is fairly straightforward because you can rely on the transaction mechanism of the DBMS. Following is an example of a possible implementation:

```
class Transaction {

int busy;
   static int count;

public :

    Transaction()
    {
    count++;
    }

    virtual ~Transaction()
    {
    count--;
```

```
if (busy)    // abort noncommitted transactions
  {
  Abort();
  }
}

void Begin();
{
#if defined (NO_NESTEDTRANS)
  if (count>1)
    return;
#endif

busy=1;
// execute SQL statement
SQL::ExecuteCommand("START TRANSACTION");
}

void Commit();
{
#if defined (NO_NESTEDTRANS)
  if (count>1)
    return;
#endif

SQL::ExecuteCommand("COMMIT TRANSACTION");
busy=0;
}

void Abort();
{
#if defined (NO_NESTEDTRANS)
  if (count>1)
    return;
#endif

SQL::ExecuteCommand("ABORT TRANSACTION");
busy=0;
}
};
```

This implementation also allows transactions to be nested if the low-level database system supports nested transactions. For low-level systems not supporting nested transactions, a counter is included in the `Transaction` class to ensure that only the outermost transaction has an effect.

10.7   Using Transactions

To ensure that the database stays consistent in the invoicing example of Chapter 7, you could modify the code to add an item to the invoice presented in Section 7.1, as follows:

```
int Invoice::addSale (Sale& item)
{
  Transaction transaction;
  transaction.Begin();

  item.invoiceNumber(number());
  if (iSaleSet.insert(item))
    {
    iTotal += item.total();
    customer.updateStatistics(item.total());
    transaction.Commit();
    return 1;
    }

  // if the transaction has not been committed, it
  // will automatically be aborted by the destructor.

  return 0;
}
```

Although this code will ensure that the database stays in a consistent state when adding an item to an invoice, one could object to this method. As already said, transactions are application-defined. The class `Invoice` is a business component that, instead of *being* the application, is *used by* the application. `Invoice` has no knowledge about the context in which it will be used. Since the transaction boundaries are defined by that context, `Invoice` cannot make assumptions about these boundaries. If `Invoice::addSale()` is used to add a single item to the invoice, then the transaction definition will be sufficient. However, if the application logic dictates that all items must be successfully added to the invoice in order for the transaction to succeed, then the previous transaction declaration will not be sufficient. A better approach would be this:

```
int Invoice::addSale (Sale& item)
{
  item.invoiceNumber(number());
  if (iSaleSet.insert(item))
    {
    iTotal += item.total();
    customer.updateStatistics(item.total());
    return 1;
    }
  return 0;
}

CreateInvoice()
{
  Invoice invoice;
  Transaction invoice_trans;

  invoice_trans.Begin();

  // ... (code for getting customer)

  // ... (code for adding items)

  if (ok_button_pressed())
    {
    invoice_trans.Commit();
    }
}
```

This time the application using the business object Invoice defines the transaction boundaries.

10.8   Nested Transactions

Most object database systems support nested transactions. As the name implies, a nested transaction mechanism allows transactions to be used within other transactions. Figure 10.7 illustrates this.

10.8.1   Basic Principles

A nested transaction mechanism operates as follows: If either of the (sub)transactions 2 or 3 are aborted, only the changes made within that aborted subtransaction will be rolled back. Rolling back transaction 3 will not affect transaction 2 or transaction 1.

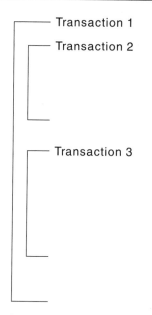

FIGURE 10.7   Nested transactions. Most object database systems allow transactions to be nested.

Committing either of the subtransactions 2 or 3 will only conditionally commit that subtransaction. Their changes will not be made permanent until transaction 1 commits successfully. Committing transaction 1 will also permanently commit all of its subtransactions. Aborting transaction 1 will roll back all previously committed subtransactions. In other words, the durability property part of the ACID test applies only to the outermost transaction.

10.8.2   Nested Transactions in Long Transactions

Traditional on-line transaction processing (OLTP) typically uses many short transactions. Many applications in the ODBMS area, however, require long transactions. Consider a CAD application in which an engineer modifies an engine. Such a transaction can easily take a whole day or more to complete.

Long transactions have different requirements than traditional transactions. For example, it is not acceptable to abort the entire long transaction because of a time-out to acquire a lock. Also, their concurrency requirements differ. In an OLTP environment, the user can easily wait for a transaction to complete to acquire a certain lock. It is less reasonable to expect someone to wait a whole day to access some object locked by a long transaction.

Nested transactions can be very useful here. This is because the effects of, for example, a lock time-out can be limited to only a small subtransaction. Judicious use of subtransactions also can increase concurrency, and in case of a failure of some kind, a rollback can be limited to only a small subtransaction.

Another way to increase concurrency in an environment using long transactions is to use concurrent versioning, which was discussed in Chapter 7. This kind of versioning allows multiple users to simultaneously manipulate some object by giving each user its own copy (version) of that object. After all changes have been entered, the different versions are reintegrated semiautomatically.

10.8.3 The Invoice Example Revisited

In an environment that supports nested transactions, the first approach sketched in Section 10.7—use transactions in adding items to invoices—would be no problem. Indeed, although class `Invoice` has no knowledge of the context in which it will be used, it does know that *at least* its body must be completed successfully. Thus this body could be considered a subtransaction. An application using this `Invoice` class can then define a wider transaction, if necessary, that states the requirement that the whole invoice must be completed successfully.

10.9 Distributed Database Systems

There remains the question of what to do if a transaction spans multiple database systems, thereby placing you in a distributed database environment. Consider someone who wants to make a flight reservation and pay for the flight by credit card. Suppose that the data about flights is kept in one database and the data about credit cards in another. Thus, although making the reservation and billing it to the credit card creates a single logical transaction, that transaction is distributed over two different database systems.

10.9.1 How Not to Do It

A first, rather naive, way to implement this transaction scheme would be as follows:

```
Transaction::Commit()
{
    for (int i=0; i < number_of_database_systems_involved; i++)
    {
    DataBaseManager[i]::CommitTransaction();
    }
}
```

Such an approach would work correctly most of the time. However, what if there are, say, five databases involved and the first three have committed successfully, but before the fourth can commit, this system experiences a failure and has to be rolled back? Because the first three transactions have already committed, their results cannot be undone, while the fourth will be rolled back and thus never be able to commit. The result: an inconsistent set of databases.

10.9.2   A Better Way: The Two-Phase Commit

A popular method for implementing distributed transactions is to use a two-phase commit mechanism [Loomis95]. In this system, a transaction coordinator controls the commitment process of all subtransactions residing on the distributed machines. Important to note here is that this entire process is the sole responsibility of the database management system. The programmer is not confronted with the internal workings of the two-phase commit mechanism. Here are the two phases of the mechanism:

1. The transaction coordinator asks each subtransaction whether it is ready to commit. To answer this, the subtransaction determines whether all of its updates have been successfully written to the log. Thus enough information has been recorded to guarantee that the subtransaction can commit, no matter what happens.
2. If each subtransaction has indicated that it is ready to commit, all transactions are committed. On the other hand, if not all subtransactions respond affirmatively, the entire transaction, including all subtransactions, is aborted.

A two-phase commit mechanism is much harder to implement than an ordinary transaction mechanism. It also can result in serious overhead, especially when a failure occurs. For example, suppose a local system goes down while the commit process is in phase 2—that is, the local system is unable to communicate to the transaction coordinator whether it successfully completed phase 1. Then the coordinator will have to wait until the system is up again before it can continue. Hence, a two-phase commit should be used only when absolutely necessary.

10.9.3   Alternatives to the Two-Phase Commit

Because a two-phase commit potentially carries serious overhead, several alternatives have been developed that have less overhead. One elegant alternative is splitting the transaction into two subtransactions and adding a third that takes care of all reconciliation issues. This mechanism can be used whenever the application tolerates out-of-synch updates [Loomis95].

For example, the transaction for the earlier flight reservation system can be easily implemented using this alternative approach. To do so, you divide the transaction into two subtransactions, one operation on each database site. You add a third transaction that will coordinate those two subtransactions. This is shown in Figure 10.8.

If something goes wrong now, the database can be brought back to a consistent state as follows:

- Transaction 1 fails: Abort the whole process. Do not start transaction 2 or 3.
- Transaction 2 fails: Abort the process. Based on the log file of transaction 1, manually undo the effects of that transaction.

```
Logical transaction:

    1. Reserve flight (on system 1)
    2. Debit credit card (on system 2)


Transaction 1 (executing on system 1):

    1. Reserve flight
    2. Make a record of the reservation to log file


Transaction 2 (executing on system 2):

    1. Debit credit card


Transaction 3 (executing on system 1):

    1. Delete log file
```

FIGURE 10.8   Distributed transaction processing without the need for a two-phase commit.

- Transaction 3 fails: This failure is no problem, as transactions 1 and 2 have already completed successfully. Manually delete the log file.

This approach has an advantage in that if some failure occurs and a database system goes down, the application does not have to wait until that system is up again. The two databases can later be reconciled. This approach has the drawback, however, that it becomes the programmer's responsibility to take care of the distributed nature of the database environment. The programmer has to implement the log file and split the transaction into subtransactions. In the two-phase commit mechanism, all of these considerations are entirely taken care of by the database system.

10.10   Other Levels of Concurrency

All concurrency aspects discussed so far have had to do with traditional database concurrency. Here, multiple processes, which may run on different computers, may want to access the same data (or objects) simultaneously. This data traditionally resides in the database.

10.10.1 Multiple Object Instances within the Same Process

A second level of concurrency involves several objects within the same process trying to simultaneously access the same data. Because of GUIs, this type of concurrency has become important. Indeed, a classical environment and a GUI environment differ mainly in that in a classical environment, the programmers dictate the event flow, while in a GUI, the end users dictate it. Thus users might choose to start two operations that work on the same data. For example, a user might start an invoice for a certain customer and then, when another customer enters, switch to the customer module in order to change some of that new customer's attributes. But what if the customers happen to be the same in both cases? In systems in which it is the transaction that acquires the lock (most SQL-based systems, for example), this situation will not be allowed. In systems in which it is the process to which the lock is granted that acquires the lock (many file-based systems), this situation can lead to inconsistencies.

Although this kind of concurrency problem can be handled on the database level, it is a typical example of a concurrency problem that is best handled on the application level. The user interface should be prevented from accessing two instances of the same customer simultaneously. One way to achieve this is by using modal dialog boxes. In this case, if the invoice screen is defined to be a modal dialog, the user will not be able to leave it as long as the dialog is not closed and the transaction is thus not finished.

10.10.2 Multiple Object Instances within the Same Transaction

Another concurrency problem can occur when a transaction tries to access and modify multiple instances of the same object in the persistent set. Consider, for example, the following program fragment:

```
Transaction mytrans;

mytrans.Begin();

Student a,b;

a.seek_id(100);
b = a;

a.set_major("Math");
b.set_city("Dallas");

a.write();
b.write();

mytrans.Commit();
```

In this case, the object is read only once from the database, but it is copied into (and manipulated by) several programming language variables. It is very hard to safeguard against the effects of such a situation. The problem is that both objects reference the same database object. Because the copying is done on the programming language level, normal database locking will be unable to prevent this inconsistency. One way to avoid this situation is to use smart pointers and implement these in such a way that a and b reference the same object in memory.

However, because both objects are manipulated within the same transaction, the program flow is completely in the hands of the programmer and can thus be known in advance. You won't have to worry too much about this kind of concurrency problem, since it can be avoided by correct coding.

10.11   Lock Notification through Call-Back Functions

An elegant way to increase concurrency—by using lock call-back functions—is implemented in the object-oriented database POET [Bartels93]. The idea is that objects can register themselves with a locking manager. This is illustrated in Figure 10.9. Whenever an object tries to obtain a lock, all objects registered in the locking manager are notified and must give permission to grant the lock. When the object is unlocked, the registered objects are notified. These notifications give the objects the chance to take appropriate actions to avoid working with outdated information. For example, when receiving the lock notifications, they can send a message to the user interface to gray this object, thereby telling the user someone is altering it. Upon notification of the unlock, the object can reread itself and redisplay itself to the screen.

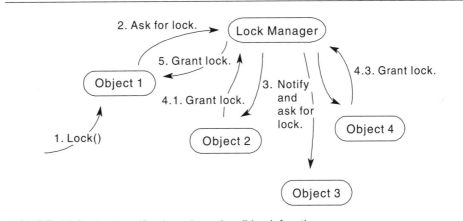

FIGURE 10.9   Lock notifications through call-back functions.

10.12 Summary

This chapter discussed the main issues involved with transaction handling and concurrency. It showed that the concept of the transaction is not limited to the database; rather it is found on all levels of the application architecture. It explained how distributed transactions can be implemented using a two-phase commit mechanism. Because this mechanism sometimes results in too much overhead, alternatives were offered. Finally, the chapter explained the concept of locking and discussed deep locking versus shallow locking.

Chapter 11

The Front End

User interaction is a critical consideration when designing applications. A complete discussion of user interfaces would require a whole book. However, this chapter touches on the most important aspects of user interfaces.

11.1   Analogy between User Interfaces and Databases

Look at user interface (UI) design from a higher level of abstraction, and you'll find that there is a significant analogy between user interfaces and databases. Both allow you to store objects (the database stores them to disk, the user interface to the screen) and to retrieve objects (from disk and from the keyboard). Whether this storage process is done to the disk or to the screen is not so important and could be regarded as an implementation aspect. It thus can be well abstracted.

The analogy between user interfaces and databases also means that large parts of what has been written in this book about `DataSet`s and `IM_Resolver`s can be (and have been) used to construct a data entry framework built on top of, for example, a GUI.

Here, too, exists an impedance mismatch between how something is presented on the screen and how that information is stored in the business model.

11.2   Separating the User Interface from the Business Model

As already stipulated, the application should be as independent of all user interface aspects as possible. It is important to have a clear separation of business model and user interface. Your application will have to behave as an information server with which several types of user interfaces—the clients—can interact.

An example of how this can be implemented is a user who wants to search for a certain object in the database. There are two parts to this implementation:

1. *What* has to be searched for
2. *How* the object must be searched for

The search command and specifying the object that you want to look for are typical user interface operations, but the logic of *how* to search for an object should be part of the application logic. For example, suppose you want to search for a certain customer. The business model might dictate the search process to be as follows:

1. If the customer's ID is specified, search on this ID.
2. Otherwise, if the customer's name is specified, search on this name.
3. Otherwise, cancel the search process.

The next subsections describe possible implementations for this search process.

11.2.1   Traditional Approach

The traditional programming approach is to include all user interface statements in CustomerSet's search function. This would result in code of the following form:

```
int CustomerSet::search()
{
  long id;
  char name[31];

  if (get_id(&id))
    return seek(f_id == id);
  else
    if (get_name(name))
      return seek(f_name == name);
  else
      {
      return -1;  // search cancelled
      }
}
```

The disadvantage of this method is that it is heavily interwoven with user interface aspects. Furthermore, it is written in a programmer-driven UI philosophy. That is, the users are obliged to first enter the customer's ID field. Only if they leave that field blank do they get the chance to enter the customer's name. Although this approach can be acceptable in an old-style character user interface, in a (user-driven) GUI one would expect to be able to directly click the name field and enter it. It also is difficult to picture using this method in a system in which the user interface and the application logic run on different machines.

11.2.2   Data-Driven Approach

A technique for designing event-driven GUI applications that is often used by many so-
called object-oriented client/server approaches is to design a class `CustomerDialog`, as
follows, and let it take care of the search functionality by making the necessary calls to the
database:

```
class CustomerDialog: public DialogWindow {

  CharEditField id_field, name_field;

protected:

  virtual void Event(UI_EVENT& event);
  // etc...
};

void CustomerDialog::Event(UI_EVENT& event)
{
  switch (event)
    {
    case SEARCH_BUTTON_PRESSED:
      {
      if (!is_empty_string(id_field->value()) {
        select * from customer where
            customer.id = id_field->value();
        {
      else
        {
        if (!is_empty_string(name_field->value()) {
          select * from customer
              where customer.name = name_field->value();
          {
        else
          {
          messagebox("Search operation canceled");
          }
        }
      }
      update_edit_fields();
      } break;
    // etc...
      }
}
```

This approach is indeed object-oriented as far as the user interface is concerned. However, this is not object-oriented software design because the user interface and the database are completely interwoven. Changes in database layout or in program requirements will result in having to rewrite large parts of the application. This example proves that using C++ as a programming language does not protect you from falling in the trap of the web architecture described in Section 3.1.

11.2.3 Using the Business Model

A better solution is to let the dialog class make calls to the business model instead of directly to the database. Then the user interface is shielded from the database layout and thus protected from changes to this layout.

```cpp
class CustomerDialog: public DialogWindow {

  CustomerSet *customer;
  CharEditField id_field, name_field;

protected:

  virtual void Event(UI_EVENT& event);
  // etc...
};

void CustomerDialog::Event(UI_EVENT& event)
{
  switch (event)
    {
    case SEARCH_BUTTON_PRESSED:
      {
      if (!is_empty_string(id_field->value())
        {
        customer->seek(customer->f_id == id_field->value());
        }
      else
        {
        if (!is_empty_string(name_field->value())
          {
          customer->seek(customer->f_name ==
                         name_field->value());
          }
        else
```

```
                    {
                      messagebox("Search operation canceled");
                    }
                  }
                } break;
          // etc...
            }
        }
```

This approach is already a significant improvement over the previous one in the way in which it uses the business model instead of relying on the database layout. However, it still has the problem that the user interface has to be concerned not only with what must be searched, but also with the "how" part of this searching process. If you want to implement a second user interface (for example, using a Web browser) onto this business model, this search algorithm will have to be implemented in that user interface, too.

11.2.4   Client/Server Approach

An approach conforming to the client/server philosophy is to implement the search algorithm as a business process, thus making it a part of the business model. Upon receiving the search event, the user interface then calls this business process. A possible implementation of this process is presented next:

```
int CustomerSet::search()
{
  if (!is_empty_string(iCurrent->id()))
    return seek(f_id == iCurrent->id());
  else
    if (!is_empty_string(name()))
      return seek(f_name == iCurrent->name());
    else
      return -1;  // search cancelled
}
```

This time, the search function works directly on the object itself, as illustrated in Figure 11.1. This object has previously been filled in through a link to the user interface (a technique to do so is to use the class DataNavigator that is described in Section 11.4). The object can be either completely or partially filled in. It is up to the search functions to interpret this information.

This time, the search function does no data entry; rather, it sees whether the person's ID is empty. If the user filled it in, this fact is interpreted to mean that the user wants to search on the customer's ID. Thus the corresponding search is issued.

8. Object redisplays   4. DataNavigator copies information into Customer object.
   in dialog.   5. DataNavigator calls CustomerSet::search().

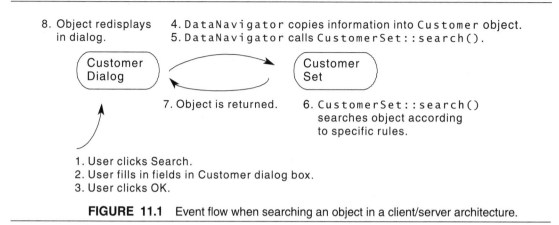

7. Object is returned.   6. CustomerSet::search()
                                searches object according
                                to specific rules.

1. User clicks Search.
2. User fills in fields in Customer dialog box.
3. User clicks OK.

FIGURE 11.1   Event flow when searching an object in a client/server architecture.

If the ID is empty, the name is examined, and if the name is filled in, it is used as the search criterion. If the name is empty, the search is canceled. All other fields are disregarded. If the search is executed, the Customer object contains the right object, provided it could be located.

The advantage of this approach is that the search operation is totally independent of the way the query information is gathered. It can be entered with a GUI or with a character-based user interface. However, it also can come from an IPC link with another cooperating process. Such a mechanism could be used, for example, to give your application dynamic data exchange (DDE) server capabilities.

With regard to the Internet, this approach could be interesting. For example, you could use a Web browser to communicate with your business model. You could achieve this functionality by giving the business model a CGI or by using ActiveX or Java. Figure 11.2 illustrates this. A total separation of concerns is achieved. That is, the user interface takes care of the details of how to enter an object and specifying *what* has to be searched, while the application (the business logic) deals with *how* an object is to be searched for.

2. Application puts data in Customer object (e.g., through COM).
3. Application sends search event.

1. Application needs   5. Object is returned.   4. CustomerSet::search() searches
   information about   object according to specific rules.
   certain customer.

FIGURE 11.2   A single search function can be used to accommodate entirely different user interface technologies. Here, the user interface is another application communicating through some IPC mechanism.

11.3   What to Put Where

The example in the previous section prompts the question of what to put in the user interface part of the program and what to put in the business model. As a rule, you should try to put all syntax knowledge in the user interface and all semantic knowledge in the business model.

Knowledge about the data itself can be handled by the user interface. However, what must be *done* with the data is the domain of the business model. This implies that all syntax checking can be (and is best) done on the user interface level. After all, the user interface has enough information to check whether, for example, a date is syntactically correct. It should be smart enough to flag February 30 as an incorrect date, for example. However, the user interface cannot be expected to know in what context this date will be used. So it cannot decide whether the date is meaningful for your application; that is, it cannot check the semantic correctness of this date. For example, the date July 16, 2044, will be considered perfectly correct on a syntactic level. However, it is up to the business model to tell that this date is not a correct date of birth (yet).

11.4   Navigating through Persistent Sets

This section offers an example of using a client/server data entry framework—a GUI built for a customer entry program.

11.4.1   The Business Object

Begin by designing the business component, which is the class `Customer` encountered in previous chapters and which is totally independent of all user interface aspects:

```
class Customer : public Person {

    friend class CustomerDialog;

private :
    double iDebit;
    double iCredit;
    Telephone iPhone2;
    Telephone iFax;
    Date iFirstVisit;
    Date iLatestVisit;
    Note note;

public :
    Customer();
    defaults();
```

```
     void reset_statistics(); // reset all objects to default value
     void update_statistics(double total, double payed, Date date);
     double debit() { return iDebit;}
     double credit() { return iCredit;}
     double increase_debit(double x) { iDebit+=x; return iDebit;}
     double increase_credit(double x) { iCredit+=x; return iCredit;}
     double balance()  { return debit()-credit(); }
     // etc...
   };
```

11.4.2 Class DataNavigator

Only when designing the user interface do you decide which *view* you want on your Customer objects. For starters, you might want to see and edit the customer's attributes
(name, address, and so on). To do this, you can draw a customer dialog window using a
resource editor, or you can hard code this dialog in a separate source file. This dialog window (data entry screen) consists of static text and several data entry fields (edit fields),
each of which has a symbolic name.

So next, when building the sample GUI for a customer entry program, you'll want to add
buttons to this dialog that allow you to edit customers, add new ones, delete current ones, and
navigate through the customer database. As this functionality is required for almost any object
set, a special data entry class can be designed. An example of such a class is DataNavigator,
which can be regarded as a data entry dialog with navigational capabilities attached.

The main objective of DataNavigator is to offer a general-purpose data management
and entry system that offers a high level of abstraction to the application developer, both in
view of the manipulation of persistent objects and of the presentation of data to the end
user. This is common functionality for many applications. Indeed, a frequent operation in
data manipulation is navigation through a persistent set. Almost all applications need at
least the following functionality: skipping forward and backward and searching, editing,
deleting, updating, and adding objects.

Because of the requirements of reusability, it makes sense to abstract that functionality by a common base class DataNavigator. Because of the interaction with the end user
in the operations mentioned previously, a user interface also must be incorporated in the
class. DataNavigator's interface is shown next:

```
     template <class T>
     class DataNavigator : public UIW_WINDOW {

     protected :
       T *_navset;
       EditField* *efld;
       // etc...
```

```
            UIW_TOOL_BAR *navigation;

            virtual VOID ButtonClick(int nr);
            virtual int Accept();
            virtual int AutoSet();
            virtual int Activate();
            virtual int Desactivate();
            int Response();

        public :
            DataNavigator(char *form, T *obj);
            virtual ~DataNavigator();
            int Add(EditField* fld);
            DataNavigator& operator+(EditField *fld);// add field to dialog
            virtual int Edit();
            virtual int Search();
        };
```

This DataNavigator class expects the set of type T to be navigable. This means that instances of type T are expected to have a function search(), which searches for a specified object (see the CustomerSet::search() function of Section 11.2.4). They also require a function next(), which allows you to skip through the set. The default PSet::next() function can be used to accomplish this functionality.

11.4.3   Derived Navigators

From the DataNavigator class, you can now derive a class CustomerDialog, which contains the customer set with which you'll want to work. In other words, CustomerDialog presents a view on the customer objects. Its implementation is given here:

```
        class CustomerDialog : public DataNavigator<CustomerSet> {

        public :
            CustomerDialog(CustomerSet *cset);
            virtual ~CustomerDialog();
            // etc...
        };

        CustomerDialog::CustomerDialog(CustomerSet *cset)
        : DataNavigator ("account.dat~CUSTOMER_DIALOG", cset)
        {
            // link the variables to the edit fields in the dialog box
```

```
Customer *cust = cset->current();

*this
    + new EditID("ID_PERSON_ID", this, &cust->id)
    + new EditChar("ID_PERSON_NAME", this, cust->name, 30)
    + new EditAddress("ID_STREET", "ID_ZIP", "ID_CITY", this,
                      &cust->address) + new EditVatNumber
                      ("ID_VATNUMBER", this, &cust->vatnr)
    + new EditBankAccount("ID_BANKACCOUNT", this,
                      &cust->bankaccount) + new
                      EditTelephone("ID_PHONE", this,
                      &cust->phone)
    + new EditTelephone("ID_FAX", this, &cust->fax)
    + new EditNote("ID_REMARK", this, &cust->note);

// automatically set all edit fields to their value in cust
AutoSet();
}
```

Note that nowhere in this code do you have to specify how to enter the different variables. No intelligence of how to enter a name, an address, an account number, and so on, is coded in CustomerDialog or the class Customer. This intelligence is contained in its own set of classes (EditString, EditAddress, EditTelephone, EditBankAccount, and so on), all derived from the base class EditField. Instances of these derived classes link the memory variables of the customer object to the data entry screen. Furthermore, they are responsible for the necessary syntax control.

Notice also that you don't have to specify the layout of the data entry screen. This screen can be designed by a separate screen painter and can be modified at any time (even after the program has been compiled). Furthermore, it is not necessary that all edit fields actually be present on the data entry form. Thus, several different entry forms can be designed (one for each type of user privilege) and can run with the same application code.

The data entry system offered by DataNavigator is completely analogous to the basic architecture used in the persistence framework. Indeed, the derived EditField objects are equivalent to the IM_Resolvers, and the dialogs are equivalent to the Data-Sets, while the business model, of course, stays the business model. Here, too, the Edit-Field classes serve in resolving the impedance mismatch that exists between the data entry screen and the corresponding objects in the business model. This once more points to the significant analogy between databases and user interfaces, which can both be regarded as views on the business model.

Another important thing to note is that the intelligence of how to browse the customer database or how to enter new objects is not part of CustomerDialog. This intelligence is completely contained in the business object CustomerSet.

11.4.4   Activating a `DataNavigator`

Class `DataNavigator` also provides for the rest of the user interface functions (for example, opening the window, performing basic event handling, and so on). By hiding most of the user interface concepts, it not only simplifies the program development, but also improves portability across different GUI platforms.

The following function illustrates how the customer navigator can be used:

```
void edit_customers()
{
    // create a new dialog
    CustomerDialog *dialog = new CustomerDialog(new CustomerSet);

    // add the dialog to the window manager
    windowManager->Add(dialog);
}
```

The output of this code is shown in Figure 11.3.

As you can see, a limited amount of code, based on a set of robust and independently verified classes, can exhibit a rich behavior, the reliability of which is based on a set of certified software components.

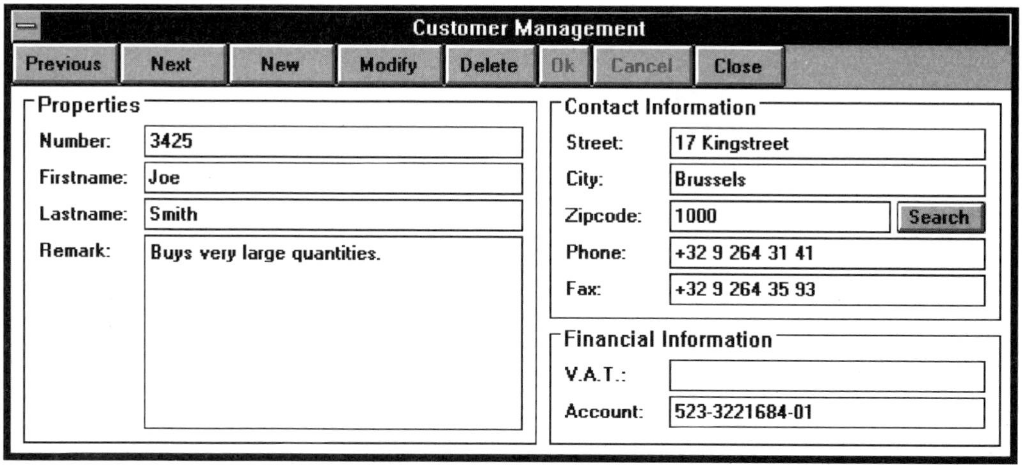

FIGURE 11.3   Illustration of the user interface implemented in class `DataNavigator`.

11.5 Summary

This chapter presented an example of how the client/server principle can be applied to the interaction between the business model and the user interface. It also showed how a GUI framework can be designed using the principles of the Scoop architecture. A class `DataNavigator` was presented that is a general-purpose data management and entry system. It offers a high level of abstraction to the application developer, with regard both to the manipulation of persistent objects and to the presentation of data to the end user.

Chapter 12

Case Study: An Electronic Telephone Directory

This chapter looks in some detail at a project that was implemented using the principles described in this book. The purpose of the project was to automate the printed telephone directory at a university and to give it a number of extensions [Carron95], thereby resulting in a simple system that allowed the outside world to reach the right person at the university.

12.1 Project Definition

The program that resulted from the project had to reflect the structure of the university. Thus it needed to present to the user a picture of the hierarchy consisting of the different faculties and departments. Here are the specifics:

- Each department belongs to a parent department and can have several other departments attached to it.
- Each department has a name, a type, a phone number, a fax number, and an address.
- People are attached to departments. Each person belongs to at least one department.
- Each person has a phone number, a fax number, and a job title for each department he or she belongs to.
- People are organized in a hierarchy. Each person has one direct superior and can have several employees.
- People are categorized in categories that are independent of the person's department or job title. The possible categories are Professor, Teaching Assistant, and Administrative Personnel.
- For each person, the system registers in which domains he or she specializes. These domains are called projects. Each project can be categorized in a hierarchy and may

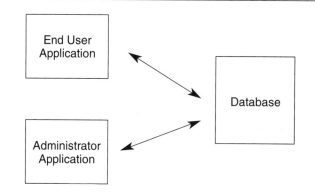

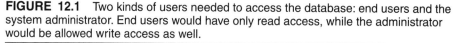

FIGURE 12.1 Two kinds of users needed to access the database: end users and the system administrator. End users would have only read access, while the administrator would be allowed write access as well.

contain several subprojects. For example, the project Informatics includes the subprojects Object-Oriented Analysis, Databases, and Artificial Intelligence. The subproject Databases, in turn, contains several other projects, such as Relational Databases and Object-Oriented Databases.

- Each person must be able to leave a message, which appears whenever someone asks for information about him or her.

For example, if a user wants to contact someone who knows something about, say, object orientation, it suffices to search through the telephone directory using Object Orientation as a key. The user will end up with a list of all employees involved with object orientation. For each, the user can find out the name of the head of that employee's department and the names of the employees (if any) who report to the person.

The data had to be accessible by two kinds of users: the system administrator and the end users (see Figure 12.1). The system administrator would be able to add new projects, add and delete people, add departments, and so on; that is, the administrator would have read and write access. The end user would be able to consult the data but would only be able to modify his or her own data; that person would have only read access to the data of others.

12.2 Comparing Development Approaches

This project was used to compare various development approaches. More particularly, several 4GL languages were tested and compared to a C++ approach [VandenBerghe95]. For many of the approaches using 4GL, the starting point was the design of the user interface and database layout. Development of these designs required a lot of discussion. One prerequisite of the project was that all applications should have the same user interface and be able to work on the same database, so the C++ developer had to take part in this discussion. Note, however, that from an object-oriented point of view, the proper way to start this project would have been to design the business model first.

12.3 Designing the User Interface

All development teams started by designing a collection of screens that would form the user interface to the telephone directory. These were drawn using a screen designer that came with the 4GL tool or, in the case of the C++ approach, the window application framework. Figure 12.2 shows several of the resulting dialog boxes. Note that some are similar in functionality or appearance (or both).

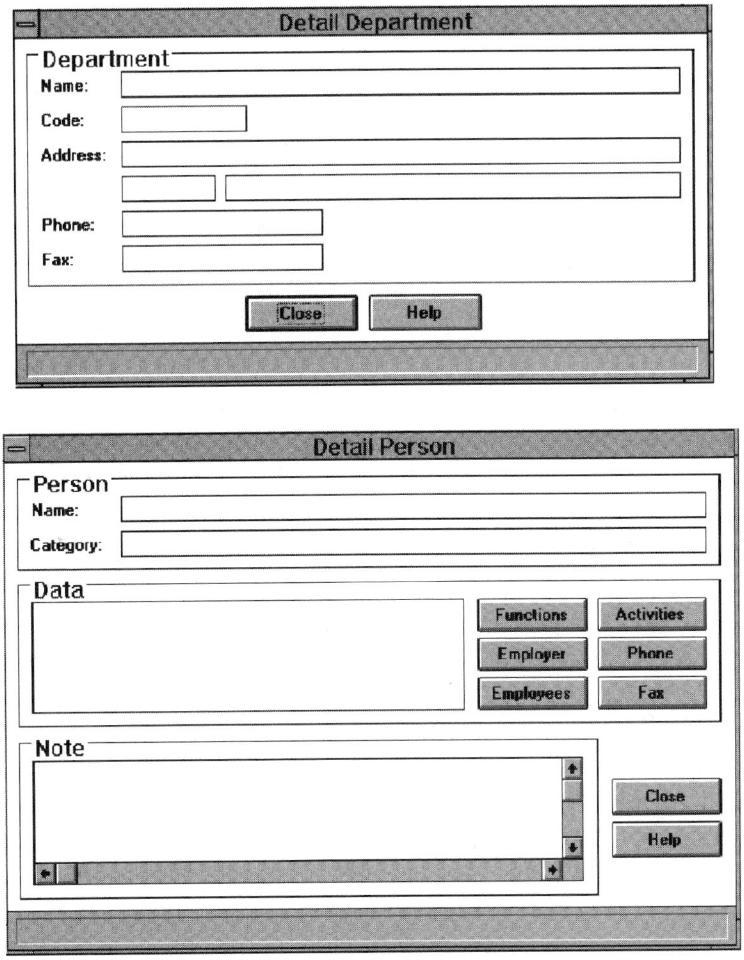

continued

FIGURE 12.2 Sample dialog windows used in the telephone directory user interface.

Lookup Department

Department

Preferences
☐ type

Structure

[Detail]

[Close] [Browse] [Help]

Lookup Person

Person

Preferences
☐ department [   ] [Search]
☐ activity [   ] [Search]
☐ category [   ]
☐ function [   ]

[Detail]

[Close] [Browse] [Help]

continued

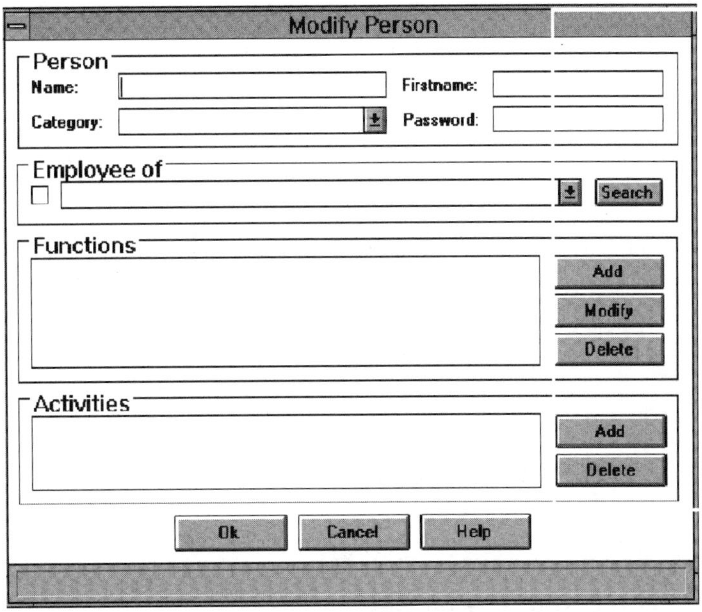
Modify Person
Person
Name:
Firstname:
Category:
Password:
Employee of
Search
Functions
Add
Modify
Delete
Activities
Add
Delete
Ok
Cancel
Help

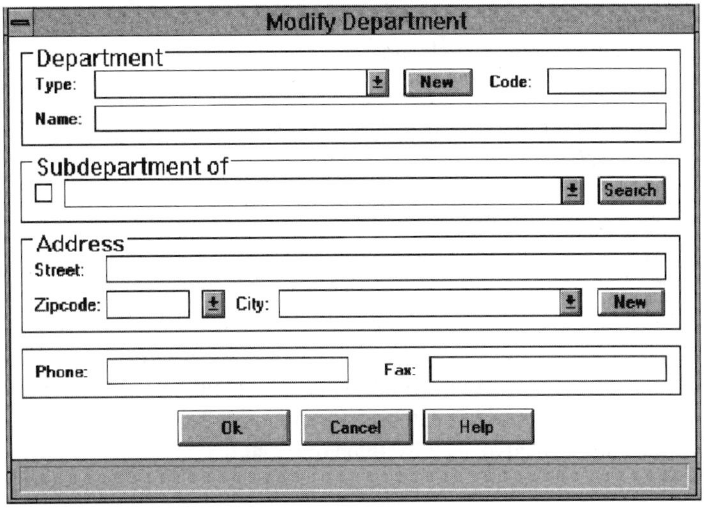
Modify Department
Department
Type:
New
Code:
Name:
Subdepartment of
Search
Address
Street:
Zipcode:
City:
New
Phone:
Fax:
Ok
Cancel
Help

continued

FIGURE 12.2 Concluded.

12.4 The Database Model

The next step was the design of the entity-relationship (E/R) diagram.[1] After a long discussion, the teams created the model sketched in Figure 12.3.

From this E/R model, the database layout shown in Figure 12.4 was derived. In the figure, primary keys are represented in bold, and foreign keys are in italic. Bold italic signifies both primary and foreign.

12.5 Designing the Business Model

The approach followed and outlined in previous sections was far from ideal and completely contradicted the basic principles of object-oriented software design. Good object-oriented design requires first the development of a stable business model, independent of all user interface and database considerations. However, this was not possible because of the approach advocated by some of the 4GLs.

But, as has already been suggested, if the model should be independent of the database layout, then the database layout should be independent of the model. In other words, the fact that the UI and the database layout had to be designed first should not be an obstacle.

---

1. Note again that proper object-oriented design would have begun with designing the business model first. The only reason the project began with the E/R model was that most 4GL approaches required this.

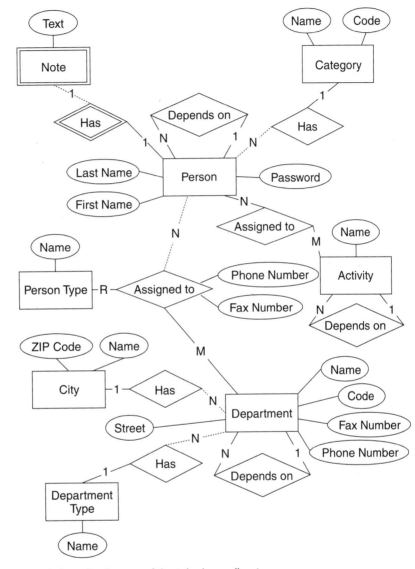

FIGURE 12.3   E/R diagram of the telephone directory.

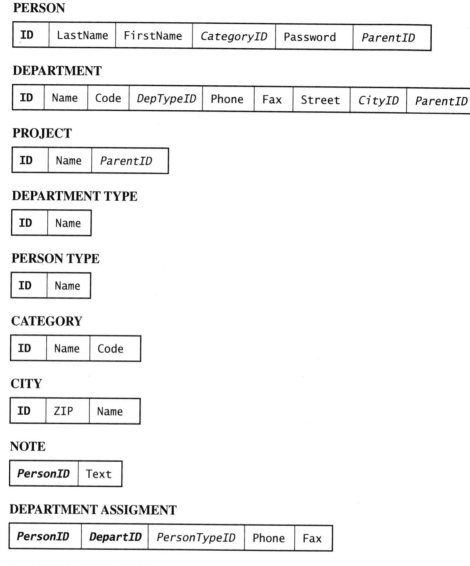

PERSON

ID	LastName	FirstName	CategoryID	Password	ParentID

DEPARTMENT

ID	Name	Code	DepTypeID	Phone	Fax	Street	CityID	ParentID

PROJECT

ID	Name	ParentID

DEPARTMENT TYPE

ID	Name

PERSON TYPE

ID	Name

CATEGORY

ID	Name	Code

CITY

ID	ZIP	Name

NOTE

PersonID	Text

DEPARTMENT ASSIGMENT

PersonID	DepartID	PersonTypeID	Phone	Fax

PROJECT ASSIGNMENT

PersonID	ProjectID

FIGURE 12.4 Relational database layout of the telephone directory application.

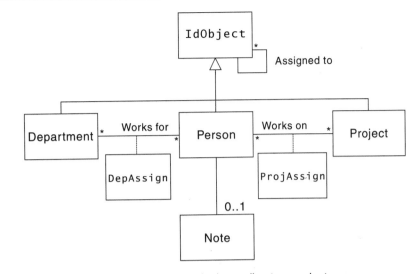

FIGURE 12.5   Business model of the telephone directory project.

In a test of this theory, the user interface and database layout design were put aside, and the analysis was started over from scratch—but this time with the development of the business model in mind. This analysis was done by someone who had not been involved in the design of the UI and database layout and so had no knowledge of either. His analysis led to the business model shown in Figure 12.5.

12.6   Comparing the Business Model and the Database Model

A comparison of the business model with the database model reveals the remarkable relative simplicity of the business model compared to the problem definition or to the ER diagram. This simplicity results because the business model is situated on a higher level of abstraction than the E/R model. Consider the city table of Figure 12.4. The city appears in the E/R model. In the business model, however, it is merely an attribute of the Person class and so won't appear as a separate class. The result is a model that is much simpler and that concentrates on the essence of the problem domain instead of representing the physical implementation thereof.

This is the major difference between the business model and the E/R model. The business model is intended to represent the workings of the system (in other words, the business in which you operate). It contains the objects that are relevant for that business, regardless of whether they are persistent. The E/R model, on the other hand, is a more

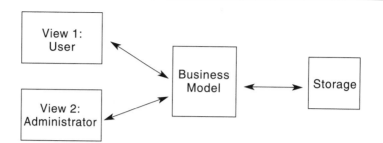

FIGURE 12.6 Two applications, one model. Instead of developing two different applications, design two views on the business model. This is a much simpler task, since all intelligence is contained in the business model.

physical concept. It contains only those objects that are persistent. Thus it does not so much represent the problem domain as it is mainly concerned with which data will be stored and how.

Even in this simple example, an impedance mismatch exists between the business model and the database model. Several business-model objects are spread over multiple database tables and vice versa; that is, certain tables contain information that will be used by multiple business objects.

12.6.1   Two Applications, One Model

There will be two applications working on the database: one for the users and one for the administrators. This translates into having two different views on the same business model. This is shown in Figure 12.6. Since all intelligence is centralized in the business model, the construction of these two views is likely to be fairly straightforward.

12.7   Implementing the Business Objects

Once the business model was designed, the next step was to design a set of C++ classes that implemented this business model. Stability and reuse were important design considerations. On first sight, designing the classes may appear complex. An examination of the their code, however, shows it was not; the result was a set of very simple C++ classes. Notice also that all classes were initially designed without the need for discussions about database or user interface aspects. Developers were able to concentrate fully on the essence of the problem. The following subsections look briefly at some of those classes.

12.7.1 Class `IdObject`

A recurring requirement in most classes is that their instances must be uniquely identifiable, for example to compare two instances. Furthermore, objects have both a name and a full name. The full name can be the same as the name, but for a `Person` object, it also can be, for example, a concatenation of the first and the last names. The full name is used when an object has to present itself to the user of the class (in a list, for example). Instead of having to reimplement the basic functionality in each class, the designer chose to use the following base class `IdObject` to implement this common functionality:

```
class IdObject {

    long _id;

  public:

    IdObject();
    IdObject(const IdObject& idobject);
    IdObject& operator = (const IdObject& object);
    IdObject& Assign(const IdObject& object);
    int operator == (const IdObject& idobject);

    long GetId (void);
    virtual char* GetName (void);
    virtual char* GetFullName (void);
    void SetId (const long id);
    void AssignId (void);
    int GetById (long id);
    virtual void Initialise (void);
};
```

12.7.2 Class Person

As an example of a first business object, class `Person` follows:

```
class Person : public IdObject
  {
  private:
    char _lastname[_LASTNAMELENGTH+1],
        _firstname[_FIRSTNAMELENGTH+1];
    Password _password;
    Category _category;
    Note _note;
```

```
public:
  Person();
  Person(const Person& person);
  virtual ~Person();

  char* GetLastname (void);
  char* GetFirstname (void);
  char* GetFullName (void);
  Password& GetPassword (void);
  Note& GetNote (void);
  Category& GetCategory (void);

  void SetLastname (const char* lastname);
  void SetFirstname (const char* firstname);
  void SetPassword (const Password& password);
  void SetNote (const Note& note);
  void SetCategory (const Category& category);
};
```

A person belongs to a certain category. To accommodate this, the designer created the class Category, presented below. Notice, however, that the Category instance is merely an attribute of Person and is not considered to be an association.

```
class Category : public IdObject
  {
  private:
    char _name[_CATEGORYNAMELENGTH+1],
         _code[_CATEGORYCODELENGTH+1];

  public:
    Category();
    virtual ~Category();
    char* GetName (void);
    char* GetCode (void);
    void SetName (const char* name);
    void SetCode (const char* code);
  };
```

Recall from the program's specifications (Section 12.1) that a person had to be able to leave a message. This message is implemented by giving each person a member object of type Note:

```
const int _TEXTLENGTH = 254;

class Note
  {
  private:
    char _text[_TEXTLENGTH+1];

  public:
    Note();
    char* GetText (void);
    void SetText (const char* text);
    void Initialise (void);
  };
```

Figure 12.7 gives the implementation of the member functions of Person.

```
Person::Person ()
  {}

char* Person::GetLastname (void)
  {
  return (_lastname);
  }

char* Person::GetFirstname (void)
  {
  return (_firstname);
  }

char* Person::GetFullName (void)
  {
  char* name = new char[_LASTNAMELENGTH+_FIRSTNAMELENGTH+2];
  strcpy (name,_lastname);
  strcat (name," ");
  strcat (name,_firstname);
  return (name);
  }

Password& Person::GetPassword (void)
  {
  return (_password);
  }
```

continued

```
Note& Person::GetNote (void)
  {
  return (_note);
  }


Category& Person::GetCategory (void)
  {
  return (_category);
  }


void Person::SetLastname (const char* lastname)
  {
  strncpy (_lastname,lastname,_LASTNAMELENGTH);
  _lastname[_LASTNAMELENGTH]='\0';
  }


void Person::SetFirstname (const char* firstname)
  {
  strncpy (_firstname,firstname,_FIRSTNAMELENGTH);
  _firstname[_FIRSTNAMELENGTH]='\0';
  }


void Person::SetPassword (const Password& password)
  {
  _password=password;
  }


void Person::SetNote (const Note& note)
  {
  _note=note;
  }


void Person::SetCategory (const Category& category)
  {
  _category=category;
  }
```

FIGURE 12.7   Implementation of class Person's member functions.

12.7.3   Class Department

Class Department has a layout similar to Person's:

```
class Department : public IdObject
  {
  private:
    char _name[_DEPARTMENTNAMELENGTH+1],
         _code[_DEPARTMENTCODELENGTH+1],
         _phone[_DEPARTMENTPHONELENGTH+1],
         _fax[_DEPARTMENTFAXLENGTH+1];
    Address _address;
    DepartmentType _type;

  public:
    Department();
    virtual ~Department();

    char* GetName (void);
    char* GetFullName (void);
    char* GetCode (void);
    char* GetPhoneNumber (void);
    char* GetFaxNumber (void);
    Address& GetAddress (void);
    DepartmentType& GetType (void);

    void SetName (const char* name);
    void SetCode (const char* code);
    void SetPhoneNumber (const char* phone);
    void SetFaxNumber (const char* fax);
    void SetAddress (const Address& address);
    void SetType (const DepartmentType& type);
  };
```

12.7.4   Class Dependency

To implement the "is-assigned-to" dependencies that exist between objects (to specify an boss-employee relationship, for example), the following special class Dependency (implemented as a template) was designed:

```
template <class T>
class Dependency
  {
  private:
    T _child,_parent;
```

```
public:
  Dependency ();
  virtual ~Dependency();

  int GetChildDependency (void);
  int GetFirstParentDependency (void);
  int GetNextParentDependency (void);

  T& GetChild (void);
  T& GetParent (void);

  void SetChild (const T& child);
  void SetParent (const T& parent);
};

typedef Dependency<Activity> ActivityDependency;
typedef Dependency<Department> DepartmentDependency;
typedef Dependency<Person> PersonDependency;
```

This class makes the connection between child objects and parent objects. It has functions that set and retrieve these objects, as well as three navigation functions. The latter serve in retrieving dependencies connected to a certain parent or child.

Note that the presence of these navigation functions has nothing to do with whether you are working with a database. Rather, they indicate only that you are working with collections. Any later decision to put this collection in a database table is just an implementation aspect and should not influence the rest of the program.[2]

12.8 Making Classes Persistent

Finally, the designer decided which classes had to be made persistent. It was decided to make objects persistent by directly deriving them from PSet, thus using the second approach described in Section 6.1. The only changes needed to the previously developed classes were to derive them from PSet and assign to them the corresponding IM_Resolvers. These changes are discussed in the following subsections.

12.8.1 Changing Class IdObject

Changes to the class IdObject, which serves as base class for most other persistent objects, are in bold in the following code:

---

2. As shown later in the chapter, the dependencies are stored in the database but in a way that is not as you might expect.

```
class IdObject : public PSet {

  proteced:

    long _id;
    DataSet ds;
    IM_long f_id;

  public:
    IdObject (char* setname);
    IdObject (const IdObject& idobject);
    IdObject& operator = (const IdObject& object);
    IdObject& Assign(const IdObject& object);
    int operator == (const IdObject& idobject);
    long GetId (void);
    virtual char* GetName (void);
    virtual char* GetFullName (void);
    void SetId (const long id);
    void AssignId (void);
    int GetById (long id);
    virtual void Initialise (void);
};
```

A corresponding IM resolver in the Ref template can be used. The actual implementation of class IdObject is presented in Figure 12.8.

```
IdObject::IdObject (char* setname)
        :ds(this, setname),
         f_id (&_id, &ds,"ID")
  {}
IdObject::IdObject (const IdObject& idobject)
        :ds(this, idobject.who()),
         f_id(&_id, &ds,"ID")
  {}

IdObject& IdObject::operator = (const IdObject& idobject)
  {
  return Assign(idobject);
  }
```

continued

```
IdObject& IdObject::Assign(const IdObject& idobject)
  {
  if (this!=&idobject)
    GetById (idobject.GetId());
  return *this;
  }

int IdObject::operator == (const IdObject& idobject)
  {
  return (GetId()==idobject.GetId());
  }

long IdObject::GetId (void)
  {
  return (_id);
  }

char* IdObject::GetName (void)
  {
  return (NULL);
  }

char* IdObject::GetFullName (void)
  {
  return (GetName());
  }

void IdObject::SetId (const long id)
  {
  _id=id;
  }

void IdObject::AssignId (void)
  {
  Configuration configuration;
  SetId (configuration.RequestId());
  }
```

continued

```
int IdObject::GetById (long id)
  {
  int found=(seek(f_id == id)==FOUND);
  if (!found)
    Initialise();
  return (found);
  }

void IdObject::Initialise (void)
  {
  _id=UNDEFINED_OBJECT;
  }
```

FIGURE 12.8   Implementation of IdObject.

12.8.2   Changing Class Person

Person is derived from IdObject, so it automatically gains persistent capabilities. All that is left to do is to add an instance of the associated IM_Resolver for each member object of Person that is to be written to the database. The new version of class Person is presented in Figure 12.9. In the figure, all changes to the previous version are shown in bold.

```
class Person : public IdObject {

  private:
    char _lastname[_LASTNAMELENGTH+1],_firstname[_FIRSTNAMELENGTH+1];
    Password _password;
    Ref<Category> _category;
    Note _note;

    IM_char f_lastname, f_firstname;
    IM_Note f_note;
    IM_Ref<Category> f_category;

  public:
    Person();
    virtual ~Person();
```

continued

```
        char* GetLastname (void);
        char* GetFirstname (void);
        char* GetFullName (void);
        Password& GetPassword (void);
        Note& GetNote (void);
        Ref<Category>& GetCategory (void);

        void SetLastname (const char* lastname);
        void SetFirstname (const char* firstname);
        void SetPassword (const Password& password);
        void SetNote (const Note& note);
        void SetCategory (const Category& category);
};


typedef IdObject_field DepartmentType_field;

class Department : public IdObject
  {
  private:
    char _name[_DEPARTMENTNAMELENGTH+1],
         _code[_DEPARTMENTCODELENGTH+1],
         _phone[_DEPARTMENTPHONELENGTH+1],
         _fax[_DEPARTMENTFAXLENGTH+1];
    Address _address;
    Ref<DepartmentType> _type;

    IM_char f_name, f_code, f_phone, f_fax;
    IM_Ref<DepartmentType> f_type;

  public:
    Department();
    char* GetName (void);
    char* GetFullName (void);
    char* GetCode (void);
    char* GetPhoneNumber (void);
    char* GetFaxNumber (void);
    Address& GetAddress (void);
    Ref<DepartmentType>& GetType (void);
```

continued

```
    void SetName (const char* name);
    void SetCode (const char* code);
    void SetPhoneNumber (const char* phone);
    void SetFaxNumber (const char* fax);
    void SetAddress (const Address& address);
    void SetType (const DepartmentType& type);
};


Person::Person()
      :IdObject ("PERSON"),
      f_lastname(_lastname, &ds,"LASTNAME",_LASTNAMELENGTH),
      f_firstname(_firstname,&ds,"FIRSTNAME",_FIRSTNAMELENGTH),
      f_category (&_category, &ds, "CATID"),
      f_note (&_note, &ds, "NOTE")
   {}

char* Person::GetLastname (void)
   {
   return (_lastname);
   }

char* Person::GetFirstname (void)
   {
   return (_firstname);
   }

char* Person::GetFullName (void)
   {
   char* name= new char[_LASTNAMELENGTH+_FIRSTNAMELENGTH+2];
   strcpy (name,_lastname);
   strcat (name," ");
   strcat (name,_firstname);
   return (name);
   }

Password& Person::GetPassword (void)
   {
   return (_password);
   }
```

continued

```
Note& Person::GetNote (void)
  {
  return (_note);
  }

Ref<Category>& Person::GetCategory (void)
  {
  return (_category);
  }

void Person::SetLastname (const char* lastname)
  {
  strncpy (_lastname,lastname,_LASTNAMELENGTH);
  _lastname[_LASTNAMELENGTH]='\0';
  }

void Person::SetFirstname (const char* firstname)
  {
  strncpy (_firstname,firstname,_FIRSTNAMELENGTH);
  _firstname[_FIRSTNAMELENGTH]='\0';
  }

void Person::SetPassword (const Password& password)
  {
  _password=password;
  }

void Person::SetNote (const Note& note)
  {
  _note=note;
  }

void Person::SetCategory (const Category& category)
  {
  _category=category;
  }
```

FIGURE 12.9 Persistent version of class Person.

Class `Category` also has been made persistent, shown as follows. This persistence allows the category to be chosen from a predefined set of categories.

```
class Category : public IdObject
  {
  private:
    char _name[_CATEGORYNAMELENGTH+1],_code[_CATEGORYCODELENGTH+1];
    IM_char f_name,f_code;

  public:
    Category();
    virtual ~Category();

    char* GetName (void);
    char* GetCode (void);
    void SetName (const char* name);
    void SetCode (const char* code);
  };
```

Storing objects of type `Category` as members of other objects was done by using the `Ref` template.

Making objects persistent has no effect on the existing inheritance tree. Also, the business objects need not specify how the mapping on the database must be done.

12.9 Impedance Mismatch Examples

This section looks at some examples in which there existed significant impedance mismatches between the business model and the database layout.

12.9.1 Changing Class Note

The first example of the impedance mismatch between the business model and the database layout was the person's `Note` (the message that he or she can leave behind) and its associated `IM_Note` instance. In the first version, `Note` was implemented, as in Section 12.7.2, and `IM_Note` was implemented as follows:

```
class IM_Note: public IM_Resolver {

private:
  Note* _note;
```

```
public:
  IM_Note (Note* var, DataSet* base, const char* nme);

  void read (Cursor& cursor);
  void to_update(Statement& stmt);
};

IM_Note::IM_Note (Note* var,DataSet* base,const char* nme)
            :IM_Resolver (base, nme,F_CHAR,_TEXTLENGTH)
  {
  _note=var;
  }

void IM_Note::read(Cursor& cursor)
  {
  char str[_TEXTLENGTH+1];
  cursor[column->name()] >> str;
  _note->SetText(str);
  }

void IM_Note::to_update(Statement& stmt)
  {
  stmt[column->name()] << _note->GetText();
  }
```

In this approach, the note was an ordinary row (of type string) in the person table. However, it was discovered that most people left their notes empty and that those notes tended to take up relatively a lot of space. So it was better to put the notes in a separate table, one that contained only notes that were filled in. There was now a one-to-zero-or-one relationship between the person table and the note table. This relationship is shown in Figure 12.10.

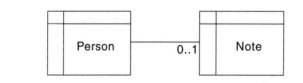

FIGURE 12.10 Person-Note relationship. To save space in the database, the Person-Note relationship was implemented using two separate tables that have a one-to-one or one-to-zero relationship.

Implementing this change in the 4GL-based applications required considerable effort because every piece of code that used a note had to be recoded. Implementing this change in the object-oriented approach, on the other hand, required only designing a new version of IM_Note. The rest of the code, including all classes using Note, remained unchanged. Here is the new version of Note:

```
const int _TEXTLENGTH = 254;

class Note : public IdObject
  {
  private:
    char _text[_TEXTLENGTH+1];
    IM_char f_text;

  public:
    Note()
       :IdObject("NOTE"),
        f_text (_text,this,"TEXT",_TEXTLENGTH)
     {}

    char* GetText (void);
    void SetText (const char* text);
    void Initialise (void);
  };
```

The IM resolver corresponding to this class follows. Notice that it was not possible to use the Ref template in this implementation because the person table does not contain a reference (foreign key) to the corresponding entry in the note table. Rather, the note was implemented in the database as a **weak object,** meaning its primary key is the same as its corresponding Person instance.

```
class IM_Note: public IM_Resolver
  {
  private:
    Note* _note;

  public:
    IM_Note (Note* var, DataSet* base, const char* nme=NULL);

    void read (Cursor& cursor);
    void to_update(Statement& stmt);
  };
```

```
IM_Note::IM_Note(Note* var,DataSet* base,const char* nme)
    :IM_Resolver (base, "NULL",F_CHAR,10)
  {
  _note=var;
  }


void IM_Note::read(Cursor& cursor)
  {
  return (_note->GetById (((IdObject*)pset())->GetId()));
  }


void IM_Note::to_update(Statement& stmt)
  {
  _note->SetId(((IdObject*)pset())->GetId());
  Note help;
  int exists = help.GetById(_note->GetId());
  if (strcmp(_note->GetText()," ")!=0)
    {
    if (exists)
      _note->write();
    else
      _note->append();
    }
  else                  // if note is empty
    if (exists)         // if an old note present
      {
      _note->erase();   // delete it
      }
  }
```

One complication with the write function of IM_Note was that it should take care that the one-to-zero-or-one relationship is maintained. Thus, if the note is not empty, IM_Note::to_update() should first check whether there is already a note for that person and, if so, replace it with the new note. If there is no note present, the new note must be appended to the table. If the person's note is empty, however, the system must check if there is still an old note present and, if so, delete it. Notice that from a logical point of view, the note is still part of a person. However, from a physical point of view this is no longer true. In the database, an explicit join must be made between the person and the note table. Hiding this knowledge in the class IM_Note makes this database layout transparent to the rest of the application. In other words, class Person, which uses class Note, did not have to be changed.

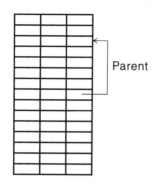

FIGURE 12.11   Dependency implementation.

12.9.2   Modeling Dependency

Another example in which there is a significant mismatch between the business model and the database was in the modeling of the dependencies between objects. In the database, an object (record) refers to its parent by means of a column that contains a foreign key to that parent. This is depicted in Figure 12.11.

In the object model, however, this relationship is modeled through a dedicated class Dependency, as follows, which refers to dependent child and parent objects:

```
template <class T,char* S>
class Dependency:public PSet
  {
  protected:
    DataSet ds;
    Ref<T> _child,_parent;
    IM_Ref<T> f_child, f_parent;

  public:
    Dependency (char* setname=S);
    int GetChildDependency (void);
    int GetFirstParentDependency (void);
    int GetNextParentDependency (void);
    Ref<T>& GetChild (void);
    Ref<T>& GetParent (void);
    void SetChild (const T& child);
    void SetParent (const T& parent);
  };
```

```
typedef Dependency<Activity,"ACTIVITY"> ActivityDependency;
typedef Dependency<Department,"DEPART"> DepartmentDependency;
typedef Dependency<Person,"PERSON"> PersonDependency;
```

Notice that although the Dependency class has a parent and a child object, the database table that stores these dependencies knows only about parent records. This means that the data about a dependency is distributed over two records in the same table.

Thanks to the IM resolvers associated with the child and parent objects, the retrieval of the objects is done automatically. Notice, however, that this is far from evident. On a logical level, three record pointers within a table exist: one for the person object and two for the dependency object (one for the parent and one for the child). On the database level, only one record pointer exists. The persistence framework takes care of the necessary management of these pointers.

To the user, the dependencies connected with a certain parent take the form of a container that can be navigated. The implementation of the navigation functions are presented next:

```
template<class T,char* S>
Dependency<T,S>::Dependency (char* setname)
                :ds(this, setname),
                 f_child (&_child, &ds, "ID"),
                 f_parent (&_parent, &ds, "PARENTID")
  {}


// Return the first dependency with the current child.
template<class T,char* S>
int Dependency<T,S>::GetChildDependency (void)
  {
  Ref<T> assist=_child;
  return ((seek (f_child == assist)==FOUND) &&
          (GetParent().GetId()!=UNDEFINED_OBJECT));
  }


template<class T,char* S>
int Dependency<T,S>::GetFirstParentDependency (void)
  {
  Ref<T> assist = _parent;
  return (seek (f_parent == assist)==FOUND);
  }


template<class T,char* S>
int Dependency<T,S>::GetNextParentDependency (void)
  {
  return next();
  }
```

```
template<class T,char* S>
Ref<T>& Dependency<T,S>::GetChild (void)
  {
  return (_child);
  }

template<class T,char* S>
Ref<T>& Dependency<T,S>::GetParent (void)
  {
  return (_parent);
  }

template<class T,char* S>
void Dependency<T,S>::SetChild (const T& childobject)
  {
  _child = childobject;
  }

template<class T,char* S>
void Dependency<T,S>::SetParent (const T& parentobject)
  {
  _parent = parentobject;
  }
```

The function `GetFirstParentDependency()` gets the first dependency that corresponds with the current parent object. This is done by performing a search on the `f_parent` `IM_Resolver`. Translated to the physical database layout, this boils down to searching the first record of the current parent object in the column *PARENTID* (see Figure 12.3).

If you take the time (and have the patience) to try to really understand the low-level database read process, you'll find that having a framework that abstracts this impedance mismatch is very valuable.

12.10 Implementing the User Interface

As the next step, the designer implemented the user interface for this specific application, which consisted of designing a controller that mapped the application view onto the model. The controller's main task was to translate all user events into a set of calls to the business model.

To hide all low-level details of GUI design and to guarantee platform independence, the designer used a commercial class library to design the user interface.[3] This framework

---

3. The Zinc Application Framework was chosen for this application, but any other object-oriented framework would have been a viable alternative.

came with a design tool that allowed the programmer to design platform-independent resources. Using this tool, he designed all windows and dialog boxes. He further developed a set of reusable base classes that allowed easy manipulation of these resources.

12.10.1 Reusable Base Classes

The two main base classes developed were `EditObjectWindow` and `HandleObject-Window`. The first allows for consulting and modifying a certain object. It can correspond to the Modify Person dialog box of Figure 12.2, for example. The second class allows for browsing a list of objects and displaying its hierarchical position with respect to the other objects of the same set. It corresponds to the Handle Person dialog box of Figure 12.2, for example. Both classes are illustrated in Figure 12.12. Their implementations are shown in Figure 12.13.

```
class EditObjectWindow : public BaseWindow {

protected:
  IdObject* _object;
  int dataid;

  void EventHandler (int objectid,int event);
  virtual int ValidateInformation (void);
  virtual void StoreInformation (void);

public:
  EditObjectWindow (int parentid,int windowid,char* resource);
};

class HandleObjectWindow : public BaseWindow {

protected:
  IdObject* _object;

public:
  HandleObjectWindow (int parentid,int windowid,char* resource);
  ~HandleObjectWindow (void);

  void EventHandler (int objectid,int event);
  virtual void DetailObject (IdObject* object);
};
```

FIGURE 12.12   Base classes to edit and consult objects.

```
EditObjectWindow::EditObjectWindow(int callerid, int windowid,
                                   char* resource)
    :BaseWindow (callerid,windowid,resource)
{}

void EditObjectWindow::EventHandler(int objectid,int event)
{
   switch (objectid)
     {
     case OK_BUTTON:
       {
       if (ValidateInformation())  // if input is acceptable
         {
         StoreInformation();
         DeliverData(GetCallerId(),(void*)_object,dataid);
         Close();
         }
       } break;

     case CANCEL_BUTTON:
       {
       Close();
       } break;
     }
}

int EditObjectWindow::ValidateInformation (void)
{
  return 1;
}

void EditObjectWindow::StoreInformation (void)
{}

HandleObjectWindow::HandleObjectWindow(int parentid,int windowid,
                                       char* resource)
        :BaseWindow (parentid,windowid,resource)
  {}
```

continued

```
HandleObjectWindow::~HandleObjectWindow (void)
{
  delete _object;
}

void HandleObjectWindow::EventHandler (int objectid,int event)
{
  ObjectList* objectlist=(ObjectList*)GetObject(NAME_PICKLIST);

  switch (objectid)
    {
    case NAME_STRING:
      {
      // GetObject() returns a user interface data entry field
      char* text= ((UIW_STRING*)GetObject(NAME_STRING))->DataGet();
      objectlist->FocusItem(text);
      } break;

    case NAME_PICKLIST:
      {
      if (objectlist->GetObject(_object))
        {
        UIW_STRING* fullname = (UIW_STRING*)GetObject(NAME_STRING);
        fullname->DataSet(_object->GetFullName());
        }
      } break;

    case DETAIL_BUTTON:
      {
      DetailObject(_object);
      } break;
    }
}

void HandleObjectWindow::DetailObject (IdObject* object)
{}
```

FIGURE 12.13   Implementation of the HandleObjectWindow and EditObjectWindow classes.

Using these standard classes, the developer derived different specific dialog classes, which define the application-specific view onto the business model. Consider, for example, the `HandlePersonWindow` and `HandleDepartmentWindow` dialog classes, both derived from `HandleObjectWindow`. Both of these classes have similar functionality:

```
class HandleDepartmentWindow : public HandleObjectWindow
  {
  protected:
    DepartmentType* _departmenttype;

  public:
    HandleDepartmentWindow (int parentid,int windowid,
                                  char* resource);
    ~HandleDepartmentWindow (void);

    void EventHandler (int objectid,int event);
    void DataHandler (int dataid,void* data,int serverid);
    void DetailObject (IdObject* person);
  };
```

```
class HandlePersonWindow : public HandleObjectWindow
  {
  protected:
    Department* _department;
    Activity* _activity;
    Category* _category;
    PersonType* _persontype;

  public:
    HandlePersonWindow(int parentid,int windowid,char* resource);
    ~HandlePersonWindow (void);

    void EventHandler (int objectid,int event);
    void DataHandler (int dataid,void* data,int serverid);
    void DetailObject (IdObject* person);
  };
```

However, comparing the `HandlePersonWindow` and `HandleDepartmentWindow` dialog classes with the database layout shows that the way they get their data differs, as follows:

- In the Person dialog box, the data in the list box (left-hand side) is constructed by concatenating the person's last and first names. Both names are fields in the person table stored in the database.

- The Department dialog box has a similar list box that contains the department's full name. This name is the concatenation of the department's type and its short name. However, this time the type is not stored directly in the department table; rather, it is referenced using a foreign key. Thus getting the department's full name requires a join between the department table and the department type table.

12.10.2   Separating the *What* and *How*

From the viewpoints of object orientation and designing robust and reusable software, it is unacceptable that in order to achieve two identical goals, two different methodologies must be applied. Nevertheless, all two-tier, client/server approaches (as most RAD techniques and 4GLs are) work this way.

With a business model approach, the dialog class limits itself to asking *what* it wants: an object's full name. The dialog asks this information of the business model (the information base), which in its turn deals with *how* to get this information. This is illustrated in Figure 12.14.

To accomplish this goal, each `IdObject` has a member function `GetFullName()` that determines how the object will be displayed in, for example, lists and reports. For the `Person` class, this function needs only to return the concatenation of the first and last names:

```
char* Person::GetFullName (void)
  {
  char* name = new char[_LASTNAMELENGTH+_FIRSTNAMELENGTH+2];
  strcpy (name,_lastname);
  strcat (name," ");
  strcat (name,_firstname);
  return (name);
  }
```

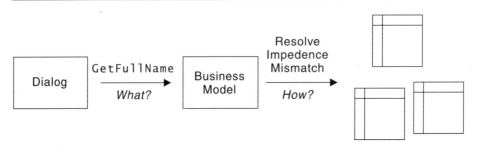

FIGURE 12.14   Separation of concerns. The dialog class is concerned only about *what* it wants. The business model contains the intelligence about *how* to get it.

For the `Department` class, the concatenation of the department type and department name will be returned:

```
char* Department::GetFullName (void)
  {
  char* name = new char[_TYPENAMELENGTH+_DEPARTMENTNAMELENGTH+2];
  strcpy (name,_type->GetName());
  strcat (name," ");
  strcat (name,_name);
  return (name);
  }
```

Note that although it is this function that joins both database tables, this join cannot be seen. The type object, in collaboration with its IM resolver, takes care of its own persistence aspects. This example proves once more that, to class `Department`, there is no difference in handling real embedded objects and handling objects that are actually retrieved through a join with another table.

12.10.3 Code Extracts

By means of illustration, the implementation of class `HandleDepartmentWindow` is presented in Figure 12.15.

```
HandleDepartmentWindow::HandleDepartmentWindow (int parentid, int
                                              windowid,char* resource)
        :HandleObjectWindow (parentid,windowid,resource)
  {
    _object=new Department();
    _departmenttype=new DepartmentType();
    ((ObjectList*)GetObject(NAME_PICKLIST))->AddObjects(_object);
    ((ObjectBox*)GetObject(TYPE_PICKBOX))->AddObjects(_departmenttype);
  }


HandleDepartmentWindow::~HandleDepartmentWindow (void)
  {
    delete _departmenttype;
  }
```

continued

```
void HandleDepartmentWindow::EventHandler (int objectid,int event)
{
  HandleObjectWindow::EventHandler (objectid,event);switch (objectid)
    {
    case NAME_PICKLIST:
      {
      DepartmentStructureList* list = GetObject(STRUCTURE_PICKLIST);
      list->Fill(*(Department*)_object);
      } break;

    case STRUCTURE_PICKLIST:
      {
      Department department;
      DepartmentStructureList *list = GetObject(STRUCTURE_PICKLIST);
      list->GetObject(department);
      list->Fill(department);
      ObjectList *objlist = (ObjectList*)GetObject(NAME_PICKLIST);
      objlist->AddObjects(_object,(IdObject*)&department);
      } break;
    }
}

void HandleDepartmentWindow::DataHandler (int dataid,void* data,
                                          int serverid)
{
  switch (dataid)
    {
    case DEPARTMENTTYPE_DATA:
      {
      ObjectBox *objbox = (ObjectBox*)GetObject(TYPE_PICKBOX);
      objbox->AddObjects(_departmenttype,(DepartmentType*)data);
      } break;
    }
}

void HandleDepartmentWindow::DetailObject (IdObject* department)
{
  // create and open new window
  DetailDepartmentWindow *window = new DetailDepartmentWindow();
  window->Open();

  // send department data to new window
  DeliverData (DETAILDEPARTMENT_WINDOW, (void*)department,
               DEPARTMENT_DATA);
}
```

FIGURE 12.15   Implementation of class HandleDepartmentWindow.

It might be a little difficult to fully comprehend exactly how the code in Figure 12.15 works without more information on the user interface framework, but the general idea of the approach should not be too difficult to follow. Only a relatively small amount of fairly simple code was required to implement the user interface. Primarily, it is concerned only with *what* has to be presented to the user and not with *how* this information must be obtained.

Notice further that in this whole process, no mention has been made that a database is being worked with. All of the user interface's communication is done with the business model. This section concludes with some examples of classes derived from EditObject-Window:

Class `EditActivityWindow`

```
class EditActivityWindow : public EditObjectWindow
  {
  protected:
    Activity _parent;
    ActivityDependency _dependency;

    void EventHandler (int objectid,int event);
    void DataHandler (int dataid,void* data,int serverid);
                        int ValidateInformation (void);

  public:
    EditActivityWindow(int parentid,int win_id,char* resource);
  };
```

Class `EditDepartmentWindow`

```
class EditDepartmentWindow : public EditObjectWindow
  {
  protected:
    DepartmentType _type;
    Department _parent;
    DepartmentDependency _dependency;

    void EventHandler (int objectid,int event);
    void DataHandler (int dataid,void* data,int serverid);
                        int ValidateInformation (void);

  public:
    EditDepartmentWindow(int parentid,int win_id,char* resource);
  };
```

Class `EditPersonWindow`

```
class EditPersonWindow : public EditObjectWindow
  {
  protected:
    Category _category;
    Person _parent;
    PersonDependency _dependency;

    void EventHandler (int objectid,int event);
    void DataHandler (int dataid,void* data,int serverid);
                    int ValidateInformation (void);

  public:
    EditPersonWindow (int parentid,int windowid,char* resource);
  };
```

The following example shows the implementation of class `EditPersonWindow`. Fully understanding this code might be difficult. However, in the interest of realism it was purposely not simplified. Note that nowhere in this code is the database or database layout visible; a complete separation between user interface, business model, and database has been achieved.

A drawback of the code in this example is that it doesn't use the `DataNavigator` class described in Chapter 11. If that class had been used, the amount of code necessary to implement the user interface would have been significantly less.

```
EditPersonWindow::EditPersonWindow (int parentid,int windowid,
                                    char* resource)
    :EditObjectWindow (parentid,windowid,resource)
  {
  _object=new Person();
  dataid=PERSON_DATA;
  }


void EditPersonWindow::EventHandler (int objectid,int event)
  {
  EditObjectWindow::EventHandler (objectid,event);
  switch (objectid)
      {
      case SEARCHPERSON_BUTTON:
```

```
                     {
                     SearchPersonWindow* window = new SearchPersonWindow(GetId());
                     window->Open();
                     break;
                     }
                  case ADDFUNCTION_BUTTON:
                     {
                     NewFunctionWindow* window=new NewFunctionWindow(GetId());
                     window->Open();
                     DeliverData (NEWFUNCTION_WINDOW, (void*)_object,
                                   PERSON_DATA);
                     break;
                     }
                  case ADDACTIVITY_BUTTON:
                     {
                     SearchActivityWindow* window = new SearchActivityWindow
                                                                 (GetId());
                     window->Open();
                     break;
                     }
                  }
            }

   void EditPersonWindow::DataHandler (int dataid,void* data,int serverid)
      {
      switch (dataid)
        {
        case PERSON_DATA:
           {
           if (serverid==SEARCHPERSON_WINDOW)
              {
              ObjectBox *tmp = (ObjectBox*)GetObject(PERSON_PICKBOX);
              tmp->AddObjects(&_parent,(Person*)data);
              }
           break;
           }
        case ACTIVITY_DATA:
           {
           Activity* activity=(Activity*)data;
           PickList* list=(PickList*)GetObject(ACTIVITY_PICKLIST);
```

```
        PickItem *item=list->GetItem(activity->GetId());
        if (item==NULL)
          {
          ActivityAssignment assignment;
          assignment.SetPerson(*(Person*)_object);
          assignment.SetActivity (*activity);
          assignment.append();
          list->AddItem(activity->GetId(),activity->GetName());
          list->Refresh();
          }
        break;
        }
    }
  }


int EditPersonWindow::ValidateInformation (void)
  {
  int valid,hasparent;

  ObjectBox* categorybox=(ObjectBox*)GetObject(CATEGORY_PICKBOX);
  ObjectBox* personbox=(ObjectBox*)GetObject(PERSON_PICKBOX);

  char lastname[_LASTNAMELENGTH+1],firstname[_FIRSTNAMELENGTH+1];
  strcpy (lastname,
       ((UIW_STRING*)GetObject(LASTNAME_STRING))->//DataGet());
  strcpy (firstname,
       ((UIW_STRING*)GetObject(FIRSTNAME_STRING))->//DataGet());

  valid=(strcmp(TrimString(lastname),"")!=0) &&
       (strcmp(TrimString(firstname),"")!=0) &&
       (categorybox->GetObject(&_category));

  if (hasparent = FlagSet(GetObject(PERSON_BUTTON)->woStatus,
                      WOS_SELECTED))
    valid=valid && (personbox->GetObject(&_parent));
  else_parent.Initialise();

  if (valid)
    {
    // if entry is valid, put the attributes in the person object
```

```
        ((Person*)_object)->SetLastname(lastname);
        ((Person*)_object)->SetFirstname(firstname);
        ((Person*)_object)->SetCategory(_category);
        ((Person*)_object)->GetNote().SetText("");


        // set the parent-child dependency. Notice the simplicity
        // of this operation. Notice furthermore the absence of any
        // sign of the impedance mismatch between B.M. and database


        _dependency.SetParent(_parent);
        }
    return (valid);
    }
```

12.11 Summary

The project discussed in this chapter produced some interesting conclusions. The independent development of the business model and database layout proved that the impedance mismatch between the two does not have to be an insurmountable problem. The designers succeeded in developing a program in which the three subparts (UI, business model, and database) were totally separated and independent of one another.

In comparison to the data-driven RAD approaches, the object-oriented approach seemed to be slower in the early project phases. This was because in these phases, much emphasis was put on developing a robust and stable business model. The RAD approach, on the other hand, seemed to produce results faster, since it could skip this stage. Near the end of the project, however, the object-oriented approach caught up with the RAD implementation, and both finished at about the same time.

When a few changes were introduced in the database model (the note column in the person table, for example), the object-oriented designers implemented these changes in hardly any time, while the RAD people started to panic.

Also interesting to note is that this application was rather simple. Since it did not contain much business logic, it was an ideal example of an application in the domain of classical 4GL tools. This observation suggests that if the designers had implemented a more sophisticated application, the object-oriented approach would have been significantly faster. Experience with large-scale, object-oriented database applications supports this postulate.

The designers created three independent application layers relatively quickly and easily. The user interface layer communicated with the business model and was thus independent of the database layout. The business model communicated with the database using the Scoop architecture. This approach resulted in an easily maintainable application, a high degree of reusability, and good platform independence, as far as both the database and the user interface were concerned.

This case study showed that software design based on an object-oriented philosophy and using an object-oriented language such as C++ does not have to be cumbersome and time-consuming. Because the designers started with a good and stable business model and used platform-independent frameworks, the resulting application turned out to be several times more robust, maintainable, and viable than could be achieved using most of the current 4GLs.

Chapter 13

Toward Open Applications

Long gone are the days when an application just had to work correctly and everybody was happy. Today, an application still has to work correctly, but it also has to be *open*. That is, other applications must be able to exchange information with the application in an easy and flexible way. This requirement contrasts with the way software was viewed in the old days. Indeed, in traditional applications, the whole application and all access to it were controlled by the vendor.

Today, the information stored in the database must be accessible for several categories of users. A company's information technology (IT) department plays a central role in managing this information. One of its tasks is to prevent each category of user from developing its own database. On the contrary, an IT solution should span the entire business structure. Applications should no longer work in isolation. Rather, the most diverse applications, covering all facets of the company, should be able to communicate with one another and operate on the same databases, thereby forming one company-wide IT network.

However, the purposes for which this data will be used may differ significantly, depending on the user. Some people will want just a report of certain results, others will want to further process the data using a spreadsheet, and still others will want to use the data in connection with some other application and some local database.

Today, because of the variety of purposes that data is used for, many categories of users try to maintain their own version of the database. They do so because either the data is not accessible in the right format or they do not know how to access the data in its current format (because of the table layout, for example). However, keeping all of the different versions of the database consistent with one another is virtually impossible and soon leads to hopelessly outdated databases.

Thus, aside from the end user's ability to communicate with the application, there are also necessary provisions that allow for retrieving information from these applications. Users will want to import this data into their office tools (such as spreadsheet and word-processing programs) or use it in cooperation with other applications.

13.1 Third-Party Access to Your Application's Data

One way users can access the data in the form of reports is, of course, via the prepro-grammed reports in your application. However, often they might need certain reports other than the preprogrammed ones.[1] Indeed, the reports a user might want are not always known at the time the application specifications are set forth, so preprogramming them is not possible.

There are two ways to provide for this contingency: either include a report generator in your application (which is often a complete task in itself) or choose not to reinvent the wheel a hundred times and instead use an off-the-shelf report generator. The latter approach has the advantage of allowing you to concentrate on the main aspects of your application.

A primary requirement of report-generating tools is that they be able to communicate with your products. This, as already said, is not always easy. However, in the early 1990s, significant progress was made in the development of standardized ways to access information. So it will be important to offer access to your data in one of the standard available protocols.

A point already made is that the existing database community is mainly relational—and becoming more so every day. Just look at concepts such as ODBC and SQL or at the increasing success of 4GL products. Thus object-oriented approaches must be able to interoperate with these relational products.

13.2 Standard Report Generators and Query Tools

A wide range of standard report generators and query tools is available. In addition, many other applications, such as spreadsheets and word processors, include support for database querying. An important standard in this regard is Microsoft ODBC.

13.2.1 Directly Accessing the Database

If you have designed your application on top of a relational database for which an ODBC driver is available, you can directly incorporate your data in applications that support ODBC. You can, for example, choose from among a wide range of off-the-shelf report generators to design reports. Thanks to the ODBC interface, your report generator can directly access the data stored in the database. Figure 13.1 illustrates this idea.

This approach has several advantages. First, because all reporting facilities are gone from the actual application, the work of the programming team is significantly reduced. Second, it allows you to design reports that were not taken into account in the require-ments analysis of the application. Otherwise, if the reporting was hard-coded in the appli-cation, a recompilation of the application would be required. Also, each new type of report would require the intervention of the IT department, thereby resulting in an extra load for that department and a loss of time for the user who needs the report.

---

1. It might even be debated whether it is a good idea to preprogram reports at all.

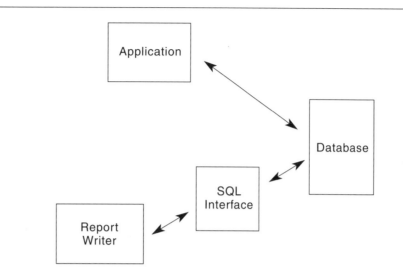

FIGURE 13.1   Using an SQL interface (such as ODBC), you can enable off-the-shelf report generators and query tools to interface directly with the database.

However, this approach also has a number of disadvantages. First, the user must have knowledge of the database layout. As already said, this layout can change significantly during the lifetime of a program. Such a change to the database layout not only means that all reports and queries that depend on this layout will have to be modified. It also implies that all users of the database system will have to be notified of the change to the database layout. Accommodating these schema changes can be an enormous task.

Second, the query can operate only on those fields that are actually stored in the database. Consider a stock-keeping program. Typically one field represents the number of items still in stock (`instock`), and another represents the minimum number of items to have in stock at all times (`min_stock`). To find out how many items to order, you must submit the following query to the SQL engine:

```
select description, supplier, min_stock - instock from stock
    where instock < min_stock
```

Although this approach works, it can be made much more elegant by adding access to a field, `to_order`, which gives this information. You then could issue this query:

```
select description, supplier, to_order from stock where to_order > 0
```

But as there is no `to_order` field, it is up to the query program (and thus to the end user) to specify this calculation. Even if for such a straightforward task this presents no real problem, there are still several objections to this method, as follows:

- Users have to know which fields are available and which must be calculated. That is, they have to know (and understand) the database layout.
- If this database layout changes, users will have to rebuild all of their predefined queries.
- While the previous calculation is not really a problem, this might be a whole different matter if, for example, you want to predict how many items you will have to order over the next two months.

The real problem with this approach, however, is that you have broken the rule of information hiding. This is discussed in the next subsection.

13.2.2 Data Becomes Information

The main disadvantage to the approach sketched in the previous subsection is that by using it, you break the rule of information hiding: The query program has to know the layout of the database. All of the intelligence is put with the users, and the database is considered as nothing more than a collection of data. This approach contrasts sharply with that of object orientation. In an object-oriented approach, the users need to know nothing about the data itself, just about the information it represents. They have no direct access to the *data* and obtain and manipulate their *information* through a well-defined interface. Thus the layout of the database—the way all data is organized in tables—can be said to belong to the private part of your information system.

For example, suppose that in the stock-keeping example a user wants to know how many items must be ordered. Instead of directly looking in the database, the user must ask for this information through a predefined channel. How this information is obtained internally is of no concern to the user. Perhaps it is directly available (such as `min_stock`), perhaps it can be calculated easily (such as `to_order`), or perhaps the system has to make a call to another database on the other side of the planet. All of these implementation details stay hidden from the user. Hence, the intelligence no longer resides with the users but with the data itself. *Data* has thus become *information*. So, for the stock object, you would have an interface `to_order` that takes care of all necessary calculations and gives the number of items to order. This time, you can issue the following SQL statement:

```
select description, supplier, to_order from stock where to_order > 0
```

However, this time `description`, `supplier`, and `to_order` should no longer be considered data members of the database; rather, they should be seen as *methods*.

By looking at data this way, you are no longer working with *data* but are dealing with *information*. Your database has gained intelligence and as a result has evolved into an "informationbase."

13.2.3 Views and Stored Procedures

Using views and stored procedures, you can take big steps toward resolving the problems sketched in the previous sections. For example, you could define a view that has a field, to_order. Thus users would no longer have to worry about doing the necessary calculations. Furthermore, by creating views, you can hide the necessary joins between the databases, to a certain degree.

Views and stored procedures are a first step in the right direction, but they do have drawbacks. Not only do they limit the portability of an application. They also work directly on the database. For complex tasks, this approach is not always powerful enough. Furthermore, as applications are ever increasing in complexity, the data needed to construct a certain piece of information may not be in a single database and may need to be gathered from several other places, such as other databases or even other applications.

Thus all calculations should be part of the business model. If the implementer of the business model chooses to implement certain functionality using a stored procedure, this is fine—provided this decision stays confined within the business model and has no influence on its clients. The stored procedure should be seen as an implementation aspect of the business model and thus as belonging to its private part.

13.3   Informationbases

Querying and reporting should rely not on the tables and columns of the database but on the services provided by the objects of the business model. This concept is illustrated in Figure 13.2. The architecture sketched in this figure has the same advantages as the approach discussed in the previous section, with an additional advantage: It is independent of the database system, database technology, and database layout. All reports and queries now depend only on the business model. The architecture is no longer centered around the request for data, but around the request for *information*. Thus the business model is a server for *information*, while the database is a server for *data*. These ideas fit well in the MVC architecture. Indeed, each report can be seen as just another view on the business model.

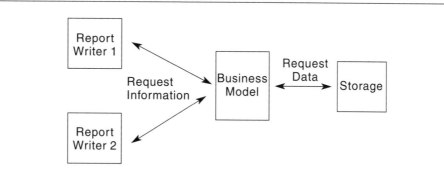

FIGURE 13.2   Information bases. By querying the business model instead of the database, you can shield the database layout from the report generators and query tools. Those tools have to be concerned only with *what* they want, not about *how* to get it.

13.4   Interoperability with Other Applications

Not only report writers or query tools may want to access the information stored in your database. Other applications, too, might want to actively consult and manipulate that information. An example of such a situation is Medidoc, a program used in the health care industry.

13.4.1   Example

The Medidoc program was developed mainly for medical doctors to automate their patient records. It keeps track of a patient's file and provides several levels of control. For example, a doctor prescribing a certain medication can check whether the patient is allergic to that medication, whether the medication might interact with other drugs the patient is taking, what the maximum dosage is, and whether that maximum is exceeded.

For simplicity's sake, consider Medidoc as providing two functions: It automates the management of the patient's file, and it has a knowledge base that actively helps the doctor treat the patient. The application is PC-based and works on top of a Btrieve file system.

There are several other products that offer computerized medical record management, but Medidoc's knowledge base is rather unique. Other developers of medical software have chosen to license this database and to incorporate it in their products. There also are applications that want to cooperate with Medidoc. In this case, Medidoc takes care of the patient's medical record and everything associated with it, while the other application handles all of the financial processing that is associated with that patient. Figure 13.3 illustrates this.

Data-Based Approach
For another application to work with Medidoc, it needs access to the database layout of the knowledge base. This approach leads to the situation sketched in Figure 13.4. However, it has several disadvantages, as follows (see also [Carroll95]):

- The other application must know the database layout. Also, it relies on it. Hence, every change to this layout affects that other application.

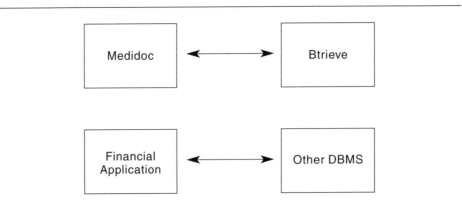

FIGURE 13.3   Integrating two applications.

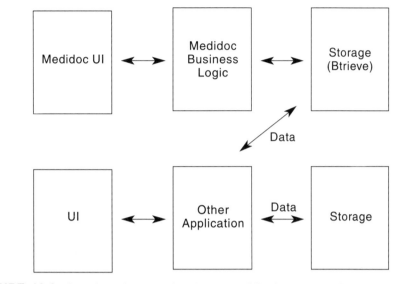

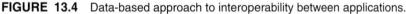

FIGURE 13.4 Data-based approach to interoperability between applications.

- Because the other application works directly on the database, it cannot take advantage of the inference engine that is built into Medidoc. It is this engine that gives the data in the database its real value. To take advantage of this information, the other application must implement this engine itself.
- The other application must work with two different database systems—its own and Medidoc's.

Information-Based Approach

To overcome the disadvantages of the data-based approach, the two applications are allowed to interoperate on the application level, rather than on the database level. This is depicted in Figure 13.5. With this approach, each application can do what it does best: Medidoc handles the knowledge base and the patient's file, while the other application deals with all financial aspects of the patient's visit.

To the users, however, a single interface has to be presented. The company selling the financial-oriented application does not want to let its customers come into direct contact with Medidoc. Rather, they want Medidoc to work in the background so that it appears, to the user, that the other application does all of the work. To achieve this goal, it was decided to let the application communicate with Medidoc using an IPC mechanism[2] (see Figure 13.6).

---

2. Because OLE did not exist at the time of the project, dynamic data exchange (DDE) was used for the IPC implementation. Today, using OLE would be a better choice.

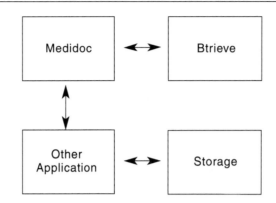

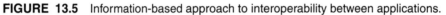

FIGURE 13.5   Information-based approach to interoperability between applications.

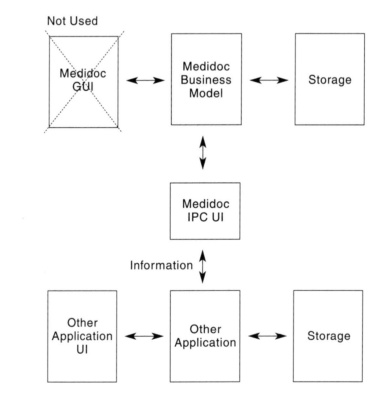

FIGURE 13.6   Adding an IPC user interface to the business model.

In this respect, the three-tier, client/server architecture (UI, business model, and storage) comes in very helpful. It makes it possible to construct another view (the IPC user interface) for Medidoc's business model that allows other applications to request the necessary services.

13.5 Implementing an Informationbase

This section looks at some possible implementations of an informationbase. The key point is that a third-party application must gain access to the business model instead of having to work on the database directly.

On Windows platforms, ODBC has become a widely accepted standard for database access. It allows a wide variety of applications to access the most diverse databases in a uniform way. So a possible way to let applications access the informationbase is to design an ODBC interface to the business model.

ODBC access to a data source requires that a driver in the form of a DLL be implemented. This driver translates the ODBC calls to calls that are understood by the back end (usually the DBMS). In this example, this back end is not a DBMS, but rather the business model. So the trick is to implement this ODBC driver so that it makes the business model act as a relational database. You can do this by making the following analogy: Tables correspond with sets, rows correspond with objects, and columns correspond with methods (thus not attributes). Instead of querying for database columns, the SQL statement actually invokes methods on the business objects. This is shown in Table 13.1.

Consider, for example, the following SQL statement:

```
select description, supplier, to_order from stock where to_order > 0
```

This statement queries the `StockSet` for those `Stock` objects for which the result returned by the method `to_order` returns a positive value. For these objects, the results of the methods `description`, `supplier`, and `to_order` will be returned (in the form of a result table).

The implementation of the ODBC driver is best divided into two parts. The first part is the actual ODBC driver to be installed on the client platform. This driver, which is implemented as a DLL, is called by the third-party application (for example, a report generator). The driver uses an IPC mechanism to pass the SQL statements on to the ODBC server that

TABLE 13.1. Analogy between relational database and business model.

RDBMS	Business Model
Table	Set
Row	Object
Column	Method (!)

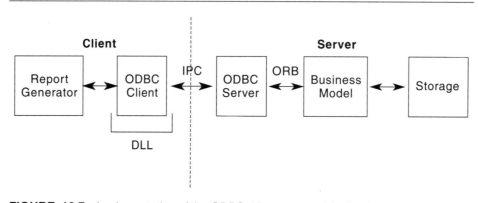

Client   **Server**

FIGURE 13.7 Implementation of the ODBC driver on top of the business model.

runs on the application server machine. The ODBC server is responsible for parsing the SQL statements and translating these into calls to the business model. The business model thus acts as a virtual database. The communication between the ODBC server and the business model is best implemented with object brokering (CORBA or COM). This architecture does not require the database or the business model to be local. Figure 13.7 shows a possible configuration.

The ODBC driver acts as another client/server user interface to the business model. This model is global for your business and plays the role that the database used to play in classical architectures. Applications now can directly communicate with that business model.

You may ask, Why not access the application through OLE? This is a viable approach if the third-party application (in this case, the report generator) supports this technique. However, in practice, ODBC support for data access is more available than OLE support and is much easier to use in conjunction with query tools.

13.6 Architecture for Next-Generation Software

13.6.1 The Object Web

A popular way to distribute information is via pages on the World Wide Web. For example, a university professor might want to use the Web to get a list of all students who enrolled in a particular course. Similarly, a student might use the Web to enroll in a certain course.

Many Web pages communicate with the database through CGI scripts (implemented in Perl, for example). However, most of these scripts contain direct SQL calls to the database, so they suffer from the same drawbacks described in Chapter 3. Hence, you end up in the same situation as with the two-tier solutions described in that chapter.

Here, too, the better approach is to use the business model utilizing, for example, Java, CORBA, and ActiveX. A good discussion of these can be found in [Orfali97]. More sophisticated Web pages can be built using JavaScript or VBScript, with calls to appropriate business objects.

13.6.2 RAD and 4GLs in a New Perspective

Although C++ and Java allow for very robust software design, they do have a serious drawback: They are complicated and require highly skilled developers who are both scarce and expensive. Further, it is often difficult to retrain an existing staff of, for example, COBOL programmers to use object-oriented programming languages. Many RAD environments, on the other hand, excel in their ease of learning. Even untrained computer users can start using tools such as Visual Basic in a matter of days.

Using component technology, you now can combine the best of two worlds: Develop your business model in a language such as Java or C++, and build your user interface in, for example, Visual Basic or even a Web browser (by using JavaScript or VBScript). To glue together the user interface and the business model, you have two options. One is to use an ORB (COM might be the best choice when working with Visual Basic). Another is to use an ODBC interface on the business model. The second approach is less performant than the ORB-based technique, but it has the advantage that you can use the built-in, two-tiered, table-screen mapping facilities that most RAD tools have. In contrast to the RAD situation described in Chapter 3, you will get a robust solution, since the second tier will be the business model instead of the database (see Figure 13.8).

It is relatively simple to build applications this way, since the programmer can fully concentrate on the *what* part, while letting the business model take care of the *how* part.

The concept of the informationbase throws a whole new perspective on the use of RAD tools. Such tools are well suited for use with informationbases. In this case, it is not the data that is central to the RAD application, but the information. And this is fine because the information layout (which describes the objects and their methods) does not change: It is the public part of the informationbase.

Thus, here again, it is not *whether* you should use object-oriented programming languages or 4GLs, but *how* you can best integrate them.

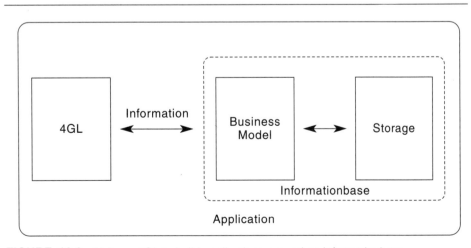

FIGURE 13.8 Using a 4GL to build applications around an informationbase.

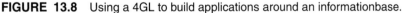

13.6.3   Distributed Business Objects

The ideas of the previous sections lead eventually to the general architecture of an application, shown in Figure 13.9. The business model, which is a collection of business objects and business processes, is accessible through an ORB. The business objects themselves, for example CORBA objects, achieve their persistence through a persistence mechanism that abstracts the persistence technology.

On top of the business model you can design several types of user interfaces, including GUIs, OLE interfaces, and ODBC interfaces. A single implementation of the business model is thus shared by many types of applications (see Figure 13.10), including these:

- Dedicated client/server applications
- Reporting tools
- Third-party applications
- Office tools (e.g., Word, Excel, and Access)
- Web pages

This component architecture combines the best of several worlds. With a central business model, you achieve a significant amount of reuse and prevent your business logic from getting duplicated in multiple applications. Also, it gives the IT department a new role: managing information by implementing the business objects and business processes. The development of the applications that need to work on this business model will shift more and more to end users. These users will use tools such as Web browsers and Microsoft Office (with Visual Basic macros) to access the information in the business model. Only the more complicated applications will require the intervention of the IT department.

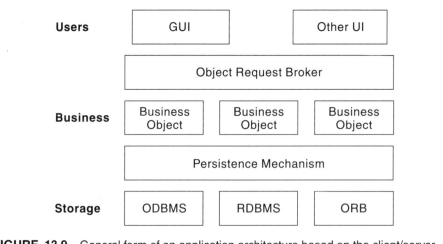

FIGURE 13.9   General form of an application architecture based on the client/server model.

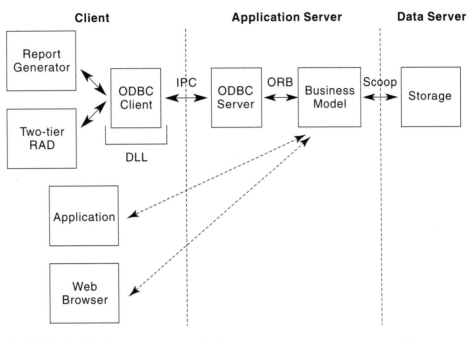

FIGURE 13.10 Many types of applications work on a single business model.

13.7 Summary

This chapter presented some ideas on how to make applications more open. It introduced the concept of the informationbase as an opposition to the database and explained how an informationbase helps to abstract the database layout and technology to the query program. It also presented some sample architectures that implement this informationbase approach. However, it is important to stress that research is still necessary to implement these ideas efficiently.

Chapter 14

Conclusion

This book looked at the main issues involved in making objects persistent. It showed that in contrast to much contemporary opinion, the database does not play the all-important role in software design. It also showed that it is neither necessary nor justified to let the database dictate the entire software development approach.

There are three major parts to the design of client/server software. Two are the user interface and the database. These are, in fact, views on the information contained in the business model. The business model is the central and most important part of the design. It implements the relevant business objects and business processes and must be designed to be independent of all user interface and database considerations.

By separating the user interface, the business model, and the database from one another, you can realize significant gains in the robustness and extensibility of the software. Furthermore, a major part of the software becomes reusable, and the software development time decreases significantly.

The book illustrated the principles involved in developing reusable client/server software using the Scoop architecture. This architecture allows you to abstract the database concept and thus work with persistent objects in the same way as with transient ones. The fact that an object is persistent is the responsibility of that object only and thus becomes largely invisible to programmers.

By hiding the database aspects almost completely, application developers can finally concentrate on the more fundamental aspect of their programs: developing a robust and stable business model. The book showed how reusable software components (business objects) can be created, regardless of whether they are connected to a database. Scalability allows you to use the same component library over a wide range of applications and platforms.

An entirely new look at the concept of databases is required. It should no longer be data that is central to your applications, but rather information. Thus it becomes possible to abstract the data storage from the applications that use it. This abstraction results in a significant improvement in development time and allows you to create applications that are more open. Hence, your software is no longer just another application; it is a provider of information. And, if necessary, this provider can be accessed in the same way as any ordinary database. In other words, your application has become an intelligent view on data, accessible as any other database. Furthermore, by hiding the database technology, you also protect the often phenomenal investments in traditional systems. The actual database itself has thus become just some low-level mechanism used to physically store the data. It has become a type of commodity product.

Appendix

DBtools-Based Implementation of Scoop

This appendix presents some source code of a (simplified) Scoop implementation based on the DBtools.h++ framework [RogueWave96].

A.1 PSet

```
class PSet {
  friend class DataSet;
protected:
  Container<DataSet*> setlist;
  RWDBReader reader;
  RWDBSelector selector;
  RWDBCriterion where_clause;
  virtual RWBoolean add_DataSet(DataSet* ds);
public:
  static RWDBDatabase db;
  PSet();
  ~PSet();
  virtual int buildSelect(RWDBSelector& select);
  virtual int select(); // cursor points to first object;
  virtual int next();
  virtual int append();
  virtual int write();
  virtual int read(); // resolve impedance mismatch
```

```
        virtual int read(RWDBReader& aReader);
        virtual int erase();
        virtual int seek(RWDBCriterion& crit);
        virtual void add_filter(RWDBCriterion& crit);
        virtual void clear_filter();
    };
```

A.2 DataSet

```
    class DataSet {
      friend class PSet;
    protected:
      RWDBTable iTable;
      Container<IM_Resolver*> imrList;
      PSet *iPset;
    public:
      DataSet(PersistentSet *pset, const char *nme);
      ~DataSet();
      RWDBTable& Table() { return iTable; }
      int add_field(IM_Resolver *imr);
      const RWCString& name() const { return iTable.name();}
      virtual int append();
      virtual int update(RWDBCriterion& clause);
      virtual int erase(RWDBCriterion& clause);
      read(RWDBReader& reader);
      select(RWDBSelector& selector);
      PSet* pset();
      long OID();
    };
```

A.3 IM_Resolver

```
    class IM_Resolver {
    protected:
      RWDBColumn *column;
      char readwritemode;
      DataSet* iDs;
      PersistentSet* pset();
```

```
public:
  IM_Resolver(DataSet *base, const char *nme, FIELD_TYPE fldtype,
              int wdth, int dec=0, char mode=FLD_READWRITE);
~IM_Resolver();
  virtual void to_selector(RWDBSelector& selector)
    {
    if (column!=NULL)
      {
      selector << *column;
      }
    }
  virtual void to_inserter(RWDBInserter& inserter)=0;
  virtual void to_updater(RWDBUpdater& updater)=0;
  virtual read(RWDBReader& reader)=0;
};
```

A.4   Resolving Impedance Mismatch

```
// Resolve IM mismatch between classes and tables

PSet::read()
{
  for (setlist.go_top(); setlist.current(); setlist.next())
    {
    setlist.current()->read(reader);
    }
  return TRUE;
}


// Resolve IM mismatch between attributes and columns

DataSet::read(RWDBReader& reader)
{
  for (imrList.go_top(); imrList.current(); imrList.next())
    {
    imrList.current()->read(reader);
    }
  return TRUE;
}
```

A.5   Building the Select Statement

```
// Build and execute select statement

PSet::select()
{
  selector = db.selector();
  // let DataSets build select statement
  for (setlist.go_top(); setlist.current(); setlist.next())
    {
    setlist.current()->select(selector);
    }
  selector.where(where_clause);
  // execute select statement
  reader = selector.reader();
  // clear where_clause
  clear_filter();
  return next();   // read first object
}


// Attach attributes to select statement

DataSet::select(RWDBSelector& selector)
{
  for (imrList.go_top(); imrList.current(); imrList.next())
    {
    imrList.current()->to_selector(selector);
    }
  return TRUE;
}
```

References

[Andleigh92] Prabhat K. Andleigh and Michael R. Gretzinger, *Distributed Object-Oriented Data-Systems Design*. Englewood Cliffs, N. J.: Prentice Hall, 1992.

[Bartels93] Dirk Bartels, "ODBMS: Key Techniques for Workgroup Computing," in *Proceedings Object Expo Europe 1993*. New York: SIGS Publications.

[Booch94] Grady Booch, *Object-Oriented Analysis and Design*, Second Edition. Menlo Park, Calif.: Benjamin/Cummings, 1994.

[Brooks87] Frederick P. Brooks, "No Silver-Bullet: Essence and Accidents of Software Engineering." *IEEE Computer*, April 1987, pp. 10–19.

[Carolan89] J. Carolan, "Constructing Bullet-Proof Classes," in *Proceedings C++ at Work '89*. New York: SIGS Publications, 1989.

[Carroll95] M. Carroll and M. Ellis, *Designing and Coding Reusable C++*. Reading, Mass.: Addison Wesley, 1995.

[Carron95] Kris Carron, *Object-Oriented Design and Implementation of a Telephone Directory in C++* (in Dutch). Department of Information Technology, University of Ghent, Belgium, June 1995.

[Cattell94] R. G. G. Cattell, *Object Data Management: Object-Oriented and Extended Relational Database Systems*. Reading, Mass.: Addison Wesley, 1994.

[Cleal96] Dave Cleal, "Optimizing Relational Database Access," in *Object Expert*. New York: SIGS Publications, March–April 1996.

[Cox86] Brad J. Cox and Andrew Novobilski, *Object-Oriented-Programming: An Evolutionary Approach*. Reading, Mass.: Addison Wesley, 1986.

[Date95] C. J. Date, *An Introduction to Database Systems,* Sixth Edition. Reading, Mass.: Addison Wesley, 1995.

[Dewhurst96] Stephan C. Dewhurst, "Decoupling and Leveraging C++ Source Code," in *Proceedings C++ World '96*. New York: SIGS Publications, 1996.

[D'Souza94] Desmond D'Souza, "Working with OMT, Part 2," *Journal of Object-oriented Programming*. New York: SIGS Publications, February 1994.

[Ellis93] M. Ellis and M. Carroll, "Inheritance-Based Versus Template-Based Containers," *C++ Report*, 5(3), March–April 1993, pp.17–20. New York: SIGS Publications.

[Gamma94] E. Gamma et al., *Design Patterns: Elements of Reusable Object-Oriented Software*. Reading, Mass.: Addison Wesley, 1994.

[Gorlen90] Keith E. Gorlen, Sanford M. Orlow, and Perry S. Plexico, *Data Abstraction and Object-Oriented Programming in C++*. New York: John Wiley & Sons, 1990.

[Heinckiens92] Peter Heinckiens, *Design of an Object-Oriented Database Interface* (in Dutch). University of Ghent, Belgium, May 1992.

[Heinckiens93] Peter Heinckiens, Herman Tromp, and Ghislain Hoffman, "A Scalable Object-Oriented Database Interface," in *Proceedings C++ World 1993*. New York: SIGS Publications, 1993.

[Heinckiens95] Peter Heinckiens and Ghislain Hoffman, "Object Persistence: The Application Programmer Perspective," in *Objects and Relational Databases*, J-Y Chung, Y-J Lin, and D. T. Chang (Eds.), Addendum to the *Proceedings OOPSLA '95. OOPS Messenger,* 6(4), pp. 164–169. New York: ACM Press, 1995.

[Heinckiens95a] Peter Heinckiens, Herman Tromp, and Ghislain Hoffman, "A Model-View-Controller Approach to Object Persistence," in R. Ege, M. Singh, & B. Meyer (Eds.), *TOOLS 17*, pp. 307-320. Englewood Cliffs, N. J.: Prentice Hall, 1995.

[Hoffman95] Ghislain Hoffman, "Foundations for an Efficient IT Infrastructure," Unisys Symposium, Saint Paul de Vence (France), 1995.

[Jordan97] David Jordan, *C++ Object Databases*. Reading, Mass.: Addison Wesley, 1997.

[Keene93] Christopher Keene, "Using Objects with Relational Databases." *Proceedings of C++ World*, SIGS Conferences, Dallas, TX, 1993.

[Khoshafian93] Setrag Khoshafian, *Object-Oriented Databases*. New York: John Wiley & Sons, 1993.

[Kristen93] Gerald Kristen, *KISS-Methode voor object-orientatie: van informatiearchitectuur naar informatiesysteem*. Schoonhoven, Netherlands: Academic Service, 1993.

[Kroha93] Petr Kroha, *Objects and Databases*, McGraw-Hill International Series in Software Engineering. New York: McGraw-Hill, 1993.

[Lakos96] John Lakos, *Large-Scale C++ Software Design*. Reading, Mass.: Addison Wesley, 1996.

[Loomis95] Mary E. S. Loomis, *Object Databases, The Essentials*. Reading, Mass.: Addison Wesley, 1995.

[ODMG93] R. G. G. Cattell, *The Object Database Standard: ODMG-93,* Release 1.1. San Francisco: Morgan Kaufmann Publishers, 1993.

[ODMG97] R. G. G. Cattell and D. Barry, *The Object Database Standard: ODMG 2.0*. San Francisco: Morgan Kaufmann Publishers, 1997.

[Odell95] James Martin and James J. Odell, *Object-Oriented Methods: A Foundation*. New York: Prentice Hall, 1995.

[Orfali97] Robert Orfali and Dan Harkey, *Client/Server Programming with JAVA and CORBA,* New York: John Wiley & Sons, 1997.

[Otte96] R. Otte, P. Patrick and M. Roy, *Understanding CORBA*. Englewood Cliffs, N. J.: Prentice Hall, 1996.

[RogueWave96] *DBTools.h++*, Rogue Wave, 1996.

[Rumbaugh91] James Rumbaugh, Michael Blaha, William Lorensen, Frederick Eddy, and William Premerlani, *Object-Oriented Modeling and Design*. Englewood Cliffs, N. J.: Prentice Hall, 1991.

[Siegel94] Jon Siegel (ed.), *Common Object Services, Volume I* (Rev. 1.0). New York: John Wiley & Sons, 1994.

[Siegel96] Jon Siegel, *CORBA Fundamentals and Programming*. New York: John Wiley & Sons, 1996.

[Stroustrup91] Bjarne Stroustrup, *The C++ Programming Language*, Second Edition. Reading, Mass.: Addison Wesley, 1991.

[Tanzer95] Christian Tanzer, "Remarks on Object-Oriented Modeling of Associations." *Journal of Object-oriented Programming*, SIGS Publications, February 1995.

[Tromp92] H. Tromp and G. Hoffman, "An Object-Oriented Message System for a Client/Server Architecture." *Proceedings MEDINFO 92*, World Congress on Medical Informatics, pp.101–105 (also as IFIP World Conference Series on Medical Informatics, North-Holland), Geneva, September 1992.

[VandenBerghe95] Bart Van den Berghe, *Design and Implementation of a Telephone Directory in Progress* (in Dutch). Department of Information Technology, University of Ghent, Belgium, June 1995.

Index